Bauwelt Berlin Annual

Chronology of Building Events 1996 to 2001: 1997

Edited
by Martina Düttmann
and Felix Zwoch

Bauwelt Berlin   Birkhäuser Verlag
Basel · Berlin · Boston

The Bauwelt Berlin Annual is indebted to a number of persons and firms
working in Berlin and commited to the city.
Through sponsoring and advertising they contributed to the making of this Berlin chronology.
The editors would like to thank

Allianz Grundstücks-GmbH, Berlin
BauNetz Online-Dienst GmbH & Co KG, Berlin
Bauwert GmbH, Allgemeine Projektentwicklungs- und Bauträgergesellschaft mbH, Berlin
Bavaria Objekt- und Baubetreuung GmbH, Berlin
Berlin Hyp, Berlin-Hannoversche Hypothekenbank AG
BLEG Berliner Landesentwicklungsgesellschaft mbH
CCS Schöning & Ruh GmbH, Berlin
Checkpoint Charlie KG Network Office Grundstücks GmbH & Co, Berlin
ERCO Leuchten GmbH, Lüdenscheid
FSB Franz Schneider Brakel
GROTH + GRAALFS Industrie- und Wohnbau GmbH, Berlin
GSW Gemeinnützige Siedlungs- und Wohnungsbaugesellschaft Berlin mbH
ITAG Immobilien Treuhand- und Vermögensanlage AG, Berlin
Jagdfeld FriedrichstadtPassagen Quartier 206 Vermögensverwaltung KG, Berlin
KME Europa Metal Aktiengesellschaft, Osnabrück
Dr. Peter und Isolde Kottmair GbR, Berlin/Munich
MetaDesign Berlin
RHEINZINK GMBH, Datteln
STADT UND LAND, Wohnbauten-Gesellschaft mbH, Berlin
Wasserstadt GmbH, Berlin
WIR Wohnungsbaugesellschaft in Berlin mbH
Wohnungsbaugesellschaft Hellersdorf mbH, Berlin

Editorial Staff	Martina Düttmann
	with Michael Goj, Hildegard Loeb-Ullmann, Galina Rave, Christoph Tempel
English Editor	Alexandra Staub
Translations	Nick Kumanoff (p. 32, 48, 98, 119, 151– 157), Jeremiah M. Riemer (p. 122 – 150),
into English	Alexandra Staub (p. 10, 16, 26, 40, 60, 104, 112),
	Melissa Thorson Hause (p. 8, 54, 66, 72, 86, 118, 121, 157 – 159, all quotes)
Design	MetaDesign Berlin
Lithography/Setting	CitySatz & Nagel, Berlin
Printing	Ruksaldruck, Berlin
Binding	Heinz Stein, Berlin

A CIP catalogue record for this book is available from the Library of Congress, Washington, D.C., USA

Deutsche Bibliothek – Cataloging-in-Publication Data

Bauwelt Berlin Annual: Chronik der baulichen Ereignisse 1996 – 2001/
hrsg. von Martina Düttmann und Felix Zwoch. – Basel; Berlin; Boston: Birkhäuser

[Englische Ausg.]. Chronology of Building Events 1996 to 2001
1997. – (1998)
ISBN 3-7643-5843-2

World distribution by Birkhäuser Publishers

© 1998   Bertelsmann Fachzeitschriften GmbH, Gütersloh, Berlin, and
              Birkhäuser Publisher for Architecture, P.O.Box 133, CH 4010 Basel, Switzerland

Printed on acid-free paper produced form chlorine-free pulp. TCF ∞

Printed in Germany
              ISBN 3-7643-5843-2
              ISBN 0-8176-5843-2

              9 8 7 6 5 4 3 2 1

There are many people, whose profession it is to talk about Berlin.

The longer they speak, the bigger they grow and the more Berlin shrinks.

Like in Rome. There, at the Forum, a man ran a hot dog stand for over twenty years.

After a time, he began thinking that people were coming because of him.

Sten Nadolny

Content

Bauwelt Berlin Annual, the second year

The story of Berlin continues: with fifteen additional chapters, the end is nowhere in sight. At this point, no one can say which of the architectural events presented here will one day emerge as the "New Berlin." The purpose of an annual is not to predict the future; it can only compare the built reality with the previously published plans to see how they stack up. We begin once more with Potsdamer Platz — not because Potsdamer Platz is necessarily the most important thing happening, but because it stands for the transformation of one place into another, into a place that it previously was not. And that is just what everyone expects from Berlin, what the city expects from itself: it permits itself to be shaken by forces generated from within and imposed from without.

What remains to be seen is the effect these forces will have. The design for the Jewish Museum, for example, was the subject of marvelous agreement between officials and public; now, as an almost-completed building, it is one of the most controversial issues the city confronts. The dome of the Reichstag, on the other hand, which encountered so much opposition in the design phase, is now taken for granted as if it had always been there. With regard to the city center, the mood is now one of cautious anticipation. Not that the speed of construction has diminished — a walk through the Spittelmarkt construction site testifies to that. Still, for the time being, Berlin is letting itself be acted upon. It plays host to Aldo Rossi and Philip Johnson, but now that their buildings are standing, it hardly notices them. The chapter Pariser Platz is not yet written, and the Schlossplatz, ah, the Schlossplatz...

What is new and completely unexpected for Berlin is the way the edges of the city are coming alive. New suburbs are growing up, though no one can say whether they will remain isolated urban episodes or whether they will give the architectural plot of the Berlin story a new twist. At the same time, another, thoroughly hopeful strand of the urban narrative is emerging: Berlin as a city on the river. Between the two new lake developments in north and south stretches a ribbon of city riverbank, rich in urbanistic opportunities and unused land, an area whose structural possibilities have only begun to be explored.

Many city novels contain rooms with a view; ours, we gladly confess, have something of this Romantic, characteristically Berlinian weakness for the unfinished, the not quite right, the chaotic — from which something can certainly be salvaged, but which at the moment is a little out of step with the times. Only when the growth spurts are over, when the city has assimilated and "digested" them, will Berlin befriend itself again; only then will the city once again find out who she is and be able to present herself to the outside as someone who knows who she is.

As Gertrude Stein wrote: "After all anybody is as their land and air is. Anybody is as the sky is low or high, the air heavy or clear, anybody is as there is wind or no wind there. It is that which makes them and the arts they make and the work they do and the way they eat and the way they drink and the way they learn and everything."
Martina Düttmann

1

Architects	
debis House	Renzo Piano Building Workshop, Paris
	Christoph Kohlbecker, Gaggenau
Office buildings	
C2, C3	Arata Isozaki & Ass., Tokyo
	Steffen Lehmann & Partner, Berlin
Project Managers	
debis House	Drees und Sommer, Berlin
Office buildings	
C2, C3	Steffen Lehmann & Partner, Berlin
Facade Planning	
debis House	Emmer-Pfenniger, Münchenstein
Office buildings	
C2, C3	IFFT/Schott, Frankfurt
Structural Design	
debis House/	
Office buildings	
C2, C3	Ingenieurgemeinschaft Boll/Arup,
	Stuttgart/London
Client	debis Immobilienmanagement GmbH, Berlin
Opening	October 24th, 1997
Address	Reichpietschufer/Eichhornstrasse/Linkstrasse
	Berlin-Tiergarten

Felix Zwoch
Potsdamer Platz, October 1997

All photos:
Vincent Mosch

The mythos of Potsdamer Platz may herewith wane. The two buildings at the southern tip of the terrain calling itself Potsdamer Platz are completed, Daimler-Benz's urban fragment is gaining contours. On the streets lining the banks of the Landwehrkanal, frontages have popped up overnight. Whose plans were the best or whose will lead to the better way is no longer a matter of debate. Renzo Piano's and Arata Isozaki's buildings are here to stay.

Their proximity suits them well. The photographer uses one as a backdrop for the other, as a frame, a peephole or a mirror. Better said: Isozaki's building, with its strange colors and its wallpaper-like facades, its narrow sides and the bulbous bridge between them looking out onto the water, almost devotedly bows to Piano's bundle of stretching shafts. These shafts, some in glass, some clad in ceramic the color of freshly-baked white bread, stand out all the better. Isozaki's Bridges of Sighs over the courtyards superbly frame Piano's facade segments, mirrored by the glass waves along the edge of the roof. Or stated otherwise: It is Isosaki's "active negligence", the stumps of his Y-supports which thrust through the glass like mightily-grown trees yet wither away on the inside because they have been blocked off and plastered over, which provides the best backdrop for Piano's well-developed proportions and the fine detailing of his facade.

The era of aerial views, formerly the only perspective from which one could take in the bustle of Potsdamer Platz, is over. The photographers have returned to earth, move among the buildings, make use of a segment of staircase to gain more height, and try out the views from there. The picture fragments, the joints between the two worlds of images, make it easy to accept the alien, without its ever ceasing to be foreign.

A stroll in the autumn of 1997 reveals the following: The new buildings matter-of-factly take their place in the chain of solitaires which line the waterfront—the State Library, the National Gallery, the Scholarship Center, Fahrenkamp's BEWAG Building. What is more, they gain from their position. They also gain from the confrontation with the construction site which spreads out to the north directly behind them. Never again will these buildings appear to be so idiosyncratic, so theatrical, so shining, so strictly circumscribed. Behind them lie the canyons, on whose edge they stand. A view into the depths, where the old part of Potsdamer Strasse begins, makes it possible to comprehend the dimensions of the underground city, a city invisible from above. The ends and the ramps of tunnels become visible and it is possible to imagine how high the embankment is which became necessary in order to preserve a row of lime trees on the old Potsdamer Strasse. If one takes a guess at the costs incurred by this measure, the trees appear to be feuilletés with banknotes. Threaded deep into the earth we see the supports of the Weinhaus Huth Building's fragile shell. The new, narrow streets, which hardly a truck is able to navigate without difficulty, have a very urban quality. They

Glass stair tower of the debis Building (architect: Renzo Piano) with the neighboring Canaris Building. From the stair tower one has a view of the Landwehrkanal and Reichpietschufer. Following pages: The neighborhood of Renzo Piano's and Arata Isozaki's architecture

The stepped-back western facade of Renzo Piano's debis Building. Also: the formwork balloon used for the dome of the Imax 3-D movie theater and the construction site for the theater and casino along the rear facade of the State Library

Arata Isozaki's office building has a wave of glass along the upper and lower edge of the facade. They mirror the facade of Renzo Piano's debis Building. The atrium within the building maintains the proportions of the narrow streets outside. Official opening: October 24th, 1997

almost remind one of New York, although the high-rises there stand along broad streets. Here, a ratio of 2:1 was stipulated. The height of one building is equal to the width of two streets, making for very different proportions and a much smaller scale than those found in Manhattan. Nevertheless, the sensation evoked is similar. The visitor wanders amongst slabs of walls, the sky turns into a square field, light falls in patches. Calm seems to have settled upon this area in such close proximity to the construction site. The colors, the movements, the sounds have all become muted. The debis Building's green glass atrium, which follows the proportions of the street, visibly mirrors this tranquility. Today, however, the aquarium is loud and lively; debis is to move in on October 24th. Boxes are piled up, red-and-white-striped tapes bar passage, a crane swings to and fro inside the building, great blasts of hot air warm the visitor from behind. Only with a wistful glance behind us do we leave this building. The following streets belong to the 17 office and apartment buildings which remain to be completed, their bulk already visible. The huge green formwork balloon of the Imax-3D movie theater hangs over and into the volumes. One street further on, the balloon has again disappeared. We see wide staircases which lead onto elevated courtyards and here, where the severed piece of Potsdamer Strasse ends, one can already make out the little piazza wedged in between the volumes of the future theater-and-casino building, which will hide the rear facade of the State Library and may one day be connected to it.

Arata Isozaki: The gorges between the buildings. The Bridge of Sighs framing the picture. The bow pointing northward. The ceramic facade's wallpaper pattern. The glass waves

In the passageways between Arata Isozaki's buildings, pieces of Renzo Piano's many-layered facade continuously become visible. The facade consists of glass, aluminum and terracotta elements in various dimensions

Entering the construction site is simple. The paths are partly paved, piles of steel reinforcements and stacks of two-by-fours bridge puddles and holes. Those used to ambling across construction sites take things in stride; they peer between two form-work panels and scamper between two swing-bys of the crane boom. At the northern end of the site a magnificent view awaits. From the second floor of the cinema center one can see the other urban frag-ment, the Sony Block, excavate itself and rise to its full height. A look down and the gaze falls into the depths which the visitor has just traversed, down into the four basements under Hans Kollhoff's and Renzo Piano's back-to-back highrises, buildings already under construction despite their not yet having been completely dimensioned. All the way at the bottom, amidst a tangle of reinforcing rods, a ballet of red, pink, green, yellow, and sky-blue hard hats is in progress. The visitor is in the third tier. "Animation, animation," is the battle cry when conjuring up a use for the huge covered square in the Sony Building. The same phrase resounds when talk is of the passage, the piazza, and the casino, theater and cinema worlds in the debis Building. How, muses the visitor, will the Theater of Life one day be able to outperform the great scenes of the construction site?

2

Architect	Daniel Libeskind, Berlin
Project Architect	Matthias Reese
Construction Management	Arge Beusterin und Lubic, Berlin
Landscaping	Müller, Knippschild, Wehberg, Berlin
Structural Design	GSE Saar
	Enseleit und Partner, Berlin,
	IGW Ingenieurgruppe Wiese, Berlin
Lighting	Lichtplanung Dinnebier, Wuppertal
Client	Land Berlin
	Senatsverwaltung Bauen, Wohnen, Verkehr
Address	Lindenstrasse 14, Berlin-Kreuzberg

Heinrich Wefing
Daniel Libeskind's Jewish Museum

An Architectonic Declaration of Independence

All photos: BitterBredt

"A bombshell" is what Klaus Humpert called Daniel Libeskind's project for the Berlin Museum "extension" in June of 1989, shortly after the jury decision which he as a jury member had helped bring about. His prediction proved right. Not simply because the solitaire with the sharp edges and jutting angles further tears apart the deeply fissured structure of the Southern Friedrichstadt area, ignoring both historical building lines and the surrounding puzzle of International Building Exhibition (IBA) results and mass-produced housing slabs. No, the closer we come to the completion of the unwieldy building on Lindenstrasse, the more it becomes obvious that the lightning streak, frozen into stone and steel, is an architectonic declaration of independence on the part of the Jewish Museum. The architect's pronouncements that he built "an integrating museum" in which Jewish and non-Jewish lines of tradition cross and penetrate each other are deconstructed by a tangle of axes which interrupt, border or erase one another. They dissolve, in the process, the concept of a museum in which Judaica is displayed along with extensive parts of the Berlin Museum collection, a collection which deals with the general history of Berlin.

Exactly this juxtaposition, though, is the concept which was stipulated when the competition for the museum was announced in 1988. A total of 165 offices took part. The competition announcement clearly stated that it was planned to, "integrate the Jewish Museum into the Berlin Museum as a Jewish section." A bit less than 1,500 square meters of exhibition space, a fourth of the new building, was allotted for the division. The new building literally stands shoulder to shoulder with the compact, two-story Kollegien House, built by Phillip Gerlach in 1735 for Emperor Friedrich Wilhelm I. Libeskind, who in his own words had "waited his whole life for" this commission, brilliantly reinterpreted the assignment with the express permission of the jury, the client, and the critics. And Berlin was enthusiastic. At the end of October 1997, Humboldt University awarded the architect, urban theorist, and "world citizen" an honorary doctorate for exactly this design.

Yet now the normative force of the symbolic has reduced the showroom for municipal history to a very specific substance. Libeskind, born in 1947 in Lodz and currently living and working in Berlin and the US, has not designed a museum in the common sense of the word, nor has he designed a mere "building extension". Rather, he has created a large-scale sculpture, five floors high, based on the plan of a shattered, exploded Star of David. The building with the shimmering zinc skin, here deeply furrowed, there slit open, does not even have its own entrance. The way in is underground, via a solemn staircase reached by going into the Kollegien House. This combined entrance is, according to the architect, a reminder of how inseparably Jewish and non-Jewish history are interwoven.

Above grade the Libeskind lightning bolt gives its historical neighbor the cold metallic shoulder, unmistakably pushing its way to the forefront both

Daniel Libeskind calls his design, "Between the Lines," lines which purposely cross and dissect each other in the plan. In the facade they appear as wounds or as ornaments

in terms of dimension, design and architectural pretention, and degrading the fine baroque ensemble with its main body and side wings to a piece of picturesque decorum. Cold in its closed-off nature and demanding attention for the furious show it presents, the new museum oscillates between distance and closeness, inclusion and exclusion, collision and attachment.

The darkest era of Berlin's Jewish history, the period between 1933 and 1945, will be presented, according to current plans, on the windowless basement. Down here, two lines cross the slightly inclined main axis of the building: one is the so-called "Holocaust Axis", a 48-meter-long line which could trace the path from the railway stations where the deportations began to the death camps where they ended, in the form of pictures, witness accounts, and documents. This line ends at an empty tower, a naked void of disturbing force. The concrete stump, neither heated nor air-conditioned, dramatically lighted from above, and with its exterior left raw, almost makes an intruder of the visitor, who, at any rate, is left completely to his own devices. Only hushed sounds, whisper-like, are meant to be audible here.

The second line in the repeatedly broken, fragmented space continuum is the 52-meter-long "Exile Axis". This line is dedicated to the flight from Berlin to Jerusalem, Hollywood, Shanghai and everywhere else and leads out into the "E.T.A. Hoffmann Garden", a sloping space with Russian olive trees rising up from 49 concrete steles. The

The museum in its urban setting with a view to the north. The E.T.A. Hoffmann Garden is in the foreground. The impenetrable concrete stump surrounds the "voided void", the overwhelming empty space

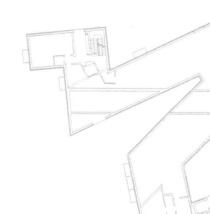

slanting stone grove is not meant to merely commemorate the poet and jurist E.T.A. Hoffmann, who
held a post in the Kollegien House as chamber law
council for His Majesty from 1816 to 1822. With
this geometric stone garden, tilted away from the
familiar horizontal, Libeskind wants to physically
recount the irritation of the emigrants' fate. "Everything seems to be perfect, ordered. But when you
walk around here, you notice how difficult it is
to orient yourself. Everything is somehow topsy-
turvy."

Such metaphorical but direct culminations,
along with the allegorical program of the architectonic sculpture itself, make the building a memorial for the banished, the murdered, and the unborn
Jews of Berlin. And in that, without it ever having
been explicitly stated, this building has become
if not the, then certainly a Holocaust Memorial in
the nation's capital.

The public's amazed and admiring silence in
the face of this architecture parlante, in view of the
new coding of the assignment, a feat which certainly could have led to an interesting debate, is
astounding. All the more as Libeskind himself, a
man who tends to cryptic, lyrical statements, clearly stated that he conceived of this building as an
"emblem" and a "symbolic beacon". "The museum
is to evolve around a void which itself permeates
the building." Not much Jewish presence remains
in Berlin, writes Libeskind, "only small objects,
documents, and archive materials which evoke
an absence rather than a presence. That's why I

The museum on Linden-
strasse.
In the background to the
left: the Berlin Museum.
The visitor has to enter
this building and
descend a staircase in
order to reach the new
museum

On the following pages:
The E. T. A. Hoffmann
Garden with its base and
concrete steles slightly
tipped away from the
horizontal plane.
Next to it the northern
courtyard which results
from the additional
distortion of the zigzag
floor plan

thought that this 'emptiness' which floats through
Berlin's contemporary culture, should be made
visible and reachable."

Libeskind takes the emptiness and strips it
down into four so-called "voids" which jut through
the floors from base to roof like a set of bricked-up
light shafts. They can be neither stepped into nor
played on but must be crossed by way of narrow
tunnels. The encapsulated emptiness disquiet-
ingly and pointedly makes reference to the fact
that something is missing — that something being
the meanings and connections which disappeared
after the destruction of Berlin's Jewish culture.

The building, with its metaphorical apparatus,
seems to support the view of the Jewish Museum's
dismissed director, Amnon Barzel, that Libeskind
won the competition exactly because his building
is full of symbols of Jewish history. In fact, the
architecture has the recollection of a rupture in
civilization clearly etched into it. It pronounces the
unspeakable. More than that, the architecture
attempts, through means of its own, to bring the
history of Berlin's Jews back into the history of the
city from which they were once so murderously
driven.

The dramaturgy of the interior spaces, the
nebulous borders of the halls, the surprising,
purposely irritating path leading through the
building, the alteration between narrowness and
wideness, between light and dark, the expressive
monumentality, a monumentality whose sheer
force was almost more present in the raw state

of the unfinished building than in the smoothed-
out finish of the completed version, all of these
prohibit the mixed use of the museum. If a use, in
the common sense of the word, is at all possible.
For this building — which is natural, one would like
to add, considering the function and Libeskind's
theory structures — has heard of nary a right angle.
The spaces consist of a spray of exploding zigzags.
The steeply climbing walls, which in the competition design tilted away from the vertical, had to, for
reasons of cost, be realigned. They are penetrated
by the nervous calligraphy of not less than 365
light slits, which transcribe a bit of the fractured
charm of the plan onto the elevation. All of this
taken together presents one with a veritable
museological challenge, to put it cautiously. Only
the future will show us if this building so laden
with meaning is even usable.

Potsdam historian Julius H. Schoeps rightfully
warned us of the enormous, "influence of the
brilliant architecture."

It is already possible to establish, long before
the opening date which has finally been set for
1999, that the exhibits belonging to the theater
section, the toy section, the fashion collection, or
the graphic collection of the Berlin Museum will
seem displaced in these walls so laden with meaning. It is no coincidence that the proponents of the
Jewish Museum's hard fought-for autonomy specifically referred to and still refer to the museum's
architecture when making their point. The chair of
Berlin's Jewish Community, Andreas Nachama, for

The main stairwell, which penetrates all floors of the building, forming a mounting path along the southern side of the longest wing

Detail of the southern facade. Inside: one of the voids, the narrow shafts meant to harbor emptiness, as seen from the ground floor, and a room on the second floor where the effect of the light bands and light spots from within become visible

example, likes to repeat his demand that the inner structure of the museum, "do justice to the design and the philosophy of the Libeskind building," which, without further ado, he designates to be one of, "the 20 most important buildings of the 20th century."

It is this enormous esteem in which the building is held which has turned the conceptional conditions of the beginning around. The overpowering architecture has taken on a life of its own and the function has been damned to follow the form. In the public mind, Libeskind's building has become synonymous with the "Jewish Museum", even though it is still not clear if there are even enough exhibits in Berlin important enough to be shown here.

This magnificent building, which is actually only an extension, makes the heavily debated autonomy of the Jewish Museum apparent.

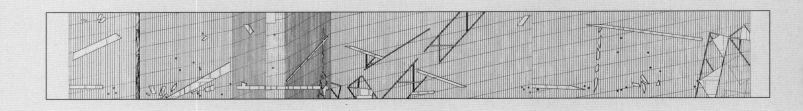

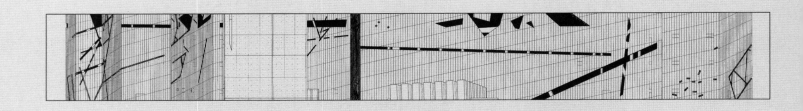

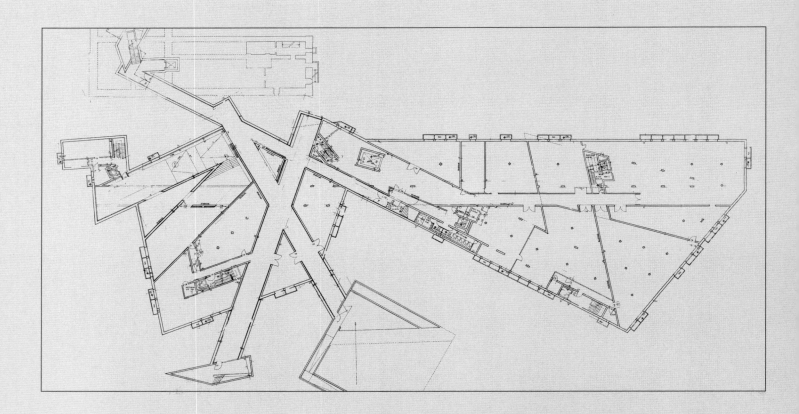

**Plans of basement and
second floor, longitudinal
section and facade to a
scale of 1:750.
North is at the top**

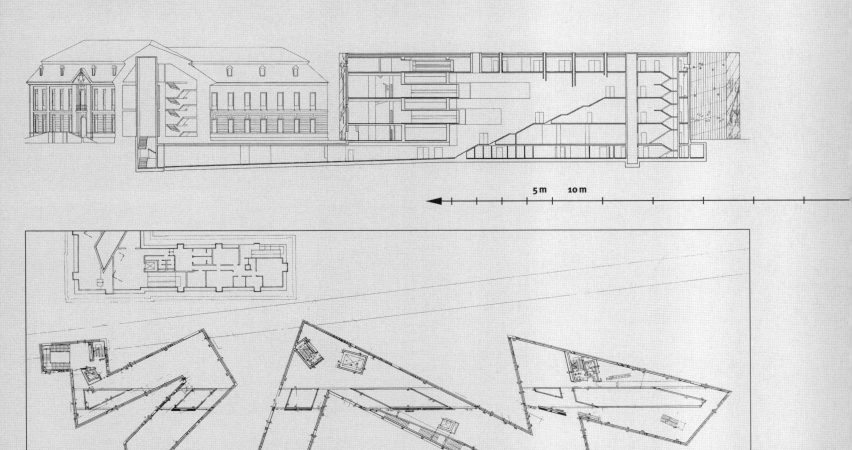

5 m   10 m

3

Architects	Foster and Partners, London/Berlin
Competition	1992
Commission	1993
Project Architect	Mark Braun, Berlin
Construction Management	Foster and Partners/Büro am Lützowplatz, Berlin
Structural Design	Leonhardt, Andrä und Partner, Berlin
Detailing, Production and Assembly of the Dome	Waagner-Biró, Vienna/Munich
Client	Bundesbaugesellschaft Berlin mbH, representing the Federal Republic of Germany
Address	Platz der Republik, Berlin-Tiergarten

Claire Borchardt
Construction of the Reichstag Dome

Conversion of the Reichstag Building into the Seat of the German Bundestag

September 18th, 1997: Topping-out ceremony for the Reichstag Building and its dome.

For many months it seemed as if the new dome had taken on its ultimate form in the city's skyline, even though the double ramp was still being held in place by scaffolding. Although the new dome is but one measure with which the old Reichstag building in Berlin is being converted into a building befitting of its new function as seat of the German Bundestag, it is by far the most spectacular.

The dome has a past. The original structure crowning Paul Wallots 1894 building was already controversial. Only a bit of iron and glass, critical voices said back then, an engineer's design and unbefitting of such an important building. In the rebuilt Reichstag of 1961 the dome became so controversial that the architect Paul Baumgarten decided to do without it altogether.

The latest dome, part of the project which the architect Sir Norman Foster reworked several times, has a new twist. One of the most important aspects of the design was to give the dome a function and not to merely let it become bogged down with its own symbolism. Thus, for the first time in the building's history, the dome's interior will be open to the public. The visitor can stride up one of the ramps, arrive at the visitors' platform and enjoy a 360° view of Berlin. The everchanging silhouettes of the city which present themselves as one ascends or descends the ramps are breathtaking, even now. A restaurant which will provide panoramas of the greater part of Berlin is planned for the

same level as the roof terrace. It too will be open to the public, even when the parliament is not in session.

In the fall of 1993, Foster Associates was commissioned to redo the Reichstag. Presentation of the new design was in the summer of 1995, followed a year later by the working drawings.

On July 7th, 1995, one day after Christo and Jeanne-Claude terminated their Wrapped Reichstag project, the building became a construction site as measures were begun to strip the building's interior to its core. Specifically, this meant the removal of all changes made by the architect Paul Baumgarten, who had given the Reichstag a contemporary interior, including five additional floors, between 1961–1969. Baumgarten's fine detailing had to be sacrificed in order to reestablish Paul Wallot's spatial concept. Wallot had planned the Reichstag as a building with four main floors and entrances on all four sides. The extra floors and galleries were removed, restoring the original floor-to-ceiling height of up to 10.5 meters. The doors were returned to their former measures of 3.5 meters by 1.6 meters and their axiality was reestablished. One of Baumgarten's architectural gestures was maintained in a modified form: In the 1960's the architect had removed the wall dividing the west lobby from the assembly room to open up the parliament to the outside world. Sir Norman Foster reinserted the wall, but as a 15-meter long, airy glass membrane which divides the public lobby from the central assembly room without visually sealing it off.

September 17th, 1997
The two visitors' ramps
are intertwined into a
double helix structure

August 28th, 1997
The interior beneath the
dome. The steel supports
of the galleries are
clearly visible

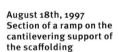

August 18th, 1997
Section of a ramp on the
cantilevering support of
the scaffolding

Photos: Rudi Meisel

In terms of function and design, Foster followed several aims as he reworked the plans for the Reichstag: transparency, vistas within the building, easy orientation, and an invitation to the public to consider the seat of the German Bundestag to be their building.

All additions from the 1960's were removed by the spring of 1996 and construction of the new interior begun.

This most importantly included the insertion of two elements: a ring of huge columns around the assembly room, which were to bear the weight of the new dome, and steel frames to hold the cantilevered galleries. In the spring of 1997 this phase of building was completed.

On April 10th, 1997 work on the dome began. Its construction on site had been preceded by a period of extensive filing on the working drawings. The members of Foster Associates often visited the Waagner-Biró factory in Vienna, where the individual elements of the dome were being manufactured, in order to follow the fascinating production process and to work out improvements or changes on the spot. Unusual was the fact that detailing of the dome and the Reichstag Building was preceded by 3,000 three-dimensional computer drawings. In addition, in order to simulate the finished situation (for example of the ramps), a large number of full-scale mockups were tried out on site. All bearing parts were prefabricated and shipped to the site by truck. The original plan, which called for their transport by boat, had to be abandoned.

The dome is a steel construction consisting primarily of tension members. The outer skin is a series of overlapping glass shingles. The main elements of the dome are as follows:

The primary bearing members, consisting of 24 curved, tapering steel ribs, triangular in plan;

two 230-meter-long ramp systems which are intertwined into a double helix structure (the system can be compared to the stairwell in the Chambord Castle on the Loire);

the visitors' platform at the end of the ramps, 16 meters above the level of the roof terraces and about 50 meters over street level;

a reflecting, conical, light-directing element which hangs from the dome's crown.

The domelike construction visible during the building phase was not the bearing arch rib construction. Because of the dome's tensile forces, a building process was chosen which at first seems illogically reversed. First to be seen was the scaffolding, from which the 13-meter-long, ten-ton ramp segments of the double helix were successively hung. This scaffolding later served to mount the main load-bearing elements, which were assembled on site and then lifted and precisely positioned into place. The ramps are located within the 38-meter diameter of the dome's 24 curved steel ribs. Seven meters over the visitors' platform the arch ribs meet at a ring which forms the dome's oculus. Once the main construction has been put into place the scaffolding will be taken down.

April 1997
Assembly room with the 12 exposed-concrete supports and the steel grid which will support the galleries

March/April 1997
Roof level; work on the ramps is begun at the lower concrete ring. Above, the protective covering, which is also used as assembly plane for the upper platform

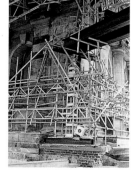

March 1997
Work in progress inside the Reichstag, temporary roofs

Photos:
Johann Sischka
Waagner-Biró (3)
Rudi Meisel (4)

The photo series shows the construction process from April to September of 1997. At first, the scaffolding and the ramps, still awaiting the steel ribs, rest on a supporting ring at their base. This ring, with an outer radius of about 20 meters, consists of 12 hollow ten-meter-long segments. (The roof opening had to be covered before the supporting ring was put into place, in order to protect the building's interior.) The base of each ramp rests on a concrete platform. The upper ramp segments rest on consoles cantilevered from the scaffolding. After they have been moved into place, they will be welded together. Each of the two ramp systems consists of 18 elements, each element will take up to two days to mount into place and connect. Then the ramps spiral upwards, their radius decreasing the higher they turn. Landings interrupt the flow of the ramps as the stringboards continue their upward motion. Finally, the visitors' platform, mounted on site, is lifted into the scaffolding and fastened to the upper ends of the ramps.

The last portion of the ramp was put into place in August of 1997. On September 18th, 1997, after both ramps were in place, Berlin celebrated the Reichstag Building's topping-out ceremony.

The Reichstag's section clearly shows that one of the important features of the new spatial concept is public access to the Bundestag. After completion, the Reichstag building will be accessible through all four of the existing entrances. The west entrance with its monumental flight of steps and

majestic ramp, an entrance which Berlin's population remembers as always closed off (and harboring the exhibition, "Questions on German History"), an entrance which in the Wallot version of the building was also the least used, is henceforth to be the entrance for public access. The west lobby is flanked by two stairwell and elevator towers. An express elevator brings visitors to the roof terrace, from where they may ascend the ramps to the dome's platform.

After passing security points, visitors arrive in the spacious west lobby, a 30-meter high room, flooded with daylight and covered with a glazed roof. An airy glass membrane forms the eastern border of this lobby. This membrane divides the public from the official space while allowing a view of the latter—a hall with the assembly area behind. Both the western and the eastern side of the assembly room are borderd by such a membrane. To the north and the south the assembly area is bordered by walls of the existing light courts. These are clad in a beige sandstone, the Reichstag stone. All new additions, by contrast, are of steel and glass.

The assembly hall, on the first (not ground) floor, is encircled by a ring of 12 exposed-concrete supports. They bear the weight of the dome and the floor above the assembly hall, where the members of the different parties sit. The historical mezzanine floor, five meters above the first floor's entrance area, continues within the building. Six individual balconies swoop from this level into the

Details from the time of the ramp's construction between April and September 1997

Below:
Installation of the second ramp segment

August 1997
Views of the city from the ramps

Photos: Johann Sischka (6)

space over the assembly room's seating area. These balconies are for spectators, the press and VIPs. Offices for the Bundestag President, her staff, the Council of Elders and the administration are on the second floor. The third floor is the final floor of the assembly room's volume. Here too are offices for the political factions represented in the German Bundestag. These rooms have large windows opening onto the light courts. Between these, centrally located and directly above the assembly hall, is the press lobby.

Here, at the roof-terrace level, the lower tip of the funnel-shaped, reflective, light-directing element breaks through the overhead glazing. Via computer-controlled mirrors, daylight is reflected deep into the assembly area below. The inside of this light-directing element contains the air-conditioning system for the assembly room; stale air is expelled through the eight-meter large oculus at the dome's crown.

The light-directing element is only part of a holistic, resource-saving energy concept. Photovoltaic cells on the southern lean-to roofs, casement windows, a power plant fueled by biological diesel, and use of the earth as a thermal storage medium are further aspects of the energy system.

The Reichstag Building, including the dome's glazing, the mirrors of the light-directing element, floors, glass parapets, and so on will be finished by August of 1998. Plans have been made to hold the May 23, 1999 election for the Bundestag President in the new building.

What is certain, is that the German Bundestag will take ceremonial possession of its house on the occasion of its 50th birthday, on September 7th, 1999.

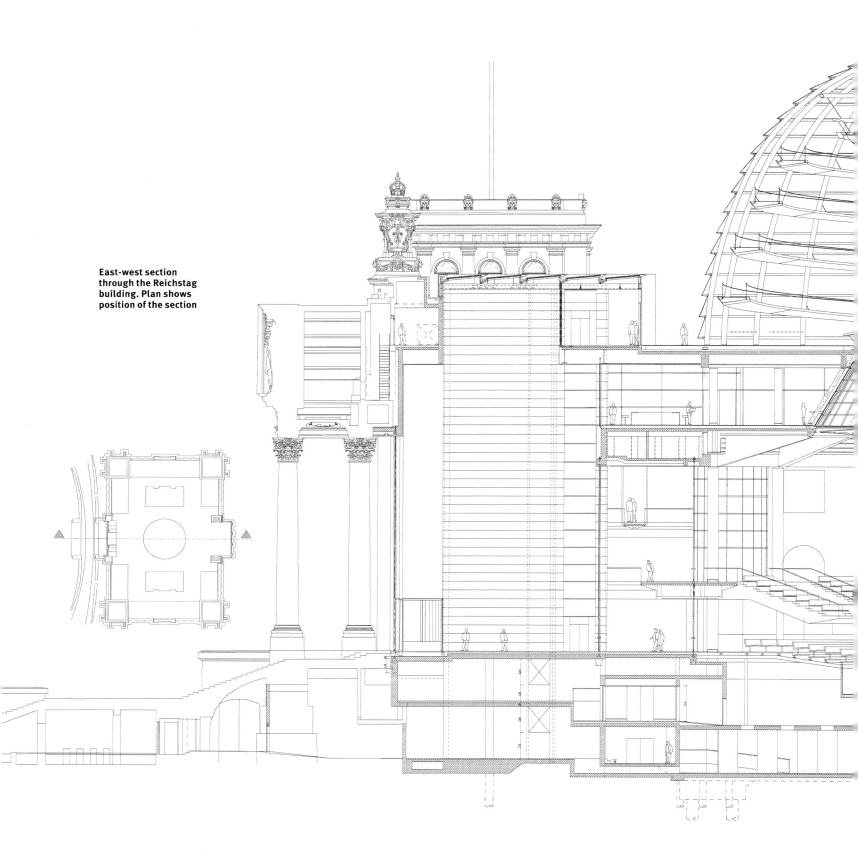

East-west section through the Reichstag building. Plan shows position of the section

September 18th, 1997
Topping-out ceremony
wreath over the dome

Photo: Rudi Meisel

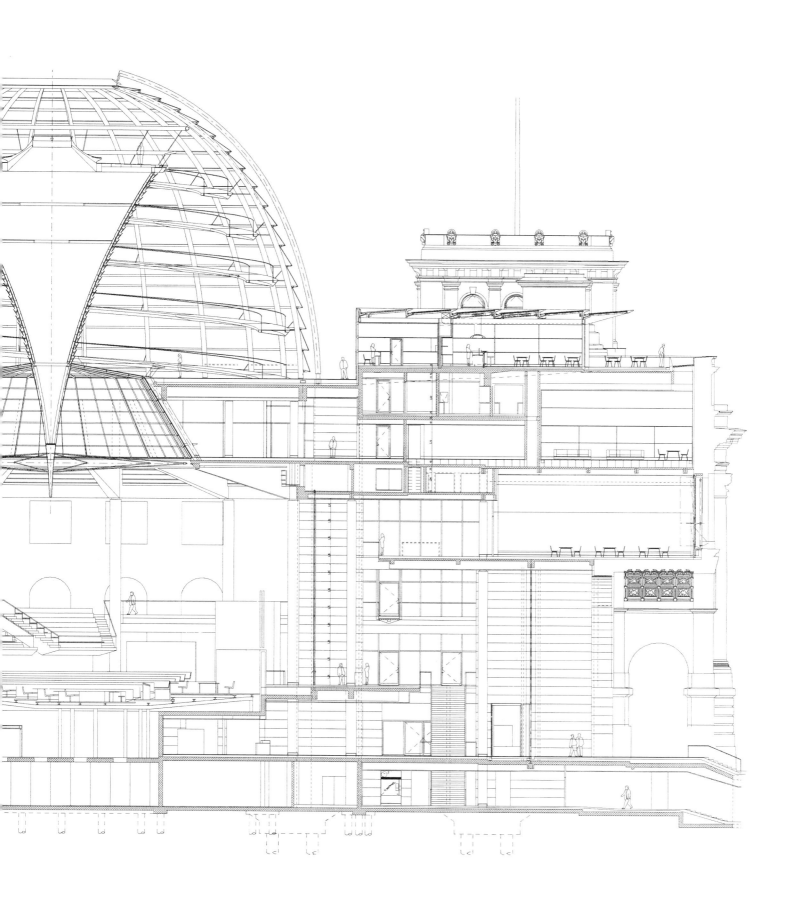

4

Master Plan and
Design

Project
Management
Client
Address

Aldo Rossi
with Massimo Scheurer, Marc Kocher
Götz Bellmann, Walter Böhm

Bellmann & Böhm, Berlin
Dr. Peter und Isolde Kottmair, Munich, Berlin
Block Schützenstrasse, Markgrafenstrasse,
Zimmerstrasse, Charlottenstrasse
Berlin-Mitte

Mathias Remmele
Aldo Rossi's "Quartier Schützenstrasse"

It seems to be a sober business relationship, but in this case we will call it a love story. Figuratively speaking. That is because in our opinion, there is no other way to describe that which distinguished the relationship between project managers Dr. Peter and Isolde Kottmair of Munich and the Italian architect Aldo Rossi.

It might have been the prospect of bustling business which seduced the Kottmairs, who have been active mainly in the Munich area, to invest in Berlin, shortly after the German reunification. Their decision to engage Aldo Rossi for all their major projects here (the realised "Quartier Schützen-strasse," as well as those planned on Landsberger Allee and Leipziger Platz) cannot be explained solely in commercial terms. Also involved were faith, love, hope, and idealism on a level hardly justifiable today. Ever since the Kottmairs discover-ed (for themselves) the Italian maestro, they have been hopelessly swept off their feet, for better or worse, by his architecture and his concepts of urbanity. With the same Baroque-Bavarian gener-osity with which they hold their legendary onsite celebrations, trucking in delicacies for everyone, they pay for his facade-extravaganzas. Their con-viction that with him they are making a historically conscious, forward-aiming, and culturally signif-icant contribution to Berlin construction has deep roots and is, whether one believes them or not, beyond all doubt.

Aldo Rossi died on the 4th of September 1997. The unveiling of the "Palazzo Farnese" facade,

planned as a splendid festivity in his honour for the following day, turned into a valediction.

The second love story might seem quite ordi-nary in comparison: the love of the architect for the city he builds in. One often hears it described this way; yes, it's an almost proper thing to be expected. As in normal life, this love includes satisfaction and disappointment, ups and downs and sometimes misunderstandings with fateful consequences. Aldo Rossi's love for Berlin, which began in the sixties and was initially devoted mainly to the Eastern half, rests on names: Hermann Hensel-mann, Bruno Taut, Peter Behrens, and inevitably, Karl Friedrich Schinkel. Rossi could only begin building much later in the West, he was commis-sioned with two apartment buildings as part of the International Building Exhibtion of 1984/87. The breakthrough he had hoped for came in 1988, with his winning design for the German Historical Muse-um. So near was the chance to leave one's stamp on the city's architectural history vis-à-vis the Reichstag, and so bitter the disappointment when the plan fell victim to reunification. The Kottmairs, "enlightened clients" as Rossi calls them, have been offering him generous compensations and opportunities to make rich expressions of his love for the city. But Rossi, who claims to know the city "as a stranger," and always tries to "understand the places and their history;" who wants to see his design for "Quartier Schützenstrasse" understood as a, "homage to the typical block architecture of Berlin at the end of the 19th century," and thus

The colorful city block. View to the north, towards Leipziger Strasse and Alexander-platz

Housefronts on Zimmer-strasse. In the middle house the family-tower motive is visible. The dark facade under the curved roof is by Bellmann & Böhm, Berlin

Photos: Christian Gahl

Courtyard facade of the Palazzo Farnese in Rome, built in 1516 by Antonio Sangallo. The facade once was modified by Michelangelo and modifyingly copied by Aldo Rossi

claims to have built something very Berlin-like here, has actually created an eccentric ensemble, an alien straight from the text books.

This thing called "Quartier Schützenstrasse" consists of a classical Friedrichstadt block defined by the Schützenstrasse, Markgrafenstrasse, Zimmerstrasse, and Charlottenstrasse. Its name was derived from the property acquisition which began in Schützenstrasse by the developers, who only slowly consolidated their holdings. When the rapidly begun rebuilding plan finally encompassed the entire block, it was decided to gauge the plan to the old system of lots, a system that no longer existed under the new ownership conditions. It was an artificial animation with many consequences for its outward charm, and was first suggested by Dieter Hoffmann-Axthelm, an unflappable proponent of the lot system. Well knowing that urban design and city history only count as long as they don't interrupt business, he argued in terms of economics: many small pieces make for flexible and varied usage, while the individualized facades encourage users to identify with "their" house. Both are good for rentals and sales. A protected 1870's apartment block on Schützenstrasse had to be incorporated into the project; another old building directly across the way was reduced to two stories during the war and proved impossible to restore, despite all efforts. Rossi reconstructed the facade and placed four full and two attic stories on top. Even if the divisions on Schützenstrasse do not, as elsewhere, just take place on the facades,

Photos:
Christian Gahl (left)
Palladium
PhotoDesign (above)

Two large and two small interior courtyards fill the block with light. The path through the smallest, ornamental courtyard behind the Palazzo Farnese

Photos:
Christian Gahl (above)
Palladium
PhotoDesign (below)

a bit of magic has still been made. The total number of facades exceeds the number of houses standing independently of each other. As far as real owner-ship is concerned, reinstating the old lots did not mean a return to a former legal status. In principle, all the houses could be resold individually, although ownership of the block is shared by three real estate holders.

Rossi's master plan, with which he laid the framework for the new buildings, was strongly oriented towards the 19th-century Berlin housing block, complete with narrow courtyards, as if this had never been criticized and for good reason. He organized his buildings around four courtyards, two large and two small ones, which come dangerously close in appearance to their notorious antecedents. They serve as access to and trail marks within the block—a novelty. Of the eleven new buildings which the master plan was supposed to melt together into a "city-within-a-city", one lot each was awarded, in a reluctant tribute to plurality, to Lucca Meda, Milan, and the onsite architects Bellmann & Böhm, Berlin. The rest is Rossi's.

Once it has been ascertained that the intentions are serious, anyone wishing information on "Quartier Schützenstrasse" receives, instead of a glossy marketing brochure, a thin, startlingly large-format book bound in thick, dark blue cardboard. Small, playfully-colored design sketches decorate Rossi's title page like labels. And, as if someone had tried to perfect the book's already unmistakable childhood charm, a turn of the page

unfolds a colorful, three-dimensional pop-up model. Above a flat silver book page the entire block made of colorful cardboard rises to a scale of 1:200 from the side, the eye encompasses the many facades; from above the roofscape and the four yards within the block unfold. No doubt the design refers to Berlin. Presented to the beholder as if on a platter, the model is so picturesque and homely that one could simply rejoice over it as a flight of fancy while forgetting that it is really a design meant to be realized. Anyone seeking to understand the design phenomenon should stick to Rossi's colored sketches. With their mostly windswept and often asymmetrical houses, these evoke even more than the model the image of an old city that has grown over centuries. A city universally considered beautiful. A city one has to consider beautiful, let us say Venice, Verona, Vicenza…

The realized buildings could not fulfill the promise of the sketches. Pushed into order, pulled straight, blown up, backed with concrete, the picture-book facades lost what had distinguished them. What as a sketch and model appeared oddly homespun, suddenly became something alienating: the quarter's varied colors and forms. What claims to be a block, one that could have emerged anywhere over time, one that consists of houses grown up, in a peaceful neighborhood, isolates itself within its neighborhood.

The intense colorfulness—the most salient characteristic—pins the block together and draws

Zimmerstrasse, view towards the south. The individualized houses signal individual plots, the unusual color scheme betrays the truth: It's all the work of one hand

*Photos:
Christian Gahl (left)
Palladium
PhotoDesign (above)*

attention to the allotment structure, which distinguishes the individual houses. But it also cuts the block off from its urban surroundings and presents itself as pure surface, as skin. The underlying forms, no matter how many, all unmistakably stem from one hand.

Aldo Rossi has not divulged the secret of his color concept. He only hinted, for instance, at the colors of antique architecture, as justification or as inspiration. And when he did speak of colors, he only named them in vague material categories, meaning he had intended particular colors for particular facade materials. A system is becoming recognizable or, shall we say, a rule of thumb: the more "artificial" the material, the more riotous the color. Frog-green and bright red signal aluminium. The strong yet relatively muted colors; eggyolk yellow, carmine red and cornflower blue are all mineral plaster. The earthy tones shading into red-brown or yellow indicate bricks. And that which appears pale on the facades is natural stone, of which there are four kinds throughout the quarter: light and dark gray, sand and pink. Finally, excepting a few special cases, one material sports its "natural" color: the silver-gray of sheet metal.

Rossi's architecture quotes (itself) and tells stories, a collage of icons and archetypes. This is most obvious where the quote is a literal one, on the facade of Schützenstrasse 8, which Rossi disguised with a copy of the courtyard facade of the Palazzo Farnese. To lend plausibility to such whims, which incidentally are not Rossi's usual

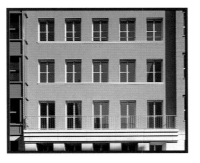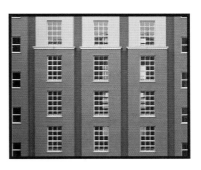

The facades: muted colors for the stucco, blaring green and red for aluminum; in addition, brick colors and zinc for the attics

*Photos:
Palladium
PhotoDesign (4)*

style, the official explanation is that with this "ironic device," Rossi laid a "counterpoint to neighboring the historically-oriented 1870's facade." A luxury department store is due to open behind the palazzo facade, and Renaissance architecture will become a means of advertisement: Michelangelo in Berlin!

Architecture insiders and Rossi connoisseurs will recognize further citations. The concave form of the tower in the Teatro del Mondo (to say nothing of its famous espresso-pot) may be hidden in the octagonal yard; five narrowly-constructed San Gimignano-towers are pressed together into one building in Zimmerstrasse 68. On the other hand a half-timbered Strasburg building type can hardly be deciphered as having been the inspiration for Markgrafenstrasse 57. The other quotations—aside from the warehouse motif in Zimmerstrasse 69, which is not by Rossi—remain purposely nebulous, like a notion or a reminiscence.

Formerly, Rossi's buildings drew their strength from reduction. In the "Quartier Schützenstrasse"—and not only there—he took the opposite path. The urge towards a multiplicity of forms is unmistakable, the efforts beyond variations in color and material impressive. The varying window shapes, the appointment of the attics, the plastic development of the facades through extroverted and reticent sections, through sills and parapets; the sometimes expressly horizontal, other times explicitly vertical division of the mostly axial-symmetric facades; and finally their own, lightly staggered

order all contribute to this effect. The great pains Rossi took with the design of his city-within-a-city were only initially devoted to the plausibility of its lot structure. Rather, the "city" was mainly dedicated to what he called a monument, so that it may have sovereignty over its use, just as it is sovereign over its environment.

If we wait until the end to inquire about the function and construction of the buildings, then we are following Rossi's priorities. His architectural sophistication has long exhausted itself in urban and facade design. One may have problems with the demonstrative indifference of his facades to what lies behind them, but at least this indifference is honest. The concrete and steel construction is without refinements and creates space for retailing, for relatively small office units, and—concentrated in three houses—for expensive apartments. What can be said? These spaces have received too many words of praise already.

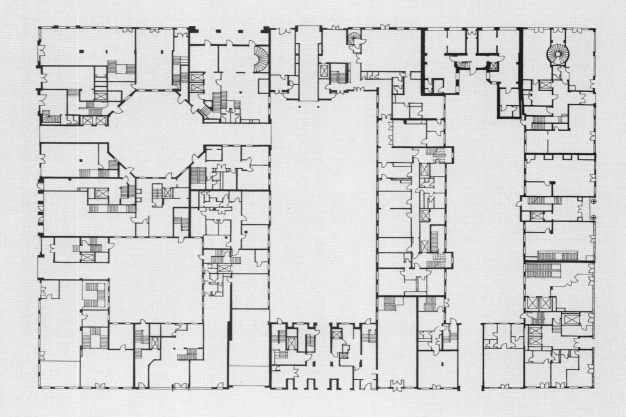

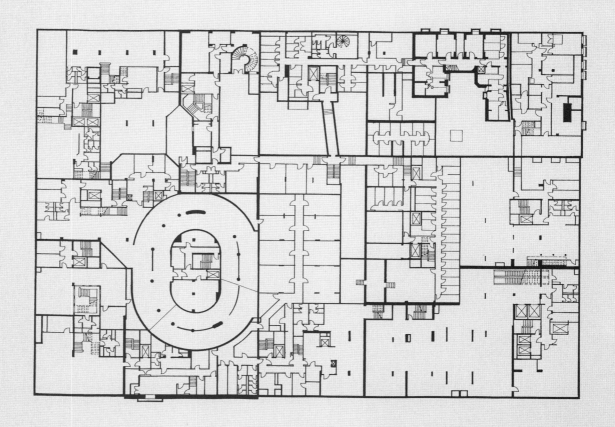

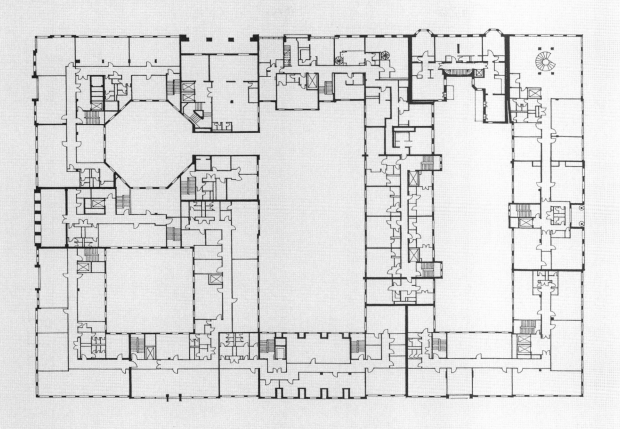

5 m   10 m

Plans of the ground floor,
basement, and first floor;
scale is 1:750.
North is at the top.
Schützenstrasse is to the
north, Zimmerstrasse to
the south, Charlotten-
strasse to the east, and
Markgrafenstrasse to
the west

5

Architects	Philip Johnson, Ritchie & Fiore Architects, New York
	PSP Pysall · Stahrenberg & Partner
Project	
Management	Christian Bjone
	Joachim Grundei
Client	CEDC Grundstücks GmbH & Co. Checkpoint Charlie KG
Network-	
Technology	CCSC Checkpoint Charlie Service Company
Opening	August 15th, 1997
Address	Friedrichstrasse 200
	Block 106
	Berlin-Mitte

Mathias Remmele
The Philip Johnson House, Friedrichstrasse 200

All photos:
Christian Gahl

We'll be held accountable and have to offer explanations. They'll ask us why this building deserves so much attention and why it's any different from the other buildings on Friedrichstrasse. We won't be able to explain it away by talking about architecture. There's no depending on architecture any more. We'll talk our way out of it by mentioning the site's uniqueness, the architect's prominence, the rumor-fueled controversy surrounding the design, and finally, a memorable lecture with the sober title, "Placing Real Estate Through Innovative Service Concepts," which was held by the investor. Those are things you can count on, things that provide support.

The emotionalism in the investor's glossy pamphlet is false, the words true: "In the beginning there was the site." The site carries a name to feed off of: Checkpoint Charlie. Only the Americans could have been so businesslike-cool, so laid-back in their superiority, so without regard for the locality when naming a militarily secured, rigorously controlled border crossing point in the divided city of Berlin. In October of 1961, shortly after the wall was built, came Checkpoint Charlie's hour of fame. No chronicle leaves it out. As things became serious the tanks stood here face to face, ready for a showdown. The exclusive border crossing point for foreigners was suddenly famous and became a symbol overnight. Ever since, it has been a de rigeur stop for visitors to West Berlin, where the Wall was shown off as a spine-chilling, exotic monument. Checkpoint Charlie—a mythical place?

The copywriters exaggerate without a second thought. Yet no doubt about it, Checkpoint Charlie is a synonym for the American presence in Berlin. It was this presence which, after the Wall came down and the armed forces left the city, was to be maintained in a civilian version: as an "American Business Center," built and managed by the speedily founded Central European Development Corporation (CEDC). The site was fitting, it was an obvious choice, and above all, it was central. The plan— back then a very trendy idea—was to use Berlin as a base from which to conquer the markets in Eastern Europe. The dreams were delayed; the word "American" has long since been deleted. The structures going up here are, as elsewhere, office buildings built for whomever.

Acquisition of the property by the CEDC didn't go quite according to plan. An attempt to obtain the mini-block containing Kleihues's "Triangle" was in vain. Yet the corporation nevertheless managed to acquire 45 former plots, spread across four neighboring quarters. The developer plans to erect five buildings here, one after the other, by the year 2000, for a total of approx. 850 million marks. Five architecture firms have been commissioned to design the buildings, two American and three German. The sites they are building on—please note the fine symbolism—are divided by nationality into an East and a West of Friedrichstrasse.

The nicest site, nicest because it occupies a whole block, was given as a direct commission to Philip Johnson. It was a deference to the old master,

View from the corner Friedrichstrasse/Mauerstrasse. J.P. Kleihues's "Triangle" is on the neighboring plot

a gesture which was heightened by the fact that the building he was to design would be the heart and crowning gem of the whole project and was to carry his name. Without a doubt it was also a fine calculation because Philip Johnson, no matter what he builds, is a guarantee for publicity.

Competitions had to be held for the other buildings.

A true "global player," David Childs of Skidmore, Owings & Merrill, is designing the "Tower Building," located south of the Johnson Building. Not yet under construction, it is the largest of the complexes by far. Facing him and also waiting to be realized will be an office building with a memorial: Berlin Wall history preserved in the "Scene of the Checkpoint." It will be built by Jürgen Engel of the Frankfurt Office of Kraemer, Sieverts and Partner. North of Engel's building and across from Johnson, Ulrike Lauber and Wolfram Wöhr from Munich have set, as the CEDC so nicely put it, a "clear and quiet accent" which is nearing completion. On the eastern part of the same block, facing onto Charlottenstrasse, Gisela Glass and Günther Bender of Berlin have designed the "Checkpoint Plaza," an apartment house which will soon be ready for occupation.

The public attention which surrounded the Checkpoint Charlie project centered, from the outset and not just coincidentally, on Philip Johnson. Berlin was flattered by his attention. The city enthusiastically took it in and saw it as a wonderful confirmation of the global importance of the site. Philip Johnson, the worldwide success, the living

legend, the genius imitator, Mies's once-was student, the figurehead of postmodernism and the promoter of deconstructivism was amply praised before he had even lifted a finger. Berlin hoped for a revelation, a new icon, at the very least a successful provocation and perhaps an alternative to "stone-faced Berlin." Admittedly, those who expected a miracle from 90-year old Johnson were the ones who don't know him and don't know that besides the architectural showpiece on his country estate in New Canaan, besides the AT&T Headquarters, the Lipstick Building and a handful of other memorable buildings, Johnson has designed a lot of mediocrities. Once Johnson presented his design and despite the fact that he had said early on that he planned to build the "most conservative" house on Friedrichstrasse, the high-flying hopes turned into the big public disappointment.

A lecture held by Johnson led to temporary confusion. In the "Berlin Lessons" in 1994 he presented a dynamically distorted creation which was not hard to recognize as a variation of his gatehouse in New Canaan, it in turn inspired by Finsterlin's architectural fantasies. This, he said, was his original design for Checkpoint Charlie. Yet in this city he hadn't been allowed to do as he pleased, the honorable Mr. Building Director of the Berlin Senate and his "stone-faced-Berlin" doctrine had thwarted all innovation in the art of building and had forced him to resort to mediocrity. Berlin would now get what it deserves: a "monstrosity." That too, he is rumored to have said.

A gag, a sly provocation, says Joachim Grundei of the Berlin office of PSP, Johnson's German partner on the Checkpoint Charlie project. The version inspired by Finsterlin or, as some found, by Zaha Hadid, was the result of a whim, an intermezzo in a sense, which was never seriously considered for realization. In reality, Johnson had never questioned either the contours of the block or the building's height as givens for his design. The first sketches for the block between Friedrichstrasse, Krausen-strasse, Mauerstrasse and Schützenstrasse show a facade divided into vertical segments of different widths. The stripes are irregularly placed and often jut into or out of the building at an angle. These slanting segments create a strangely nervous impression, as if something had gone amiss or as if the building were about to tumble down like a poorly balanced house of cards. Johnson presented his, if you will, deconstructivist-kissed design in two versions, one in glass and one in stone. The design suffered from a timid indecisiveness and from half-heartedness as evidenced by, for example, the odd contrast between the expressive motion of the facade and the conventional, steeply-pitched roof above.

A comparison of the first sketch with the real-ized plans makes clear that there was no starting over. Johnson and Grundei put their eggs into the further-development-and-final-touches basket. Their work seems to be marked by tendencies to unify and to calm down the original design. A move towards respectability, towards petty convention-

ality can hardly be overlooked. The touch of decon-structivism turned more into a brush with postmod-ernism and the debate over stone or glass as a building material was decided in favor of both. The vertical segmentation was maintained as a deter-mining element although the architects got rid of the original facade's wild back and forth move-ment. Only a few of the slanting elements survived. They now all have the same slope and are always glass clad. Four of the seven elements extend out of the building's volume at the lower level and are topped off by a fat aluminum tube. They serve as a canopy and to mark the entrances.

The finished facade of the Johnson house is characterized by the alternation of stone and glass, not by the slanting elements. The glass parts, which were also used for the corners of the building, may be more numerous, yet it is the stone-clad, towerlike parts which seem to dominate. They rage over the eaves height of the building by a story and jut out farther than the glass elements between. They create a rhythm in the facade, dif-ferentiated by the width and type of fenestration. The stone towers appear serious and massive, just as if—or let's put it more cautiously: a little bit as if—they were holding back the building behind, aided in this task by a tremendous ledgelike stone band which marks the eaves level over the fifth floor.

This effect is especially pronounced on Mauer-strasse, where the solitaire reacts to the trapezoi-dal shape of the block with an almost elegant sway of facade. Here the stone girdle becomes a hoop

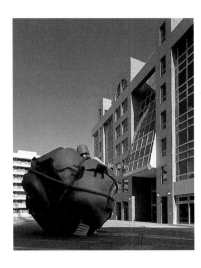

which holds back the towers like the staves of a barrel. If the stone stubs which extend higher than this encompassment and which are further emphasized by the receding glass bands between are really meant to remind one of turrets is an open question. The two quadrant windows, however, have not been enthusiastically received.

Over the ground floor is a second, less pronounced band. A wide, whitish-gray metal panel, it is limited to the area between the stone towers, tops off the base of the building, and visually separates the lower-floor commercial area from the upper-floor office levels.

Certainly, if one looks at the sometimes-stone, sometimes-glass facade segments of the Philip Johnson House, one could arrive at the conclusion that the play in materials is part of an excitingly directed game of transparent-and-closed. The architects refute such expectations. In this facade, glass by no means refers to transparency. The small aluminum profiles within the glass areas not only frame and organize the windows, which are grouped into bands, but also frame opaque glass panels which have been underlaid with gray. Located over and under the windows, these panels articulate the division of the building into stories.

The house is surrounded by an aura of cool seriousness and well-tended boredom. Except for the greenish shimmer of the windows everything is in shades of gray: the glass panels are lead gray, the blazed granite is light gray with a hint of violet, the metal panels and window profiles are whitish

gray, and the aluminum tubes over the entrances are silver gray. These shades of gray meet without meshing, and neither contrast nor harmonize with each other.

The strangely dull natural stone, originally meant to be sandstone, doesn't reveal much about its history. The truth is that Grundei, the architect, and CEDC manager Schmeller voyaged to a far corner of the Brazilian woods in search of the ultimate stone cladding. Having collected various samples, they traveled to the East Coast of the United States, to Mr. Johnson in New Canaan. There the samples were sighted and discussed and a decision was made in favor of the ultimate stone, the one-and-only. Ordered, quarried and shipped, the Brazilian granite landed in Carrara, Italy, where it was cut into facade-portioned pieces and surface treated. Then it was carted to the center of Berlin, Friedrich-strasse 200. And there it now hangs.

The three below-grade and eight upper floors of the Philip Johnson House, arranged around two interior courtyards, were designed to contain office space exclusively. The city ordinance mandating the building of apartments was circumvented with the "plaza." As is usual, the underground parking garage, and storage and mechanical areas are located in the basements, shops and restaurants are located on the ground floor, and the top seven floors, up to the recessed roof story, are filled with office space. Each floor contains six independently leasable office units, each of which is between 250 and 680 square meters large. The interior design

The "atrium" in the
middle of the crossing
paths serves as entry
hall. Functioning as the
building's calling card,
the passageways have
purposely been left
void of commercial
establishments

The square in front of
the building on Mauer-
strasse. Traced on the
ground is the outline of
the former Bohemian
Church

of the offices is based on a grid of 1.35 meters and, as is standard practice now, will be finished in accordance with the tenant's wishes and needs.

A 30 cm high, double-floor construction contains the building's technical infrastructure, thus avoiding the need for suspended ceilings and creating a better climate in the building. The showpiece of the mechanical concept is, however, an element which can "heat, circulate air, and cool all in one"—a new patent developed by one of the engineers. The windows, by the way, can be opened.

The way into the Philip Johnson House is from all four sides. The entrances on the longer sides, facing Friedrichstrasse and Mauerstrasse, have been emphasized by making them larger. At the Mauerstrasse entrance one passes Claes Oldenburg's "Houseball" sculpture on a small plaza. The pavement of this plaza has been marked—so much history is meant to be seen—with the plan of Bethlehem Church (also called the Bohemian Church), which was destroyed in the war.

Two interior streets which cross at right angles to each other, and on which are located the elevators and stairwells, allow passage through the building. In contrast to other buildings on Friedrichstrasse, these throughways have been kept free of shops in order to preserve their distinction and nobility. Obviously meant to be a sort of calling card, and noticeably in the spirit of an American high-rise lobby, the visitor is received by a stony-stern ambiance. At the crossing point of the corridor axes and on the exact position of the northern

courtyard, the corridors turn into a three-story hall, a sort of internal square, covered by skylights. The investor calls this, again prone to misunderstandings, an atrium. This space, Johnson let it be known, was inspired by Tessenow's swimming hall in the Stadtbad Mitte. The airy lightness of the model turned into stony monumentality exuding the cool noblesse of a mausoleum in the copy. The multivision video wall, a tested remedy against too much reverence, once again shows what this building is all about.

What is to be done when, in light of the increasingly obvious overabundance of office space, neither the building itself, nor the site, nor the prominent architect can guarantee that the place will be booked? When, "today you can't earn money with money"? The "state of the art" in real-estate marketing is innovative service concepts with which a building attends to its potential tenants. The heart is the Checkpoint Charlie Intranet. Just plug in, the network computer is at your command, "cc-Online Service" needs you and feeds you and gives you what you want whenever you want it. BBS = "Best-Buy-Service" is as effective for your private wishes as is E+S "Economy through Scale" for your business affairs. Need bundling and advanced technology = magic. LCR = "Least Cost Routing" offers the least expensive route for every telephone call and in case you lose track of things in the face of this confusing array of offers just turn to S.P.O.C.

Oh yes—he's your Single Point of Contact.

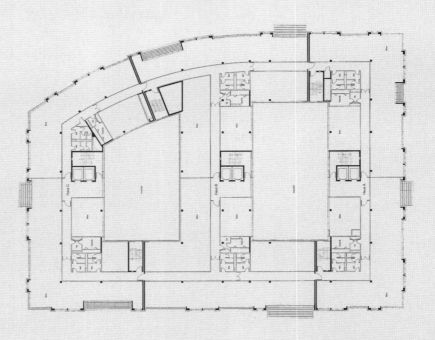

Plans of the ground floor,
a typical upper floor
(shown is the 4th), and
roof (7th) floor, as well as
a longitudinal section,
all to a scale of 1:750.
North is to the right,
Friedrichstrasse is at the
bottom of the drawing

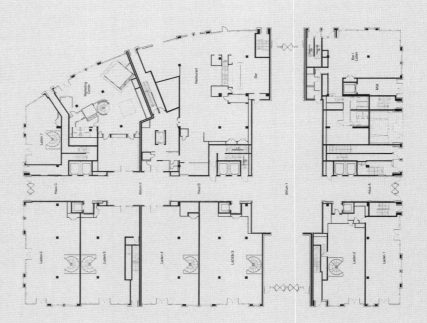

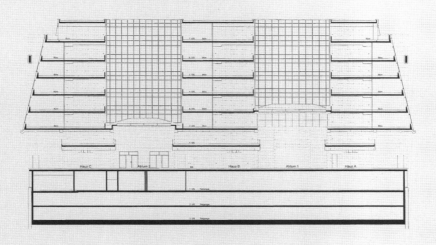

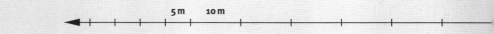

5 m   10 m

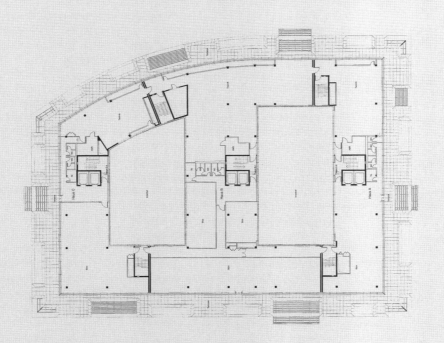

Philipp Moritz Reiser
At the Spittelmarkt

is a good place to stop for a while, especially now in the spring of 1997, before the new buildings begin populating the empty place. It is not even the real Spittelmarkt where we are standing, just an address that calls itself "At the Spittelmarkt" and invokes something that has not existed in years. Actually there are two streets, Beuthstrasse and Seydelstrasse, which meet here at a sharp corner. Because the gore between them is still largely undeveloped (excluding the new Concordia-Haus which either looks lost or, shall we say, mistakenly preserved) one might think here, yes, here was the place of the former Spittelmarkt, which we know was a triangular square that originally lay outside the city walls. Besides its classical name, refering to a hospital, there is little else people know. Were not the hospitals always beyond the city's gates? Did they not always have churches nearby and later became important and acquired a central role in the very heart of the city?

The so-called Spittel Colonnades (a partial copy of the colonnades built in 1730) give us no hint whatsoever. They stand far away on Leipziger Strasse, on the former Dönhoffplatz, but do not belong anywhere.

Way back then, the square got its shape from the tip end of an 18th century bastion and has remained in memory ever since as a triangular square. Thus the eyes' forgivable error of believing the former Spittelmarkt to have been in the undeveloped gore south of Leipziger Strasse. Actually, it lay farther north, where Leipziger Strasse's eight lanes turn a corner and lead over the flat new Gertraudenbrücke. The old bridge bearing the same name still exists a stone's throw distance to the north. The Spittelmarkt has left its name behind but today the historical location and its name fall separately.

A photographic stroll around the square with the borrowed name shows the buildings surrounding it. Even though they stand one next to the other, they seem so isolated, as though they will only be staying a while or had temporarily accepted such a neighborhood because of the famous address, which attracts visitors as well. Or as if each one of them were the outset of a different story, which began here only through chance. Nothing in the city's layout prepares the approach to the square, and if it weren't for all the buildings looking down at or into it nobody would know exactly where he was. But up there the Morgenpost lettering gets into the picture and the Springer highrise still stands planted at the edge of the Wall that no longer exists. The Springer publishing house still imagines the Wall being there, because it was defiance of the Wall that placed the building where it is. Everybody saw it there, sparkling gold colored, signaling. The towers on Leipziger Strasse lean into the void as well. The neighboring highrise has already been meticulously restored, securing the further existence of the others, and we cannot, we will not do without them; they formed the picture from the other side for so long. Now, as the surrounding street walls have not yet been closed,

The square to the south
of the historically
authentic Spittelmarkt.
Every direction opens up
vistas of a different
architectural history.
Behind the glass facade,
the new Federal Printing
Plant; in the courtyard,
the pews of the demol-
ished synagogue, set up
as they were after the fire

Photos:
Barbara Müller (2)
Johannes Uhl (2)
Erik-Jan Ouwerkerk (1)

the artificial Mendelsohn building at the corner
of Zimmerstrasse butts in as well. Rising above
the low bar that distorts the entrance to Leipziger
Strasse is the television tower, far away at Alexanderplatz.

So we know where we are. If we take into
account the new building of the Federal Printing
Plant along Kommandantenstrasse, it's even an
important place. The office building by Wolfgang
Schuster (BHHS & Partner) appears as a collage of
architectures, completely untypical in light of the
mandated closure of the street facades and of its
hidden uses, but glassy-bright, especially now
with the desert sands at its feet. Inside they print
that great German money of which one shouldn't
have too much, but not too little either. In the
shadow of the safe, reachable through the driveway of the new Barmer Insurance office building on
Axel-Springer-Strasse, we find ourselves in a yard
with high grass and birch trees the way they grow
in Berlin between unused railroads; with pews
set up, the pews of the Liberal Synagogue Lindenstrasse. When it was destroyed, part of its outline
remained behind, as if sawed off. The plaques
along the driveway say this was how the pews
stood without a roof after the fire. Now, they do so
once again (design: Zvi Hecker, Micha Ullman, and
Eyal Weizman). From the gateway the view goes
back to the unshakably heavy building along
Wallstrasse with its round arch windows visible
beyond grass and commercial cardboard. The Axel
Springer Building directly adjacent, looking newly

Windowed courtyard facade of the Axel Springer Building. Two prefabricated buildings, the left neighbor newly clad. To the east, a white building built in 1991 but sporting a 1960's exterior. Behind is a green housing oasis. And the building site around Hans Heinrich Müller's main station

Photos:
Barbara Müller (8)
Johannes Uhl (1)

refurbished, confuses the view. Its regularly punched facade towards the opened courtyard, isn't this exemplary Berlin architecture of the present?

Confusion all over, those two houses which close the still-empty square to the north, aren't those flat buildings twins? We assume the original stands to the right and that a shimmering new raincoat was later thrown over its neighbor, but that, nobody can confirm. To the east appears the house on Neue Grünstrasse, still without neighbors and on an empty part of the street; a municipal housing project of 1991, brick pedestal, windows in rows. Directly behind, a nearly suburban residential area begins, with staggered four-story buildings under trees amidst very lush greenery, once built in and against the shadow of the Wall. Next to it, at a small distance, there stands a piece of Berlin's industrial history. Franz Schwechten's power station, built in 1905, is seeing plenty of concrete laid behind its impenetrable construction site fences. From Neue Grünstrasse one only sees the main station by Hans Heinrich Müller. This building councillor, reputed to have beautifully played violin, erected his strict, quiet BEWAG buildings all over Berlin from 1924 to 1933. One meets them like old friends.

Strange and beautiful and at a distance to the Federal Printing Plant: the white house with upright-format windows. It seems as if there were two stories above the roof's edge. Characters spelling out "Fashion Center Berlin Mitte" appear over the entrance and once again, big, on the side wall.

Totally East German and totally historical, the Western stroller tells himself, mistakenly: Its name before reunification was Muratti Haus and it only became a fashion shop in 1993. The new architect from Wattenscheid, as the informed custodian knows, discovered the beautiful lettering in a Finnish magazine and imported it to Berlin. The next reconstruction will follow soon and will stretch the building's front to the street. The many small firms and the mannequins sitting around in the display window facing the yard, the sewing machines and racks with serial fashion ("Ladies' fashion for all, straight from the factory") will move out for now. Next door appears the wall of the old Federal Printing Plant, yellow brick, raised roof, in between a brick wing with a white panel in front. The wall's sections add up to something like a picture (which will not exist much longer) that forces itself upon the photographer, precisely because it is so hard to decipher.

From the other side as well, from Alte Jakobstrasse, one cannot really tell what is happening to the old industrial building. The view rests on the idyllic flower pots, set in a row on the courtyard wall of the only squatted building on the square. Inhabitants sit out in front with their dog. How must they feel among the fences, the barriers, the planks, the cranes, the piles of unlaid pipes, while above and beneath them everything is being improved, added on, stuck on, smoothed out and rented out. It won't be much longer until the magnificent "domicile at the Spittelmarkt," the

Sustained time, unusual
neighbors: The Fashion
Center Berlin-Mitte next
to the Federal Printing
Plant, the turquoise fire
wall, the metal-sheeted
gap between the bronze
grid and the historic
facade

The Concordia Building has settled in the midst of the construction site to signal that its developer is committed. He intends to build nothing short of a "small government quarter", and the "Luisenhof"

Photos:
Barbara Müller (1)
Johannes Uhl (4)
Christian Gahl (1)

Luisenhof, will be standing on Seydelstrasse, with its peaceful, double-skinned facade, loggia on loggia; behind it a broad assortment of one- and two-room apartments (architect: RCA P. Coenen, Cologne). From the rear, noise flares from Alte Jakobstrasse, construction like mad here too. New facades crowding in next to one another, the Concordia Bau und Boden AG, with its administration building standing so courageously amid the desolation, is responsible for the Luisenhof; and Concordia is also building a "little government quarter along Spree Island." The first new building of the complex at the corner of Seydelstrasse is already inhabited; other office buildings, a bit further up Alte Jakobstrasse, will be completed shortly. Back to Neue Grünstrasse, the new houses must be visible somewhere. We find them in a courtyard, as the newly-built facades force their way from two sides into the tiny idyll of the Luisenstadt Congregational Yard of St. Peter, barely screened by chestnut and lime trees.

Long before construction and excavation began, the Kontorhaus am Spittelmarkt, Neue Grünstrasse 17/18 stood like a beacon in the storm. This trade building, which was built around 1900, was perfectly, no, if not perfectly, then exceedingly lovingly restored down to the elaborately painted walls and ceilings of the staircase, the brass details in the entrance, the three courtyards, one past the other, all the way to Alte Jakobstrasse. A high, dark, skylit roof was placed overhead, which the photographer refused to acknowledge, but which

the city and the office of historical preservation allowed. The Kontorhaus Spittelmarkt, finished since October 1994, was the first to awaken affections for this peculiar locality.

Soon, two slab-construction buildings will define the triangle between Seydelstrasse and Beuthstrasse. The clients, the Federal Printing Plant Mitte and the debis real estate corporation, simply call their project Spittelmarkt, just like the adjacent subway station. Zaha M. Hadid is responsible for the preliminary design, while the architecture offices for its execution are Hentrich, Petschnigg & Partners (HPP), Hamburg/Berlin, Hans Strauch, HDS & Gallagher Inc., Boston, and Dieter Schneider & Partner, Berlin. The tall, twenty-story slab is placed in line with the Leipziger Strasse highrises, and is accompanied by a ten-story wing. Both wings extend southwards and define the new city block. Three perpendicular rows behind create narrow courtyards between them. Here, on the street, the Berlin height limit of 22 meters once again holds sway, even on Seydelstrasse, where all the balconies of the existing apartment edifices have their little balcony-idylls facing the street. The visitor to the carcass is sceptical, even though a hundred-year-old facade was obligingly preserved and embedded in the new building and even though the word "Glück," happiness, appears on the window lintels. "At home downtown" say the brochures for the future apartments in the rows between the yards. "As far as Downtown goes", thinking of nearby Friedrichstrasse, of the future

From the building complex between Seydelstrasse and Beuthstrasse, one highrise wing arises to line up with the buildings along Leipziger Strasse. Below: the Spittel Colonnades. Next to each other: the old and new Gertrauden Bridges

government quarter, and the prominent cornerstone laying for the "House of the German Economy," the visitor is ready to agree.

Through Neue Ross Strasse back to Wallstrasse. Catercorner across appears the new facade of the art'otel at the Ermeler-Haus by architects Gernot and Johanne Nalbach. Otherwise the visitor strolls along a nearly constant street-scene with many historic buildings on both sides either restored or under protection as monuments. We pass the "Wall Courtyards" to the left, then the empty display windows of the Hellerau workshops. The wild mix only begins again on Neue Grünstrasse, with a gem from 1840, Nr. 23, just around the corner. Across the street is the milky-bronze colored, patterned house of the Ingenieurbau GmbH, where a metal sheet stamped with hexagonal holes daringly closes the gap to the old building. A sky-blue light shines in from the neighboring yard.

The original Spittelmarkt, nothing more than the place currently bearing its name, was full of famous neighborhoods which lie farther away in the imagination. A bit along Lindenstrasse is the Berlin Museum with the almost-complete Jewish Museum by Daniel Libeskind. A jump over the Grünstrassen Bridge, with a small detour to the left—we concede, Leipziger Strasse is still to be crossed — and the visitor is greeted by the Nikolaiviertel, the Red City Hall, and the empty center of Berlin. The square which soon will no longer be a square spreads outwards in rings. Its non-composition is its promise.

"Wherever massed stone meets fleeting streets, their elements arising from very different interest, random creations ensue, which are accountable to no one." Thus wrote Siegfried Kracauer. This he called his "unaffected Berlin," which, like a landscape, "unconsciously holds its own."

7

Architects of the Facade	Patzschke, Klotz und Partner, Berlin
Architects of the Building	AIC, Munich
Interior Design	Ezra Attia, London AD Living Design, Stockholm
Project Management	Altstadt GmbH
Client	Fundus Fonds-Verwaltungen Jagdfeld Hotel Adlon Nr. 31 KG
General Contractor	Bredero Projekt Berlin GmbH
Opening	August 23th, 1997
Address	Unter den Linden 77 Berlin-Mitte

Vicki Baum's "Grand Hotel" — a Collage
Hotel Adlon

Grand Hotel, Behind the Scenes

*Photos: PR Office
Kempinski Hotels (1)
Michael Krone (1)
Erik-Jan Ouwerkerk (1)*

There's a lot of talk about the new Hotel Adlon at Pariser Platz—some of it enthusiastic, some reserved, some ironic, some disparaging. Only just opened and not yet occupied by its guests, the hotel is still unmarked by all that is brought in from the outside by those who come there. And so it has no answer for the many voices, nothing but its new architecture and its old name. That name, in turn, sets the standard against which the hotel is measured before it even has a chance to prove itself. What goes without saying for a grand hotel is the silent functioning behind the scenes, the perfect mechanism backdoors, the making of the show. The players in the performance "grand hotel" are joined by the architecture, the spatial atmosphere, the furnishings, the theatrical sense of time, the service, the technology, and the guests, above all the guests: the one-time visitors and those who come again and again, the called-for prominency, the snobs and the unknowns who may later contribute to a new legend. The figures in the ca. 50-year-old texts by Vicki Baum quoted here are Herr Kringelein and Doctor Otternschlag, the one entering a grand hotel for the first time in his life, the other living there apathetically for years. The figures in the photo series are the present-day actors behind the scenes. In the following, the hardware of the modern-day Hotel Adlon—the number of rooms, restaurants, bars, and banquet rooms, the marble, wallcoverings, wood, and paint—are all listed in their proper order.

The Hotel Adlon offers
79 deluxe rooms
93 superior rooms
94 executive rooms
30 business rooms
9 business suites
5 Unter den Linden suites
5 studio suites
3 junior suites
5 Pariser Platz suites
3 Brandenburger Tor suites
2 presidential suites

All rooms have
1 air-conditioning unit
1 stereo-TV
2 telephones
1 telefax
2 PC outlets
1 room safe
1 minibar

The presidential suites offer
1 dining room for 12 persons
1 salon with grand piano and
fireplace
1 library
1 study
2 bedrooms, 2 baths
1 whirlpool
2 saunas
1 kitchen

The whole house is an eyeful with
… a monumental staircase of white marble … the
"Balcony of the World" on the bel etage … the
glass dome with gold and royal-blue mosaic …
vaulted coffered ceilings with gold-leaf intarsia …
the restored elephant fountain from the Goethe-
hof of the old Adlon … walls of cream-colored
native Jurassic stone … antiques from 18th and
19th-century England … Empire style furniture,
brass tables with intarsia, decorated candelabra
… a Tiepolo copy painted on the library ceiling …
plane wood and green marble in the ballroom,
as well as three magnificent chandeliers …
checkered floors of black slate and white marble
in the winter gardens … bordeaux-red leather
upholstery and walls of whitened oak in the American Bar … hand-painted leather in the Bundes-
zimmer with the coats-of-arms of the Federal
States … colonnades, wall paintings, and mosaics
reminiscent of Roman baths in the classicizing
Wellness Center … ceiling-high French windows
in the rooms and furniture of cherry and myrtle
wood … luxurious suede upholstery … throws and
draperies of yellow, beige, and gold-colored
damask … chairs and armchairs in fine horsehair
… walls and doors with cherry and rootwood
veneer … baths in black granite, light marble, and
wood paneling … doorknobs of gold-burnished
brass … the Adlon Basket ("Adlon Putzkorb").

For leisure, guests have a
choice of
1 restaurant/bistro
1 lobby lounge
1 American Bar
2 winter gardens
1 club bar
1 mezzanine lounge
1 ballroom
6 private dining rooms

For business, the hotel offers
3 auditoriums
1 business center with
2 perfectly equipped offices
3 conference rooms

For shopping is available
1 shopping arcade with
12 shops and boutiques
1 hair salon
1 florist

Recreational facilities consist of
1 Wellness Center with
1 indoor pool
1 whirlpool
1 steam bath
2 saunas
2 solariums
3 massage and fitness rooms
1 pool bar

The music from the tea-room in the new building beat in syncopation from mirror to mirror along the walls. It was dinner time and a smell of cooking was in the air, but behind the closed doors of the large dining-room there was still silence and vacancy. The Chef, Mattoni, was setting out his cold buffet in the small white room. The porter felt a strange weakness in his knees and he stopped a moment in the doorway, arrested

by the bright gleams of the colored lights behind the blocks of ice ... Here the jazz band from the tea-room encountered the violins from the Winter Garden, while mingled with them came the thin murmur of the illuminated fountain as it fell into its imitation Venetian basin, the ring of glasses on tables, the creaking of wicker chairs and, lastly, a soft rustle of the furs and silks in which women were moving to and fro. A cool March air came in gusts through the revolving doors whenever the page-boy passed guests in or out ...
Doctor Otternschlag behind in his corner shivered and yawned. He looked between his patent-leather shoes at the carpet that everywhere covered the stairs, passages and corridors of the Grand Hotel; he was sick of its straggling pattern of yellow pine-apples mingled with brown foliage on a raspberry-red ground.

Photos:
Erik-Jan Ouwerkerk

Room No. 70 was the right thing. It had mahogany furniture, a cheval glass, silk upholstery, a carved writing-table, lace curtains and a picture of pheasants on the wall. Also a silk down quilt on the bed. Kringelein incredulously felt its lightness, its smoothness and its warmth three times in succession. On the writing-table stood a most superior bronze inkstand in the form of an eagle whose jagged outstretched wings sheltered two empty inkpots.

Outside the window there was a chill March rain, a smell of petrol, and the sound of motor traffic. Opposite, an electric sign in red, blue and white letters occupied the whole facade. As soon as it had run along to the end it began again at the beginning. Kringelein watched it for six minutes. Down below in the street there was a medley of black umbrellas, light-colored stockings, yellow buses and arc lights. There was even a tree that spread its branches not far from the hotel, but its branches were very different from those in Fredersdorf. This Berlin tree had a little island of soil in the midst of the asphalt and round the plot of soil there was a railing as though it needed some protection against the town. Kringelein, surrounded by so much that was strange and overwhelming, found something friendly in this tree.

So there he stood in the lounge of the Grand Hotel — Otto Kringelein, book-keeper, and the glasses of his pince-nez eagerly devoured it all. He saw men in dress coats and dinner-jackets, smart cosmopolitan men. Women with bare arms, in wonderful clothes, with jewellery and furs, beautiful, well-dressed women. He heard music in the distance. He smelt coffee, cigarettes, scent, whiffs of asparagus from the dining-room and the flowers that were displayed for sale on the flower-stall. He felt the thick red carpet beneath his black leather boots and this perhaps impressed him most of all. Kringelein slid the sole of his boot gingerly over its pile and blinked. The Lounge was brilliantly illuminated and the light was delightfully golden; also there were bright red-shaded lights against the walls and the jets of the fountain in the Venetian basin shone green. A waiter flitted by carrying a silver tray on which were wide shallow glasses with a little dark-gold cognac in each, and in the cognac ice was floating; but why in Berlin's best hotel were the glasses not filled to the brim? ... The guests as are to be seen in a big hotel during the morning are all solid and industrious business men. They sit in the Lounge and conduct their business in all languages, selling stocks and shares, cotton lubricating oil, patents, films, and real estate — and also plans, ideas, energy, and even life itself. They make a heavy breakfast and leave the breakfast-room full of cigar smoke ...

Director	Jean K. van Daalen
Acting Director	Carsten K. Rath
Head Housekeeper	Christine Woelke
Technical Director	Martin Hilbert
Chef	Karlheinz Hauser
Sommelier	Philippe Bouffey
Head of Reception	Matthias Beuge
Head Concierge	Ralf Räther
Back of the House Manager	Stefan Huemer
Head Steward	Carsten Friebe
Banquet Service Director	Michael Sorgenfrey
Adlon Basket Weaving Master	Jürgen Althaus

All photos:
Erik-Jan Ouwerkerk

Nobody bothers about anyone else in a big hotel. Everybody is alone with himself in this great pub that Doctor Otternschlag not inaptly compared with life in general. Everyone lives behind double doors and has no confidant but his reflection in the looking-glass or his shadow on the wall. People brush past one another in the passages, say good morning or good evening in the Lounge, sometimes even enter into a brief conversation painfully raked together out of the barren topics of the day. A glance that travels up does not reach the eyes. It stops at your clothes. Perhaps it happens that a dance in the Yellow Pavilion brings two bodies into contact. Perhaps someone steals out of his room into another's. That is all. Behind is an abyss of loneliness. Even the honeymoon couple in Room No. 134 are parted as they lie in bed by a vacancy of unspoken words. Many wedded couples of boots and shoes that stand outside the doors at night wear a distinct expression of mutual hatred on their leather visages, and many have a jaunty air though they are hopeless and lop-eared.
Translation by Basil Creighton, 1950

8

Investing in Berlin

Interview with Klaus Groth, Industrie- und Wohnbau Groth + Graalfs GmbH, on Sept. 29th, 1997

What draws you to Berlin as an investor?
Which hopes led you to come here before the fall of the Berlin Wall;
what future did you see for Berlin after 1989?

My connection to the city? I can tell you exactly when it started and why I'm still drawn to Berlin. The first time I came here was in 1960. I was at the Verwaltungs-akademie [Management Academy] in Kiel. Back then we had to take a field trip to Berlin as part of our political education. What we experienced in those ten days seemed absolutely incredible to us. All of a sudden we found ourselves enraptured by the dimension of this city, with its theaters, its night life; its East Berlin and the tension between the two halves of the city. One evening, the subway had long since stopped running for the night, three of us were walking through the downtown area and then and there three people swore to themselves, "When we're financially independent we're coming to Berlin."

And when exactly did you come? In 1971 I had my first business dealings here. It was a project on the upper Kurfürs-tendamm. But I had more ambitious plans, I wanted to build a Hyatt Hotel on the prominent corner property where the Grundkredit Bank stands today. The project wasn't realized but the dice had fallen.

From November of 1977 on, I had a small office in Berlin, two rooms on Uhlandstrasse. In 1980–81 I came to stay permanently. Back then, Berlin was at its lowest—from my point of view. The government had been toppled, the political situation was unstable, Kufürstendamm was boarded up, people threw stones at you. For my first big event in the tumultuous district of Kreuzberg I—raised in the north—showed up in a dark blue suit with a white tie. That, of course, was a bad move. Four hundred people booed me.

Back then I asked myself for the first time: What tolerance does this city demand? And what tolerance can I count on? Sometimes I lay awake nights wondering how I'd deal with it all the next day. What would I wear, was the city asking that I change? I said to myself, you want to have an influence on what's happening, you want to exercise all the creative power you have and the city has to take you as you are — and it did. In 1982 I got together with Dieter Graalfs; inwardly well prepared, I feel …

The tolerance you refer to, do you feel it today in the same way?

Berlin has become even more tolerant. Building in Berlin has become accepted, in part due to the campaigns of the Verband Freier Wohnungsunternehmen Berlin/Brandenburg [Association of Free Housing Enterprises Berlin/Brandenburg]. Take for example our campaign "Building for Berlin" in the 1980's and "Building for the Year 2000" in the past years. It was an incredible challenge, to strengthen the independent existence and the self confidence of this walled-in city through small steps. Our project on Rauchstrasse for instance, which was part of the International Building Exhibition [IBA]; that was a milestone in what can be done with small steps. The IBA offered us the chance to work with many international architects, despite the fact that we were dealing with relatively small building volumes. Hans Hollein, Rob Krier, Aldo Rossi, Giorgio Grassi, Charles Moore, they all came to Berlin back then and we were able to employ them later on as well.

Not that it was easy. If we had an appointment with the banks in Frankfurt because of a larger investment we were told that clients from Berlin aren't competitive and that they don't have a clue what market means. It took a lot of energy to convince them of the contrary. The only really prominent building in an urban sense which we built during that time was the Grundkredit Bank on Kurfürstenstrasse. The attraction of my job, for me, lies in the prospect of shaping the city and contributing to its development and change and using all the creative possibilities my job has to offer.

And when the Wall came down and the possibilities to shape the city suddenly became so much richer, how did you react?

First of all we, like everyone else, let our feelings take hold, but after that we reacted very swiftly. We made two basic decisions. First, we decided to predominantly stay in housing. That's been our main focus for the past 30 years and it's the area in which we have the most experience. Also, we were convinced that the need for housing would grow immensely. Second, we decided to also concentrate on commercial projects. We immediately secured properties, good sites in the center of the city. For example on Cicerostrasse and on Torstrasse. We also bought an old building, which has since been restored, on Friedrichstrasse.

If you look back at the past eight years, which things have changed?

Several things which we considered extremely important back then, unfortunately couldn't be realized. Something which we had our hearts set on was the joint planning of Berlin and Brandenburg [fusion of the two states was rejected in a referendum held in 1995 — translators note]. It would have meant better control over the structure of Berlin's edges and would have prevented, or at least delayed, the big shopping centers which were built on the green fields surrounding the city. In that, we didn't succeed. The competition between the two states is on, that was to be expected, and we're right in the middle of it.

What also changed: 1990/91 they showered us with predictions for enormous growth rates for Berlin. They didn't come true. One reason for that was certainly that the federal government's move from Bonn to Berlin was delayed in 1991. Another reason was market changes the world over. How many international investors wanting to build came to Berlin back then — almost all of them have since withdrawn, both because of economic instability and a tighter money flow in their own countries. The third reason is changes in need prognoses. From mid-1993 onwards we were suddenly working with totally different figures. Yet projects which were decided on in 1992 can't be stopped in 1995, they're long since under construction. So the volume was in the making and we now have an overabundance of office and service space and an extraordinarily relaxed market for housing, such as Berlin hasn't seen since 1945. Now everyone could be cheering, but instead they're disappointed because there's a surplus.

Ridiculous. The market is relaxed now but let's talk again in the year 2001. Because of the reduction in housing construction from 100 to 10 we'll have a bottleneck like no one can imagine now. The demand will be there. I can tell you today that what the government's currently doing in this area will result in a bitter backlash in 1999, 2000 or 2001. In the office sector the surplus will recede more gradually, especially in the peripheral areas. In the inner city, I'm certain the demand will already exceed the supply by next year.

But what have these eight years brought you? We were very lucky to be able to successfully realize two large development areas: Kirchsteigfeld and Karow-Nord, both large-scale, low-rise housing projects. Kirchsteigfeld is pretty much completed and a large part of the apartments in Karow-Nord are also occupied. Karow will be completely finished by the middle of next year at the latest.

Both of these ventures were the result of public-private partnerships on the basis of urban planning contracts. That seems to be usual nowadays. What direction are we moving in? Where is the balance between the responsibility of the public sector and that of the private investor? The public-private model isn't as complicated as many people think. And it isn't really new. Look at the Preussische Ansiedlungsgesetz [Prussian Settlement Law] of 1887 and of 1904; even back then, a very similar cooperation between the public and the private sector was made possible. 1971 saw the Städtebauförderungsgesetz [Urban Development Promotion Acts], which allowed for development contracts, enabling private enterprises to take over important public tasks.

The Massnahmen [Measures] law of 1990 again gives us the opportunity to form extensive contracts between the public sector and private companies, to date with great success. The public sector is able to pass on large parts of the preparation and implementation of a project to private companies, where they're organized according to principles found in private industry. That means tasks can be dealt with concurrently, while the public sector is forced to deal with them one after the other. We prepared projects in 15 months which otherwise would have taken four years. Of course that saves money. What you need in order to make such a system work is high transparency and, of course, everyone involved has to be able to absolutely trust each other. On the other hand, this system has raised some doubts too. The public sector, in order to work more economically, cuts back on its employment. Through the public-private constellation the public sector loses task areas, with which it could have maybe held jobs. It's a competitive situation, which in 1992 would have been unthinkable. But the indisputable success, in terms of quality, speed, and cost-cutting, demands that these measures be made law.

A recreational question: Does an investor have a cultural responsibility? Without a doubt. Building is culture, it reflects the times, it has a historical and a societal dimension. That's the only way I can think as a developer. Try to precisely define what is asked of a particular building. It's not that easy. But if you don't stipulate a building's profile and its philosophy, then your planning has no culture. Building philosophy means, to state it simply: What should the finished building tell a stranger standing before it? When I think of how long we discussed the substance of the CDU [Christian Democratic Union] Building, the philosophy of a building for such a large people's [political] party …

Everyone knocks the architect. That's totally wrong. It's the client who should be criticized. He's the one who authorizes the design.

But what about the architect's responsibility? Seen with old-fashioned eyes which seek the technical detail, one could find something missing here and there …

In order to be fair, you have to differentiate. We stress the developer's job, which is why we're passionately conservative and old

fashioned, in the sense of the old master builder. That's why we have to struggle and why we can't avoid responsibility for things when something really goes wrong. Point number two: What we do, we do for others. No one has the right to show off, neither we nor the architect. Yet the architect comes under pressure if he can't find someone who'll take over the master builder role. He has to deal with the market, with the allotted volume, with economic demands, and with the constructive simplifications of a general contractor. Put into such a straitjacket, there's not a lot he can do. For that reason, our company has always worked without a general contractor. The person who coordinates the trades sits in our offices. We bring together, that's our strength. That's why we say that in many localities we've managed to create architecture which really stands out. Kirchsteigfeld is for me one of the best examples of master building. What commitment, what passion was manifested there, not just by us as client representatives with a whole collection of architects but also by the architects among themselves. We're great defenders of the open workshop process. And what we accomplished with our two suburbs! As far as I'm concerned, the extraordinary architectural variety in Kirchsteigfeld, the quarters which were developed, the design of the interior courtyards, the well-done facades of the public and private spaces, they're all the result of discussions between 10, 12, 14 people sitting at a table for days on end.

You're the head of the Verband Freier Wohnungsunternehmen [Association of Free Housing Enterprises] in Berlin/Brandenburg. Subsidized housing is being severely cut back, but aren't free-market rents unaffordable for many? What does the future hold?

The period of almost wholly subsidized housing construction in Berlin is ultimately over. Despite severe cutbacks in the construction of subsidized housing we can expect further decreases in the future. We have to adapt to the changed situation and keep the market in mind. Conditions for housing construction as a whole have gotten worse. Consider, for example, the special write-offs allowed under the Fördergebietsgesetz [a law defining areas to be promoted] for new construction, which have been reduced by 50% and as of 1999 will disappear altogether. Though the planned tax reform has been stopped for the present, the conditions for building investments have been unfavorable long since. And yet, we currently have an objective need for housing, which hasn't appeared as a demand only because of the poor economic situation. That will change when the government moves from Bonn to Berlin. The Association estimates the real need for housing at 22,000 apartments annually in Berlin and 20,000 in Brandenburg.

What about privatly owned housing?

Ownership of housing is rare in Berlin. When you consider total housing, the rate of ownership is only 9%. In the Federal Republic it's 40%, in the rest of Europe it's as high as 62%. We're counting on tremendous need, especially with people moving here from West Germany. That's especially true for the inner city areas. Here we're expecting a structural change and a complete shift in the social class of the population. Just think of what's happening at Potsdamer Platz, where thousands of new jobs are being created. Just think of the embassy employees and those of the associations, of the media and last but not least the federal government. These people have a salary structure which is atypical for Berlin and they'll be moving here. We're already experiencing a demand for posh condominiums in price classes of between 6,500 and 8,000 marks or between 7,500 and 10,000 marks per square meter. In special cases the demand is for considerably more luxurious apartments. But up until now Berlin hasn't had been able to supply such apartments which could be put on a level with those of Munich, Hamburg or Düsseldorf.

Can you think of a solution?

We have to principally create owner-occupied real estate — and we have to continuously raise the rate of ownership.

We also have to move new housing construction away from subsidy programs and into the realm of privately financed housing. But for that we need creativity and a willingness to communicate on the part of politicians and administrators. We need a better economic framework and what we absolutely need is a rigorous implementation of the planned deregulation of building-and-planning laws. Above all, what we're really lacking are adequate properties.

The Berlin Senate has to speedily designate and develop new sites. It's high time the riverside properties in the inner city were developed, underused areas more densely built up, and government properties offered at favorable conditions in order to construct privately financed housing. The Senate has finally reacted and is working on a catalog of unused sites, along with the districts. A list should also be made in the near future of potential housing sites along the riverbanks. And yet I expect that it will take a while before private builders have the courage to invest in a stock of expensive apartments. Up to now, the inexpensive rent structure in Berlin has worked against such a measure.

That's a really central point. When rents in Germany as a whole are considered, Berlin's rents are 48% lower than those of comparable big cities; 28% lower than Kiel's, 25% lower than Bonn's. During negotiations with Bonn, the climate suddenly improved as soon as the average rent rates were compared. But for Berlin it's a problem. As long as we have this low rent average for existing buildings we won't be able to create much of a demand for new housing units.

A client or investor is always criticized as someone who earns off of everything. Could you find definitions for the terms investment, stake, risk and profit, so that they are generally comprehensible?

First the developer-client: I had the opportunity of observing once, how a community council which had lain dormant for 20 years was faced with a new mayor, a phenomenal man, 50 years old and endlessly experienced. Within two months he presented the council a totally new development concept for the city. What this mayor initiated as a developer was, for me, truly sensational. I wasn't interested in the money aspect of the discussion, the funds were communal; I was interested in the influence an investor can have on design and the chances he can take if he is willing to.

When talking about risks and earning money, we have to differentiate between divergent company structures. There are people, we'll call them lucky devils, who somewhere see how it's done; they become independent and are successful, but only once or twice and then it's over. Then there are people who build over a longer period of time, take in the results and don't worry about things after that. And then there are companies such as ours, which risk larger development projects.

The process of viewing the site, deciding to buy, developing, planning, construction, marketing, renting and managing takes five to eight years. With the Klingelhofer Triangle it took 17 years to get from plan to realization! During this time you have to live with the project, it accompanies you financially. And when you buy the property you have no idea what margin you'll achieve at the end. You can only say as a businessperson, hey, I think I can do it — develop this project so that it will contribute to the stability of the company and increase the company's assets. If you have 150 employees, over 300 freelancers and a considerable amount of properties, then you need to increase your capital assets and you need reserves in order to provide security for your employees.

We have to expend canvassing costs which don't always pay off, as not every project works out. We pay for preliminary studies which entail a great deal of steps; that too is canvassing. But all that is part of business life. Projects such as Kirchsteigfeld and Karow carry unknown risks. In order to work on such a project, you need reserves from the very beginning. If you have one deutschmark of that reserve left over at the end, you're happy. As a rule, you spend the money. But if I weren't able to spend a mark or two more for good design, then I wouldn't want to be a developer any more.

A final word: Your visions for Berlin?

Take a mental walk through the Berlin of the year 2002. The Parliament is in session in the Reichstag, the Chancellor's offices and parliamentary offices are occupied, the Bundesrat [Federal Council] has taken over the Prussian Herrenhaus [Gentlemen's House], and 180 embassies, at least as many associations and around 5,000 lobbyers have their seat in Berlin. Think of the impulses coming from the big new centers: Friedrichstrasse, Checkpoint Charlie and Leipziger Strasse, and above all Potsdamer Platz. Even today, contracts exist for Potsdamer Platz's future offerings which will bring five to seven million visitors annually to Berlin, including overnight stays. I can just see the bustle of activity on the new riverside streets and in the new housing areas. An excellent traffic network links points within the city and between the city and the suburbs. Four new railway stations make Berlin the line between Northern and Southern Europe and put it on the Paris-Moscow axis. The states of Berlin and Brandenburg have grown together into a joint economic region and have ventured into the Eastern European market right in our back yard. Thanks to the Transrapid [train], Hamburg is only 50 minutes, Leipzig an hour away. Let's forget all this disgruntlement, who's talking about empty pots of money, empty pots mean full pockets, the bacon's just on the wrong side of the fence.

Berlin has to solve its problems with its own possibilities. The city has to entice companies in the right market segments to move here. For example in transportation, medicine, biotechnology. Telekom has laid 62,000 km optic fiber cables; no other city in Europe has so many free channels. The next generation has boundless possibilities. All those who are complaining should go hibernate until the year 2001. When the government and the Parliament come to Berlin they'll find the city as lovable as it is. And then there'll be a new capital city contract. Of that, I have not the slightest doubt.

Photos: Thilo Rückeis

Claire Borchardt
Windows '97

City Rooms with a View

"Usually we think of the self as someone who looks out of his own eyes like a window, viewing the world spread out before him in all its expanse. And so there is a window that opens up onto the world. Outside is the world. And inside? The world too, what else?"
Italo Calvino, Palomar, 1983

Erik-Jan Ouwerkerk has photographed people at windows, people in Berlin, people who are visualizing the city and who live in the place where Berlin is most like the city they visualize. This is my window, say the photos, and the window shows that piece of the city that has become a part of me in some way or another, for a thousand different reasons. The individual window initiates the dialogue between the person inside and the section of the world he has chosen, or which, if he was unable to choose, he has accepted as his own; but many of the people in the pictures could in fact choose.

What is a door compared to a window? A door excludes: one click and the world is shut out, one has escaped it. A window, on the other hand, displays what is outside, untiringly, imperturbably, idiosyncratically. Streets recede into unending perspectives, a tree presses up against the glass, the supposedly soundless urban silhouette stands out against the sky. But the view is not soundless: noises penetrate, isolating themselves at times in the quiet of the room. As one grows accustomed to them they become inaudible again; they become the "news of the world," like the trains that travel through the quiet gardens of Westend. The windows distance the inhabitant from the world, because the world is still there.

The observer at the window reassures himself of his view. The weekly open-air market at Maybachufer, for example, is a reliable scene and as good as immutable. The construction site at Checkpoint Charlie, on the other hand, casts its shadows in anticipation of the buildings that will one day stand there, the quiet ossification of the noisy scenery. You live with it or you move away. There are the devotees of the train tracks and the multistory intersections. She would like to insist, says one inhabitant of Schönhauser Allee, that hers, yes indeed her view—streetcars below, tracks above—is the best in all Berlin. There are the champions of the rear courtyard, where sometimes the slit between two buildings lets in just enough world to make a picture. And then there are those who derive their well-being precisely from living in the unlivable or the forgotten, behind Passage IV in the industrial courtyard or in the middle of the Stralauer peninsula. There is the memory of the view over a Wall that no longer exists. A window is like the page of a book: it only contains this and that. For more, you have to lean out or turn over a new leaf.

Architects never draw the view from their windows. But even if they don't know the future residents, they know the view before they design; and if they are good—and if they can—they place the windows accordingly: emphasizing this one, minimizing that one, hanging the view like a picture

Maybachufer in Neukölln

City views from left to
right: Rosenfelder Ring,
Knesebeckstrasse across
train and S-Bahn tracks,
a strip of the Wall on
Wollankstrasse,
Friedrichstrasse at
Checkpoint Charlie

**Schönhauser Allee/
Danziger Strasse
in Prenzlauer Berg**

**From left to right,
Sorauer Strasse
in Kreuzberg,
Krausnickstrasse
in Mitte,
Bergmannstrasse
in Kreuzberg,
Zwinglistrasse
in Tiergarten**

Ohlauer Strasse
in Kreuzberg

From top to bottom:
Lausitzer Strasse
in Kreuzberg,
S-Bahn station Savigny-
platz in Charlottenburg,
Kreuzbergstrasse

Right:
Bregenzer Strasse
in Wilmersdorf

Strausberger Platz,
looking toward
Karl-Marx-Allee

From left to right:
Glückaufstrasse
in Marzahn,
Luisenplatz in
Charlottenburg,
Jewish elementary school
on Waldschulallee,
Emser Strasse in
Wilmersdorf

**Alt-Stralau in
Friedrichshain**

**From left to right:
Stresemannstrasse
in Kreuzberg,
Heinrich-Roller-Strasse
in Prenzlauer Berg**

in the room. The kitchen window, on the other hand —
where one spends hours cutting and stirring, lost in
thought; where one involuntarily sees everything and
in spirit has almost become a part of the street — never
becomes a picture.

In most cases, the photos show city-dwellers who
went looking for a story at their windows, and the windows are ones that project stories into the room.
Many window stories have already been told: Alfred
Hitchcock made the "Rear Window" his main character, while E.T.A. Hoffmann described the Gendarmenmarkt in Berlin from the "cousin's corner window."

Another story altogether are the "rooms with a
view," for which the new green suburbs were built in
Berlin. But even these views are not the same. In the
old villas, the doors and windows stand open and the
green bursts in; that is my tree, says the resident, that
is my flowerbed, and the outside world begins beyond the fence. The nearer you get to the residential
developments at the edge of town, however, the
more the world of the city disappears; green views
open up, and once you've arrived on the outside, the
moments of beauty become similar or the same. One
lives half inside and half outside, light and green
come from both sides, and the windows tell morning
and evening stories.

Martina Düttmann
Living in the New Suburbs

For a variety of reasons, it is still much too early to consider the new suburbs a part of Berlin. It is also too early to speculate as to what qualities they will one day be loved or praised for, or how they will at some point be incorporated into the mental image everyone is always making of Berlin. For the time being, they are simply there, nestling against the boundaries of the city.

Generally speaking, the new suburbs are growing up on the north and south edges of the city: in Karow (just beyond Weissensee) and Buchholz (at the edge of Pankow), in Staaken (at the end of Heerstrasse, where for decades everyone knew there was a border crossing), in Altglienicke (still on the other side of Adlershof), and in the Rudower Felder to the extreme south. No one disputes that they are necessary, though the tremendous demand for housing that produced them and accelerated their planning is presently allayed. But the tides of the urban housing market turn much too quickly to stay the course of the new suburbs. The new developments enrich the range of available forms of living with a new variation, one that is still unaccustomed in Berlin. They do not represent new editions of Grunewald, Lichterfelde, or Westend, whose clientele was already established when they were built and which today have grown, as it were, into nearly century-old trees. Nor do they constitute an alternative to the Märkisches Viertel, which, though conceived as a suburb on the edge of the Lübarser Felder, was never viewed or described as such.

Country living close to the city: these are the expectations the renters bring with them—the clientele first provided for—as well as the buyers, of whom there have been fewer up to this point. They are also the expectations to which the development companies have reacted, along with the planners and investors. "Close to the city" might as well be correct, for nothing is more important to the developers than the availability of public transportation to convey the urban exiles back into the city center. Living in the new suburbs is not like the holiday dacha, an addendum to the weekday dwelling, or the fortified weekend garden retreat, green oases extending deep into the city center. Living in the new suburbs at the edge of the metropolis is something that has to be learned.

Or to put it another way: what lifestyle images inspired the urban planners, architects, landscape designers, and above all the developers—who, whether public or private, are in the business of financing images. What do they say in their brochures? Community, garden city, park city, suburban development, living close to the city, country living, etc.—all these linguistic approximations seek to evoke a conception whose reality is still not very clear to anyone.

The plans for the new suburbs have been extensively published; in fact, the plans are far better known than the suburbs themselves. The latter, in turn, can be seen as of this year: one can view them, over the course of two days, for they are too far apart and offer too much for a single day tour.

Rehwiese and Neu-Karow

Photos: Erik-Jan Ouwerkerk

All the preliminary descriptions resembled each other, the procedures were almost identical. Both state and private investors wanted diversity, so there were integrated workshop sessions in which everyone was allowed to say anything about everything to anyone, and every architect ended up participating in some way or another. Green spaces in every form were in demand, as were building types of all kinds; every conceivable claim and dream had to be satisfied, whatever it might be. All this was implied in the plan descriptions, and fed the incredulity of the reader.

Now, however, the houses are standing: the rows, the meanders, the free-standing block houses, the urban villas, and whatever else. They are there to be seen, and the visitor, aware that all was

conceived as diversity in unity, that everything was intended everywhere and that nothing was overlooked, is left surprised and speechless in a spectrum of the different milieus now emerging.

Of course the new suburbs still sit like models placed into a larger three-dimensional representation of the city; they represent clearings in the green carpet that surrounds them and appear as perfectly crafted stage sets, though as yet no one knows what play will be performed.

Yet surprisingly enough, they differ from one another even now. Does the rural landscape withstand the rational will of the planner better than the city center? Is Berlin strong enough in all its parts to cunningly undermine the homogenizing force of an epoch (which in any case will be followed by another)? Nothing is certain. All we know is that from now on, a number of Berliners will look out the window morning and evening and, with the city at their back, live with the seasons. They will occupy the gardens outside their doors—so perfectly planted before anyone even thought of moving—and slowly grow into a world whose dimensions are not yet exactly defined, even for them. And at the end, they will be residents of this suburb or that one, whose individuality they will cherish as their own.

Französisch-Buchholz

Neu-Karow

Aalemannufer

Staaken

Rudower Felder

Altglienicke

74

10.1

Clients	Arge Karow-Nord: Groth + Graalfs, Berlin; Gehag, Berlin; Süba, Berlin
Urban Design	Moore, Ruble, Yudell, Santa Monica/California
Landscaping	Müller, Knippschild, Wehberg, Berlin
Housing Units	5,100
Social Infrastructure	10 daycare centers, 2 elementary schools, 1 Gesamtschule (comprehensive school), 2 youth centers
Commercial Area	approx. 13,000 m²
Total Area	approx. 250 acres
Green Space	60 acres
Public Transportation	S-Bahn station Karow, bus lines 150, 158, 350, 358
Date of completion	1997/98

All Panoramaphotos:
Suzanna Lauterbach

Neu-Karow

The first of the new suburbs to be finished will be Neu-Karow in the northeast of Berlin, in the Weissensee district. The first dwellings were occupied in 1995, and by mid-1998, rental housing construction will be completed. The houses intended for sale—condominiums, duplexes, and row-houses—are growing somewhat more slowly. Neu-Karow consists of two parts (section 2 and 3) north of the historic village center, and from here the landscape climbs gently. The street system adopts the existing path structure and uses it to develop a geometry of its own, an orthogonal grid with a few diagonals. The most important of these, the Achillesstrasse, connects the two parts. At the intersection of Achillesstrasse and Bucher Chaussee lies a commercial complex, which opened in November 1997 with 50 retail stores. Along Achillesstrasse there also extends the brick facade of the first elementary school, where classes have been held since August 1995. Four kindergartens are in operation, while the cornerstone of the comprehensive school was laid in January 1997. The perfectly coordinated infrastructure also included the early completion of sidewalks, green spaces, planted interior courtyards, tree-lined streets, and green and paved squares, as well as ponds and ditches for collection and seepage of surface water. The house types show a comparable variety, alternating between rowhouses, courtyard houses, free-standing multiple-family villas, and open blocks.

Architects

Dietrich Bangert, Berlin
v. Beulwitz Architekten und Planer, Berlin
Brandt + Böttcher, Berlin
Maximiliano Burgmayer, Berlin
Casa Nova, Berlin
Dörr, Ludolf, Wimmer, Berlin
Eckert, Negwer, Sommer, Suselbeek (ENSS), Berlin
Eyl, Weitz, Würmle + Partner, Berlin
Faskel + Becker, Berlin
Feddersen, von Herder + Partner, Berlin
Ferdinand + Gerth, Berlin
Fissler + Ernst, Berlin
Hermann + Valentiny, Berlin
Heueis + Fritsche, Berlin
Hilmer + Sattler, Munich/Berlin
Horst Hielscher, Berlin
Höhne + Rapp, Berlin
Kammann + Hummel, Berlin
Krüger, Schuberth, Vandreike (KSV), Berlin
Liepe + Steigelmann, Berlin
Moore, Ruble, Yudell, St. Monica/California
Neumeyer + Schönfeld, Berlin
Henry Nielebock, Berlin
Joachim Ramin, Berlin
Jan, Roosje und Rolf Rave, Berlin
Carola Schäfers, Berlin
Schmidt-Thomsen + Ziegert, Berlin
Stefan Scholz, Berlin
SRRS Schulze-Rohr, Ruprecht, Schlicht, Berlin
Thomas Sieverts, Bonn
Wiechers + Beck, Berlin
Johannes Wiesermann, Berlin
Alexander Williams, Berlin

East edge of the develop-
ment, view into the
interior courtyard of the
9th Elementary School by
Liepe + Steigelmann, with
multiple-family villas on
Achillesstrasse behind

Auepark with pond

Courtyard on Röländer
Strasse with daycare
center by Horst Hielscher

Balloon square by Jan,
Roosje, Rolf Rave

10.2

Clients	ARGE Süd; several Immobilienfonds, Coordination: BEB Berliner Eigenheim-Bau
Urban Design	Engel und Zillich, Berlin, competition 1992
Landscaping	Bos, B + J Buse, Kossel, Breuckmann, Kienle
Housing Units	2,880
Social Infrastructure	5 daycare centers for a total of 540 children, youth center, three-track elementary school with special track for learning-disabled children (three daycare centers for a total of 340 children completed by late 1997)
Commercial Area	ca. 12,000 sq. m (ca. 10,000 sq. m completed by late 1997)
Total Area	approx. 130 acres (incl. Rosenthaler Weg)
Green Space	25 acres
Public Transportation	Tram 50, bus lines 251, 259
Date of completion	1997/98

Triangular main plaza on Rosenthaler Weg with row buildings to the right and residential and commercial building to the left, both by Frank Friedrich

Panoramaphotos: Suzanna Lauterbach

Buchholz

The suburb Buchholz to the north of Berlin in the Pankow district is still under construction, though the characteristic, very urban-seeming triangular plaza on Rosenthaler Weg has apparently been completed since the spring of this year and the first tenants moved in already in January 1997. Until 1913, the area was officially known as Französisch Buchholz; the name, which is still used even today, refers to the Huguenot settlement of the area after 1713. The strict parallel layout of the parcels dates from that period and has been preserved ever since; it likewise serves as an ordering principle for the new urban design. The suburb extends between the old village green and the Blankenfelde landscape; quite unlike Neu-Karow, it is most decidedly conceived as a piece of the city (albeit on the periphery). The figure of the meander, constructing a striking opposition between the closed street fronts facing north and the open fronts with broad gardens on the south side, already evokes an urban flavor; four-storied buildings predominate, and the broad strip of green between the old town center and the "Krugpfuhl" has the dimensions of an avenue. Accordingly, the urban planners speak of the "city edges" at the periphery of the area, which they contrast with the space of the landscape. As in all of the suburbs designed using integrated planning procedures, here too a wide variety of building types and architectural forms are represented.

Architects:

Engel und Zillich, Berlin
Erling, Ewald, Graf, Neumann, Berlin
Fabrik 40, Berlin
Faskel und Becker, Berlin
Feddersen, v. Herder und Partner, Berlin
Frank Friedrich, Berlin
Klaus Kammann, Berlin
Krüger, Schuberth, Vandreike (KSV), Berlin
Maschlanka, Berlin
Meyer, Ernst & Partner, Berlin
Hans-Jürgen Mücke, Berlin
Richter Architekten, Berlin
Helge Sypereck, Berlin
Schröder, Berlin
Schattauer + Tibes, Berlin
Schaper und Noack, Berlin
Hannes Sauer, Berlin
C.-A. v. Halle, Berlin

10.3

Clients	Bauwert GmbH, München,
	Bavaria Objekt- und Baubetreuung GmbH, Berlin
	Grundstücksgesellschaft Cosmarweg
	91–121 mbH & Co. Beteiligungs KG
	Trigon Consult GmbH & Co Staakener Felder KG
Urban Design	Schiedhelm und Partner, Berlin
Landscaping	Stephan Haan, Berlin
Housing Units	1,116
Social Infrastructure	2 daycare centers
Commercial Area	200 sq. m
Total Area	3,000 sq. m
Public Transportation	Bus lines X49, 132, 137, 149, 657
Date of completion	Spring 1998

North boundary of the Bauwert site. Buildings by architects Feige + Döring

Garden City Staaken

The Staakener Felder, on the western edge of the city near Heerstrasse, adjoin both residential areas with low-lying buildings and areas still used for agriculture. The impression of the rural predominates, though the area is not far removed from the western part of greater Berlin and is only a stone's throw from the old town of Spandau. The overall urbanistic plan establishes a system of circulation that allows the construction of separate, individual areas. The planned development skillfully combines a village-like structure with a configuration of blocks open on one side. A total of four investors are cooperating to give a new quality to this somewhat contradictory area near the former border. Two separate building groups are intended to lie north and south of the village of Staaken, but even the southern area itself, which to a large extent is already finished and occupied, reveals two quite different interpretations of living on the urban periphery. On the one hand there is the garden city, in the literal sense, punctuated by a series of small gardens between houses with a maximum of four stories, open to the surrounding green space on all sides with continuous balconies, terraces, and steps. And then there is the very idiosyncratic version of the symmetrical, five-story multiple-family villa—a free-standing building type here is linked to its neigboring villa. The repertoire of green areas extends from the meadow and small park to the tenant garden.

Architects

ASP Nolte, Plaßmann, Reese, Kassel
Augustin und Frank, Berlin
Bendoraitis, Gurt, Meissner, Berlin
Emch und Berger, Berlin
Feige + Döring, Berlin
Hansen & Kellig, Berlin
Georg Heinrichs, Berlin
Reinhard Müller, Berlin
Barna von Sartory,
Martin Focks, Berlin
Schiedhelm + Partner, Berlin
Bernhard Winking, Hamburg

10.4

Clients	GEHAG, Berlin; Stadt und Land Wohnbauten-Gesellschaft mbH, Berlin, R+S Bau, Berlin, Bavaria Objekt- und Baubetreuung GmbH, Berlin
Urban Design	Martin + Pächter, Berlin
Landscaping	Ariane Röntz, Berlin; Regina Poly, Berlin
Housing Units	approx. 1,800
Social Infrastructure	3 daycare centers, 1 elementary school, 1 gymnasium
Commercial Area	ca. 5,000 sq. m
Total Area	115 acres
Green Space	35 acres
Public Transportation	Bus lines 171, 260, 738
Date of Completion	1st and 2nd building phases December 1997

Garden front of a
comb-shaped house on
Waltersdorfer Chaussee
by Arno Bonanni,
Architekten

*Panoramaphotos:
Suzanna Lauterbach*

Garden City Rudow

The Rudower Felder at the south edge of Berlin are part of a park area that remained untouched until 1989 as a substitute for the Brandenburg landscape beyond the border. The building plan sets the new development between a park in the north and a transregional landscape area in the south. The east-west course of the Lieselotte-Berger-Strasse marks the backbone of the new development, laid out on a strictly orthogonal plan and consisting of street edges, rows, blocks open on one side, and a sprinkling of cube-shaped urban villas. A villa district is planned for the east edge at Schönefelder Strasse. In its strictness, the arrangement is modeled on the Berlin Siedlungen of the 1920s. A diagonal path of green traces aboveground the course of a future subway line (from end station Rudow to S-Bahn station Schönefeld). The intersection of the diagonal with the main axis is marked by a straight-sided plaza as center and shopping area of the new development. Some of the houses have been occupied since 1996, and about two-thirds of the dwellings will be completed by the end of this year, as well as the three daycare centers. Construction on the elementary school has begun. The houses are mostly four-story, with flat or shallow pitched roofs; their architecture, though planned by a number of different firms, subordinates itself to the urbanistic structure, and the development appears as if cast from a single mold.

Architects

Blase + Kapici, Berlin
Arno Bonanni, Architekten, Berlin
Borck, Boye, Schaefer, Berlin
GEHAG, dept. Technik, Stefan Reinsbach, Berlin
Liepe + Steigelmann, Berlin
Maximiliano Burgmayer, Berlin
Martin + Pächter, Berlin
Mussotter + Poeverlein, Berlin
Nalbach Architekten, Berlin
Plessow, Ehlers, Krop, Berlin
Schattauer + Tibes, Berlin
Volkmar Schnöke, Berlin
SRRS, Wolfgang Schlicht, Berlin
Peter Träger, Berlin
Werkplan, Berlin

View northward into the
block Elly-Heuss-Knapp-
Strasse with buildings by
Liepe + Steigelmann and
Blase + Kapici

View from the west
into the Jeanette-Wolff-
Strasse with buildings
by SRRS and Liepe +
Steigelmann

10.5

Client	Stadt und Land Wohnbauten-Gesellschaft mbH, Berlin
Urban Design	PLANWERK, Heinz Tibbe, Carlo Becker, Berlin
Housing Units	2,433
Social Infrastructure	4 daycare centers, 1 elementary school, 1 gymnasium
Commercial Area	3,000 sq. m
Total Area	2,100 acres
Green Space	approx. 250 acres
Public Transportation	S-Bahn station Altglienicke, bus lines 160, 163, 260
Date of Completion	Late 1995 to mid-1997

Residential area 1.2 from the southeast. Free-standing block houses by architects Musotter + Poeverlein, Kneffel, Heide und v. Beckerath

Panoramaphotos: Suzanna Lauterbach

Altglienicke

The development area Altglienicke is located on the south edge of Berlin in the Treptow district, between Adlergestell and Waltersdorfer Chaussee. An early publication states, "Altglienicke is intended to develop into a place of many places," i.e. to consist of a number of separate areas with individual features, resulting in an urbanistic mosaic that gives precedence to the old town center. The site plan clearly manifests this goal, and viewing the many already finished districts in residential area 1 confirms the concept. South of the railroad line that cuts through the area are curved street spaces à la Bruno Taut lined with four-story houses with single-pitch roofs, a small town idyll with facades patterned in dark clinkers and light yellow plaster. A single high-rise stands in their midst, while next to it a series of L-shaped houses line the street, their striped facades reminiscent of the 1920s. The courtyards behind accommodate gloriously austere freestanding block houses on a square plan with clinkers. Parallel to the railway and the green corridor that accompanies it stands the impressive "Langhaus" and a meander construction; there is an arcade house with Italian flair, and a few other Italianate houses without the flair. The rows of houses further away, in sectors designated by letters of the alphabet, pop up again and again in different colors behind the small, old single-family homes in their bed of green.

Architects

Assmann, Salomon, Scheidt + Schmidt, Berlin
Borck, Boye, Schaefer, Berlin
Braun & Voigt und Partner, Berlin
Dähne + Dahl, Berlin
Frank Dörken, Volker Heise, Berlin
Findeisen und Partner, Berlin
M. E. Gehrmann und Partner, Berlin
Grünberg und Partner
Heide und v. Beckerath, Berlin
Hillig und Witte, Berlin
HOPRO Bauplanung, Brandenburg
Jeromin, Berlin
Kennerknecht, Berlin
Kneffel, Hamburg
Kny und Weber, Berlin
Liepe + Steigelmann, Berlin
Maedebach, Redeleit + Partner, Berlin
Meik, Berlin
MKH Mahraun, Kowal, Heieis, Berlin
Mussotter + Poeverlein, Berlin
Pieper + Partner, Berlin
Pininski, Berlin
K. Manfred Pflitsch, Berlin
Plessow, Ehlers, Krop, Berlin
Georg Procakis, Berlin
Joachim Ramin, Berlin
Dieter Rühle und Partner
Eckhard Schmidt, Berlin
Yamaguchi und Essig, Berlin

Residential area 1.3,
"Langhaus" from the
northwest. Architects:
Dähne + Dahl

Below: Residential area
1.1, buildings by
architects Borck, Boye
und Schaefer

Photos by the Architects

10.6

Client	Bauwert AG, München
Urban Design	Martin + Pächter
Landscaping	EXTERN, Berlin, Stephan Haan, Berlin
Housing Units	536
Social Infrastructure	2 daycare centers
Commercial Area	ca. 750 m²
Total Area	15 acres
Green Space	approx. 3 acres
Public Transportation	Bus lines 131 und 136, 231, 331, carferry Aalemannufer – Jörsstrasse
Date of completion	Spring 1997

Courtyard looking south toward Aalemannufer, with a row of houses by Martin + Pächter, to the left, and Feige + Partner to the right.
Looking back: In the background, a transverse structure by Feige + Partner

Photos: Christian Gahl

Aalemannufer

The housing quarter at Aalemannufer is not one of the large-scale development projects and thus is actually a stranger to this series. It consists of only 26 buildings, built by a single developer far off the beaten track at the edge of Hakenfelde, which in turn lies at the extreme edge of Spandau. Construction was begun in 1994 and is now finished but for the two daycare centers. A few ingenious planning strategies were implemented: the terrain was slightly raised toward the north, thus lengthening the streets between the houses and making them appear even longer, as well as allowing the parking spaces at the north edge toward the power plant to be inserted under the street in open pallets. Rather than distributing the volume of construction among the architects in blocks, each firm was allowed to build two urban villas on the water, one free-standing and one connected row of houses. The development owes its quality to the fact that no building is like any other, yet all appear related—through the white color, the allusion to modernism, but even more through the diversity and the rich variation of the cool vocabulary of the 1920s. The development is a felicitous solution to the problem of "building on the water," even though the Uferstrasse draws the houses away from the idyllic Havelstichkanal, and the ferry crossing over the Havel to Tegelort is located at some distance. The ferry, on the other hand, serves to partially compensate for the far out location of this small piece of town.

Architects

ASP Planungs- und Bauleitungs-gesellschaft mbH, Nolte, Reese + Partner, Kassel
David Chipperfield Architects, London
Feige + Partner, Berlin
Gregotti Associati Int., Milano
Kramm + Strigl, Darmstadt
Martin + Pächter, Berlin

**Terrace houses on
Uferstrasse by
Martin + Pächter**

*Panoramaphoto:
Suzanna Lauterbach*

**Outside: North facade
by Kramm + Strigl
Inside: West facades
by Martin + Pächter and
David Chipperfield**

**Urban villa by
Kramm + Strigl, next
to it the building profile
by David Chipperfield**

All photos: Christian Gahl

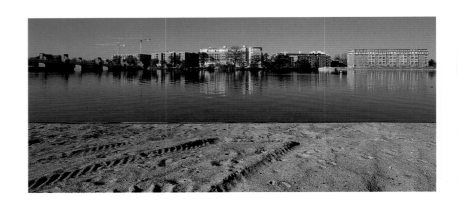

Uli Hellweg
Berlin—City on the Water

A Journey to New Urban Shores

Photo: Christian Gahl

The urban planning debate of recent years in Berlin has focused intensively on the Berlin of stone, on street profiles and urban density. The potential latent in the confrontation between the stone edges of the streets and the natural edges of the city's waterways, however, has hardly been considered. Only now is the magical boundary between land and water, between city and river—the richness of the urban shoreline—being recognized anew as an urbanistic and architectural opportunity.

Berlin owes its early development as a city to the waterways of the aboriginal river valley. The spreading tangle of rivers, streams, creeks, and lakes constituted a natural barrier that protected the double town of Berlin-Cölln like an outer moat. The waterways provided merchants with a relatively quick and safe mode of travel, prized already in the Middle Ages by the Hamburg-based "Kirchliche Bruderschaft aufwärtsfahrender Schiffer" (Ecclesiastical Brotherhood of Upstream-Bound Seafarers). The strategically important confluences of the Havel and Dahme with the Spree were protected by the fortresses of Spandau in the west and Köpenick in the east, while trade routes crossed the Spree at an easily-defended ford. Here, the sister towns of Berlin and Cölln grew up around the resting places on the sandy banks of the Spree islands.

The settlement history of Berlin unfolds amidst the bodies and ribbons of water. Berlin, Cölln, Köpenick, the Spree village of Lietzow (later Charlottenburg), Tegel, Spandau, and Potsdam are the most important orientation points in the development of the water city of Berlin. Attractive sites on the waters of the Spree, Havel, and Dahme were favored for the construction of princely, and later royal, palaces.

As early as 1702, royal barges towed by pairs of horses transported persons and goods twice daily between Berlin, Lützenburg (now Charlottenburg) and Spandau. On October 27th, 1816, more than 20 years before the first steam locomotive toiled between Berlin and Potsdam, the steamship Prinzessin Charlotte von Preussen provided regular passenger communication between the two residential cities. Beginning in the mid-19th century, however, the ever-expanding network of streets and railroad tracks superimposed itself like a spider web over the ribbons of water, relegating them to second-class transport routes. The passenger boat remained a viable alternative for greater distances only for a few decades, until here, too, the railroad won the upper hand. Travel by passenger boat was increasingly limited to sightseeing excursions.

The 19th-century decline in the importance of rivers and waterways as an urban impetus resulted in part from increasing pollution. Sewer systems and water purification failed to keep up with the growth of the big city; rivers, creeks, channels, and moats became fetid drainage ditches on which the town turned its back, while riverbank sites were increasingly appropriated by industry and trade. Today, the rivers and canals are still lined by many

Underground: Satellite image, TU Berlin, 1990

View northward from the old city of Spandau. In the foreground the citadel with the Eiswerder peninsula beyond and the new south bridge over the Spandauer See in the background

Left: The first new buildings in the Havelspitze district, viewed from the east bank

*All air-photos: Tom Peschel
All panorama-photos: Suzanna Lauterbach*

acres of warehouses, vacant lots, logistics installations, and commercial operations, structures which have long since lost their relation to the water and which now separate the city from its origin.

The Wasserstadt on the Spandauer See

The pioneer project in Berlin's remembrance of its shores is the lakeside "Wasserstadt" (Water City) on the Spandauer See. Conceived in the days of the Wall, it was intended to relieve an overcrowded district of the divided city.

For over a century and a half, the area on the Upper Havel was cut off from the urban development of Spandau. In 1839, the westward expansion of the city led to the transfer of the Moabit powder mill to the north of the old city of Spandau, immediately adjacent to the Spandau citadel. During the division of the city, a large part of the area was blocked by tank depots, emergency supply reserves, and barracks.

The development "Wasserstadt Oberhavel" has initiated Berlin's most important urban ecological project, with the reurbanization of over 500 acres of abandoned and depleted land and the cleanup of contaminated soil and ground water. More than 7 km of lakeshore trails around the Spandauer See have been provided for recreation and leisure. By the year 2010, approx. 12,700 dwellings for 30,000 residents will have been constructed. In addition, space is available for 20,000 jobs in the service and business sectors.

The urban concept, developed in 1992 by the architects Hans Kollhoff, Christoph Langhof, Klaus Zillich, and Jürgen Nottmeyer, elaborates a self-contained city on the water. The configuration of blocks, squares, parks, and promenades is oriented to the model of Lenné and Hobrecht, the Berlin urban planning type of the 19th century. In addition to the Havel—as the central "water square" which is spanned by two new bridges—historic ditches and canals from the old fortification of Spandau as well as new ornamental canals traverse the urban districts. The range of types for the definition of boundaries between land and water extends from park-like riverbank lawns and stone promenades to street and lake bridges to the green shore of the Havel.

Currently, 3,500 dwellings in the districts Havelspitze, Parkstrasse/Schultheiss, and Pulvermühle are finished or under construction. In April 1997, the first residents moved in; the south bridge (now "Spandauer See Bridge"), an important link between the two halves of the Wasserstadt, is due to open in December 1997.

The critics were sure of their case against the Wasserstadt on Spandauer See, an ambitious project pushed through in a coup de main by Wolfgang Nagel, the Berlin building superintendent at the time. The slackening of the housing market and the perpetual budget crisis were and are grist for the mill of criticism. In actual fact, however, since 1996 the original concept has continued to be developed in a number of essential areas.

11.1

WASSERSTADT AM SPANDAUER SEE
QUARTIER HAVELSPITZE

Clients	Grundstücksgesellschaft Wasserstadt Oberhavel Quartier Havelspitze GbR, Bavaria Objekt- und Baubetreuungs GmbH (LBB) in cooperation with Siemens (SBB), Berlin
Urban Design	Kees Christiaanse ASTOC, Rotterdam
Landscaping	Gustav Lange, Hamburg, WES & Partner, Hamburg Ariane Röntz, Berlin
Housing Units	1.600
Social Infrastructure	1 daycare center

View westward from the Salzhof grounds

Architects:

Kees Christiaanse
J.S.K. Perkins & Will
Josef Paul Kleihues
Otto Steidle
AG SIAT mit Albrecht

The most important modification has to do with the relation of the project to the adjoining urban and landscape spaces of Spandau. The Wasserstadt on the Upper Havel has become the Wasserstadt on Spandauer See. No longer does the project view itself as a kind of ideal city on the water, introverted and isolated from existing urban structures; rather, it has become an element and an impetus of Spandau's development, both urbanistically and with regard to the politics of housing. Differentiated according to the different qualities and features of its nine districts, the Wasserstadt will need to be defined anew.

From the Havel to the Stadtspree

In Spandau, the Spree flows into the Havel—and no one notices. From the mouth of the Spree, across from the old city of Spandau, large commercial areas, power plants, and industrial complexes extend on both sides of the Spree valley, interspersed only on the south bank by small gardens and damp meadows. At the sluice Charlottenburger Schleuse, from which point the commercial areas continue on along the Westhafenkanal, the Spree turns southward and becomes the watershed separating the park at Charlottenburg palace from Tegeler Weg and the city.

Looking upstream from the palace bridge at Charlottenburg, the Spree becomes the western Stadtspree ("city Spree"). Old and new commercial buildings along the banks alternate with houses from the 1870s, the spaces between them sporadi-

cally filled in. The attractive locations facing south, in particular, are occupied by large commercial enterprises and power plants, such as the Kraftwerk Charlottenburg or the businesses on the Darwinstrasse. At the confluence of the Spree, Landwehrkanal, and Charlottenburger Verbindungskanal, the river police and a concrete-dismantling plant share the best locations on the water. A gem was and is the former garbage loading station by Paul Baumgarten of 1936, now the home of the Kleihues architectural office.

Here, where good intentions of a stroll along the river are foiled by the security measures of police and entrepreneurs, begin the curves in the Spree so characteristic of the urban image of Berlin. Three times the river bends markedly to the north, three times to the south, before it divides into the two arms on whose banks the double town of Berlin-Cölln originated 800 years ago.

Six Bends in the Spree — Six Water Sites

The Spree first curves to the north between the Kaiserin-Augusta-Allee in the Hutten district of Moabit and the commercial area at Pascalstrasse in the south. On both banks of the river, a series of new administrative buildings have grown up in the last few years. The pioneer project on the south bank of the curve, the twin institutes of the Technische Universität and the Fraunhofer Gesellschaft, already anticipates the mistakes that now characterize the entire area and turn it into one big missed opportunity. Like its successors, the building is

11.2

QUARTIER PULVERMÜHLE

Client	GSW Gemeinnützige Siedlungs- und Wohnungsbaugesellschaft Berlin mbH
Urban Planning	Nalbach + Nalbach, Berlin
Landscaping	Häfner & Jeminez
	Alkewitz & Armbruster
Housing Units	1.126
Social Infrastructure	2 daycare centers, 1 elementary school with gymnasium

Cube houses by ENSS
and Nalbach Architekten,
Berlin

Architects:

Bernd Albers
Theodora Betow
Hentschel & Oestreich
Eckert, Negwer, Sommer,
Suselbeek (ENSS)
Faskel & Becker
Geske & Wenzel
Jahn & Suhr
Mayer, Ruhe, Voigt,
Wehrhahn
Nalbach Architekten
Klaus-Rüdiger Pankrath
Plessow, Ehlers, Krop
Carola Schäfers
Benedict Tonon

conceived as a solitary structure; despite the quantity of glass, its circular form is introverted and avoids dialogue with the riverbank. Most of the buildings behind Pascalstrasse on the south side of this Spree curve are too far from the river and remain unconnected to each other. The rigid monostructure, the paranoid security measures (above all of the twin institutes), the dead-end circulation, and the high level of vacancy give the whole scene a cheerless and desolate quality.

Unfortunately, the situation on the Moabit side is not much better. Here the buildings stand at an interesting distance to the water, but this urbanistic advantage was bought at the price of permission for investors to privatize the riverbank itself. Accordingly, the waterline remains disjointed and is accessible to the public only on a narrow, heavily traveled strip along the Kaiserin-Augusta-Allee. While the inhabitants of the densely built Beussel district sense rather than see the water, the insurance agencies, office tenants, and architecture and construction firms may divide up the most attractive banks of the Spree among themselves.

The Gotzkowsky-Brücke marks the eastern end of this Spree curve. Continuing south into the next bend, the shoreline streets Wikingerufer, Hansaufer, and Bundesratufer represent what is probably the most attractive residential location in the Moabit district. Closed block edges, tree-lined riverbank streets, and promenades show a unity as convincing as it is characteristic of the waterfront architecture of the 1870's.

The opposite, south bank of the Spree approaches the Landwehrkanal to within 250 meters. This unusual area between two waterways is the site of tile and bicycle shops, insurance agencies, shipping companies, and auto dealerships with generous parking lots. Only the eastern section of this Spree bend shows its potential with the street Schleswiger Ufer.

Beyond the Lessingbrücke, crossed by the busy thoroughfare of Stromstrasse, there appear the red terracotta facades of the most remarkable new commercial buildings on the Spree. Here, where the Kampfmeyer mills once stood, the 1988 Focus Teleport building by the architects Ganz and Rolfes symbolizes the transition from a production to a service oriented society. The 200-meter-long buildings of the former Bolle dairy, built in the mid-19th century and now under historic preservation, were skillfully integrated into the new complex by the architect Wolf-Rüdiger Borchardt and now accommodate a hotel, restaurants, and businesses.

The old dairy represents the link between Focus Teleport and the service and office complex of the pizza company Freiberger, built in 1994 by the architects Kühn, Bergander, and Bley. The complex is U-shaped and architecturally rather forbidding; but while the cylindrical building heads of granite and glass seem indeed to have been superimposed on their Moabit surroundings, their unequivocal positioning toward the river nonetheless serves to ennoble it. Here, where beer gardens and

Views of the Spree
upstream, from west to
east: Kraftwerk Reuter,
first Spree bend in
Moabit behind Pascal-
strasse, second Spree
bend in Moabit with
Bolle grounds and the
future Ministry of the
Interior

dance clubs once delighted summer visitors, the
officials of the Ministry of the Interior will soon
perform their duties.

In contrast to the commercial district on Pascalstrasse, the buildings on this bend of the Spree
create urban spaces and waterfronts that under-
line the dynamic curve of the river. The riverbank
edges are stone-hard and urban; they contrast
starkly with the Holsteiner Ufer on the opposite
side, with its green slopes and manorial residences
from the 1870s. Despite the monostructure of the
commercial complex, the riverbank promenade is
almost always lively. The inhabitants of the dense
residential quarters of Moabit appreciate the
attractiveness of this riverbank, owing not least of
all to the popular children's play ship that has
docked here.

Behind the S-Bahn station Bellevue, the Spree
leaves the Tiergarten. Before doing so, however, it
brushes the Bellevue palace, the seat of the Federal President. The three-winged complex, built in
1785 after plans by Daniel Boumann for Prince
Ferdinand, the youngest brother of Frederick the
Great, turns its northeast side rather incidentally
to the Spree. The elliptical expansion to the southwest, currently under construction by the architects
Gruber/Kleine-Kraneburg, will further weaken the
relation of the complex as a whole to the river. The
Spree is now relegated entirely to the rear.

On the opposite bank of the Moabiter Werder,
770 dwellings, a daycare center, and an elementary
school are intended to make the move to the capital more palatable for federal employees. The
meandering configuration of the residential complex echoes the curve of the Spree and opens up
green spaces toward the water.

The Republic on the Water
A few hundred meters upstream, there appears a
gigantic construction site with the Spree diverted
into an artificial bed and piles of Brandenburg sand
on the banks. Only Sir Norman Foster's elliptical
glass dome over the Reichstag reminds us that
here we are at the center of the republic. This
place, like no other, is connected with the myths
and tragedies of German democracy. Here Philipp
Scheidemann proclaimed the Republic on November 9th, 1918; here the Nazis staged the burning
of the Reichstag on February 27th, 1933, in order
to abolish democracy a month later. Here the
peoples of the world watched the citizens of Berlin
on September 9th, 1948. And 47 years later, Berlin
and its visitors celebrated a two-week-long festival
around a Reichstag wrapped by Christo and Jeanne-
Claude.

Ever since the conflict between Lenné and
Schinkel over the master plan for the Pulvermühle
area in Moabit, this bend in the Spree has had a
magical attraction for planners and architects. The
history of the place is full of fantasies of urbanistic
and political power; thus the challenge was all the
greater to find a solution for the Bundestag and
the buildings of the federal government. With the
"Band des Bundes" ("Bond of the Federation")

Diverted Spree and Reichstag construction site

extending east-west over both banks of the Spree like a clasp (competition winners Axel Schultes and Charlotte Frank), one such figure was found, lying crosswise to all the compromising north-south axes.

The horizontal arrangement results in a unique approach to the river. The bend of the Spree is bridged in two places: gently and openly in the west, with a view into the Kanzlergarten and the Bundeskanzleramt (Axel Schultes, Charlotte Frank), and in a closed, urban fashion in the east, at the transition from the "Alsenblock" to the "Luisenblock" (both by Stephan Braunfels), where the assembly halls, parliamentary factions, and offices are accommodated. Here the construction approaches the river directly and profiles a water portal with a bridge and a square ("Spreeplatz") unlike anything in the city center of Berlin. The north boundary of the "Band des Bundes" toward the river is formed by the Spreebogenpark designed by the Swiss landscape designers Toni Weber & Lucius Saurer; its sloping disposition opens up a wide view of the Spree and the opposite bank with the Humboldthafen and Zentralbahnhof.

Yet even the clever and interesting urbanistic solution of an east-west rather than a north-south axis will not solve the old problem of the south-to-north gradient on this curve of the Spree. While Lenne's scheme still called for a unified urban district with the Spree bend as an ornamental element in the center, the actual historical development with features such as the Lehrter Bahnhof, the Humboldthafen, the prison, and the Ulanen-Kaserne led to a value discrepancy between the Lehrter Strasse district in the north and the elegant Alsen area south of the river with its diplomatic villas and embassies. Even the new Zentralbahnhof by von Gerkan, Marg und Partner on the north side of the Spree will, for all its steel and glass, represent an obstacle as insurmountable as the traffic arteries at Humboldthafen, already fully overloaded at the time of the Wall.

Zentraler Bereich

The Zentraler Bereich (Central Area) extends from the new Zentralbahnhof to the Landwehrkanal in the south. Its end is marked by the debis Building by Renzo Piano on the Reichpietschufer, which runs into the Landwehrkanal like the bow of an oversized ship. Unfortunately, this motif represents the limit of the attempt to incorporate the canal into the ensemble. Instead of creating, for example, a small harbor lagoon such as was typical of the Landwehrkanal until the infilling mania of the post-war period, or the construction of a cutoff canal to the casino, music theater, and adjacent residential buildings, the planners made a half-hearted effort with flat, transparent, contourless paddle ponds. The theme of the city on the water is reduced to the decoration of "monumental" architecture.

Yet no artificial waterway in Berlin was more significant for the city's urban development than the approx. 10-km-long Landwehrkanal, constructed

Tiergarten, Großer Stern, and debis grounds at the Landwehrkanal

1845–50 after plans by Joseph Peter Lenné. The canal more or less follows the course of the Schaafgraben in the area between the current debis site and Tiergarten. At the beginning of the 19th century, the Schaafgraben was the most popular recreational site in Berlin outside the Potsdamer Tor. Beginning in the 1840s, the summer houses and restaurants developed into Berlin's first green suburb ("Untere Friedrichstadt") on the water. Everyone who was anyone in art, culture, and science lived between Tiergartenstrasse and the Landwehrkanal: Lenné, Friedrich Hitzig, Iffland, Drake, the brothers Grimm...

Barely a half a century later, this first suburb between water and park was overrun by the growth of the big city. The residents moved on to Grunewald, Wannsee, Nikolassee, and Schlachtensee. The houses were bought up by speculators and replaced by larger complexes or state buildings such as the Marineamt on Reichpietschufer. Only the Villa von der Heidt, located between the Landwehrkanal and an old arm of the Schaafgraben (visible even today in a small protrusion of the Landwehrkanal), survived the urbanistic transformation—as the Chinese embassy.

Lenné's Water City

From the area between the Landwehrkanal at the south of the Central Area and the Alsensspreebogen in the north, the most urban part of the water city of Berlin extends eastward to the confluence of the two waterways at the Lohmühleninsel. In preparation for the building of the Luisenstadt, Lenné canalized the Schaafgraben to provide drainage for the Köpenicker Feld. In Lenné's system of ornamental axes and boundaries, the Landwehrkanal acquired decisive significance as a promenade leading from Luisenstadt to Moabit.

Today, high-traffic shoreline streets straitjacket the Landwehrkanal up to Hallesches Ufer; only in Kreuzberg does the canal once again display its opportunities and potential. In context of the IBA 1984/87, the decaying blocks along Fraenkelufer and Paul-Lincke-Ufer in SO 36 were saved from demolition; through careful urban renewal and urban infill, the city of the 1870s was rebuilt and a piece of Lenné's urbanistic vision created once more.

But even the IBA was unable to reconstruct the most important water axis of the Luisenstadt: the Luisenstädtischer Kanal. This 2-km-long connecting channel, built after Lenné's plans in 1848 and filled in again in 1926, was the urban backbone of Luisenstadt, "the soul of the whole," as Lenné called it. In 1890 the journalist Wilhelm Lösche gushed: "An arrow-straight, sky-blue canal... This is the Holland of Berlin, the extreme southeast at Kottbusser Ufer... Wherever one follows the line of a major street, one runs into water. Most of the streets are straight as an arrow, parallel to one of the canals, all of them with beautiful, new, sky-high houses; the banks of the canals and pools themselves are extravagantly wide, so that in comparison to these huge areas,

even the gigantic facades of the new buildings shrink down into low frames."

The Landwehrkanal represented one element in a comprehensive water management system for regulating the Spree. Until the mid-19th century, riverbank locations outside the historic city center were threatened by flooding and thus were not suitable for urban development. Only with the construction of canals, drainage ditches, and sluices as well as additional weirs and dams could the danger of flooding be averted and additional building land be recovered on the banks.

The Historic Water City of Berlin

The historic city center, on the other hand, had been secured against flooding since the end of the 17th century. Friedrich Wilhelm, Elector of Brandenburg, had employed Dutch architects to build a fortification whose military function would soon become obsolete; in the process of construction, however, radical improvements were made in the drainage system. The creation of moats, sluices, and flood ditches made it possible to build on riverbank locations within the fortified city from 1658 on and thus established the precondition for the merging of the towns Berlin and Cölln. The Huguenot Samuel Chappuzeau, who visited the towns on the Spree in 1669, wrote: "Berlin is a very fine city of medium size, admirably built and fortified, though it stands on sandy ground... The streets on both banks of the river are straight and always clean, as are all the houses here. A number

of private persons have built fine dwellings entirely in the Dutch style, houses which could be considered palaces. They stand close to the princely residence, from which they are separated by a canal. As a result, this part of the city is the friendliest and the most beautiful."

In the decades that followed, the water city of Berlin continued to grow. Under the direction of J. A. Nering, the new Mühlendamm was constructed, along with a new harbor with silos and warehouses on the Kupfergraben and the sluice at the Packhof. The most important impetus for urban planning on the water, however, was provided by the construction of the palaces on the Spree, particularly the remodeling of the Schloss (City Palace) by Andreas Schlüter beginning in 1698 and by Johann Friedrich Eosander von Göthe after 1706.

When the fortification work was completed, the three-story Baroque houses of the bourgeoisie adorned the banks of the Spree and Kupfergraben, above all in the areas of the palace, the sluice canal in Cölln, and the first urban expansion of Friedrichswerder after 1658. The more austere two-story houses of craftsmen, merchants, and fishermen stood along the fortification moats and at the Stralauer Tor.

By the end of the 17th century, a new urbanistic element had appeared on the water: the ornamental bridge. In 1695, Nering rebuilt the Lange Brücke as the first representative bridge in the city. It was crowned by Schlüter's famous statue of Friedrich Wilhelm, Elector of Branden-

The Spree between
Jannowitzbrücke and
Warschauer Brücke, with
the new Trias office
building

View to the southeast
from the Oberbaum-
brücke toward the
Elsenbrücke and the
Treptowers

burg. Though only just completed in 1683, the
fortification was torn down again in 1732, a situation which not only opened up new prospects for
urban expansion, but also necessitated the construction of new bridges, including the Fischer-
brücke, Jungfernbrücke, Opernbrücke, Inselbrücke,
and Waisenbrücke. In 1778, the cartographer
C. L. van Oesfeld recorded no less than 35 bridges
within the excise wall.

After the wars of independence, a recovering
Prussia asserted herself in numerous building
projects in the city center. Spree Island became the
theater for imperial self-representation: in addition to the continued expansion of the palace by
Friedrich August Stüler and Ernst von Ihne, it was
above all the Museumsinsel that was to yield to the
creative will of the Hohenzollern. In 1830, in the
course of construction for Karl Friedrich Schinkel's
Altes Museum, the connecting channel between
the Spree and the Kupfergraben was filled in, a canal which ran adjacent to the Lustgarten and dated
from the time of Memhardt's fortification. The name
for the site of the four museums built there between 1830 and 1930 remained "Museumsinsel"
(Museum Island). The inhabitants of Berlin proudly
refer to the historicist ensemble as their "Athens
on the Spree."

In the middle of the island stood the City
Palace, a center of gravity for the various urban
structures between the Museumsinsel in the north
and the medieval city around Mühlendamm in the
south. Since the destruction of World War II, the

demolition of the Palace in 1950–51, and the redevelopment of the Fischerkiez, Spree Island has lost
all urban coherence. Today, the riverbank scenes
on the Spree, Spreekanal, and Kupfergraben represent a disconnected sequence of different urban
epochs and ideologies. Public accessibility is ar-
bitrary and sporadic. The banks between the construction site of the Haus der Deutschen Wirtschaft
on Mühlendamm, the Marstall, the Palast der
Republik, and the cathedral are either closed or
have become dead ends, as with the riverbank
colonnades of the Neue Galerie, which have been
walled up in the most beautiful location.

Only in the area of the so-called Fischerinsel
are the banks accessible over wide stretches. Here
they stand in noteworthy contrast to Märkisches
Ufer on the opposite side: facing the beacon of
socialist modernism with its 21-story highrises are
the last witnesses to an urbanism that inspired the
18th-century traveling English writer John Toland
to coin the phrase "Berlin—Beauty on the Water."
From the beginning of that century, stately bourgeois palaces had been built in the suburb of Neukölln am Wasser, a few of which are still preserved.
In the 1960s and 70s, bourgeois houses from the
18th and 19th centuries were inserted into the
gaps, moved to make room for modernist prefab
panel construction in other locations such as the
Friedrichsgracht or Fischerkiez.

Without a doubt, the extreme of ignorance
is represented in the area of the historic Mühlendamm. Here, an eight-lane street follows the

The grounds of the Treptowers with Puschkinallee and Treptower Park

View of the Stralau peninsula from the east

course of a fortification moat and thus creates a de facto urban boundary on the very site of the historic center of the double city of Berlin-Cölln. Before the regulation of the Spree allowed the sister cities to grow together, and even for a long time afterward, Mühlendamm constituted the social and economic center of Berlin.

Stralauer Spree

Southward from Mühlendamm extends the Stralauer Spree with the suburb of the same name. In his famous novel "Der Stechlin" of 1898, Theodor Fontane described it as a rural suburb with gardens extending to the water, "where a few late mallows or sunflowers bloomed."

Only a few years later, the Stralauer Spree was built all the way up to the banks. Gas plants, pump stations, dwellings, and commercial buildings occupied the shore along with bathing establishments and boating clubs. Following the war and the construction of the Wall, the river between the Michaelbrücke and the Oberbaumbrücke became forbidden terrain, a border strip between two political worlds.

The development of the streets Holzmarktstrasse, Mühlenstrasse, and Stralauer Allee into an eight-lane thoroughfare has effectively marginalized the almost 4-km-long strip on the northeast bank between Michaelbrücke and Elsenbrücke, rendering it inhospitable and forbidding. The Osthafen is still the most urban of the uses represented there.

To the southwest, the left bank of the Spree presents a disparate image in which the beginnings of urban life on the water alternate with vacant lots, recycling depots, and storage places for building material. The traces of IBA 1984/87 appear unmistakably between the commercial district on Köpenicker Strasse in Kreuzberg and the Oberbaumbrücke. Modernized old buildings in bright colors, the red brick and yellow clinkers of commercial buildings with black window frames, and the green Spree terraces convey an impression of Kreuzberg diversity on the water. The Deutsches Architekturzentrum (DAZ) in particular, renovated and extended by Claus Anderhalten and Assmann/Salomon/Scheidt, is an outstanding example of the quality of historic waterfronts, others of which still await investors.

The splendid Oberbaumbrücke, built in 1894 and renovated in 1992–95 with the assistance of Santiago Calatrava, provides a view of the Osthafen on the north bank and the commercial and warehouse buildings on the south bank of the Spree. The highly attractive landscape of the Lohmühleninsel, where the Landwehrkanal branches off from the Spree, is used as a storage depot by a concrete company. Behind the urbanistically impressive ensemble of the "Kunstfabrik" ("Art Factory" with artists' ateliers) and cultural forum "Arena" on the Treptow side, the new TwinTowers and Treptowers extend to the Elsenbrücke. At the Warschauer Brücke, a new, primarily service-oriented city district is being developed in the approx. 30-acres

11.3

WASSERSTADT AN DER RUMMELSBURGER BUCHT
QUARTIER STRALAU STADT

Clients	Veba Immobilien AG
	Brau & Brunnen/BHP, Bauforum GmbH & Co. KG
	Concordia Bau+Boden AG, Cologne/Berlin
	DePfa Immobilien Management AG
	Zschokke GmbH, Berlin
Urban Planning	Herman Hertzberger, Amsterdam
Landscaping	Atelier Loidl, Berlin
Housing Units	1.951
Social	
Infrastructure	3 daycare centers
	1 youth leisure facility
Area Size	78 acres

The new buildings of the Quartier Stralau Stadt on the Stralau peninsula, seen from the Lichtenberg banks

Architects:

**Arnold & Bezzenberger
Architektengemeinschaft
Bartels + Wittwer
Braun & Voigt und
Partner
Bremmer-Lorenz-
Frielinghaus
Herman Hertzberger
O&S Architekten AG mit
Schenker & Stuber AG
WLP – Werner Lehmann &
Partner
Inken Baller
Vollmer & Larisch**

large area of the former Narwa electrical plant. With its 30 floors and 120 meters height, the Treptowers are the tallest office building in Berlin. They mark the water-gate of the city between the rural and urban Spree to the southeast of the city center.

Wasserstadt Rummelsburger Bucht
Looking outward from the city, the unusually long, straight section of the Spree between Mühlendamm and the "Zenner" ends at the Elsenbrücke. The Zenner, a historic attraction in Treptower Park, drew many inhabitants of Berlin, and not only in the summer. Before the regulation of the Spree, curious sightseers came here in droves to view the event of "land under water" of the Stralau peninsula from the elevated vantage point of the Zenner.

On the Stralau peninsula and the area north of the Rummelsburger See (an old arm of the Spree), a new water city is under construction. By the year 2010, approx. 5,000 dwellings, schools, and daycare centers, as well as service and commercial areas to accommodate 12,000 jobs, will be built in the approx. 340-acres development area under the direction of Wasserstadt GmbH. Its proximity to downtown Berlin and to large recreational areas such as Treptower Park and Plänterwald, as well as its excellent public transportation connections, make this development an extremely promising location for future residence and business.

Here the identities of the new water districts are rooted in history. Stralau, an old fishing village on the peninsula, is familiar to every citizen of

Berlin from the Stralauer Fischzug, the city's oldest folk festival. At the beginning of the 19th century, the fishing village of Stralau developed into a holiday site for summer visitors, and in the second half of the century into an industrial center for glass production and machine building.

The master plan for the Rummelsburger Bucht development, designed by Klaus Theo Brenner, Herman Hertzberger, and the landscape architect Karl Thomanek, combines urban and suburban building forms in the interest of an "urban landscape." The banks are made accessible to the public again, partly as promenades, partly as pedestrian paths through the landscape.

The buildings stand in the western part of the Stralau peninsula ("Stralau-Stadt"). Imitating the construction of the 1870s, they are placed perpendicular to the bank and visually integrate the water into the "hinterland" (unfortunately, the canals originally planned were unable to be realized). To the east and the south, the new construction alludes to the historic image of village and landscape.

On the Rummelsburger side, "Hofgärten" ("Court Gardens") designed by Theo Brenner open southward toward the bay. Here, 540 dwellings are currently under construction, as well as a series of commercial and service areas. Despite their formal severity, the U-shaped structures by the architects Pudritz + Paul formulate a downright Baroque gesture toward the water. Together with the construction on the Stralau side, Rummelsburger See re-

11.4

Client	Ziel Baubetreuungs GmbH
Urban Design	Klaus Theo Brenner, Berlin
Landscaping	Thomanek & Duquesnoy, Berlin
Housing Units	approx. 600
Social	
Infrastructure	2 daycare centers

"Hofgärten" on the Lichtenberger Ufer, seen from the Straulau peninsula; rearward view of the Stralau-Stadt district.
At present, the "Hofgärten" are the most attractive new residential complexes on the water

Architects:

Pudritz + Paul, Berlin

ceives an architectural frame that transforms it into an urban lake with a diversity of shores and waterfronts. An additional 1,000 dwellings are planned for this side of Rummelsburger Bucht, as well as an office park in the eastern part of the area. The fate of the former Rummelsburg prison is still unclear. Already Fontane, who made fun of the name of the bay, remarked: "But the place itself is beautiful, and names don't mean a thing."

At present, a total of 1,400 dwellings are under construction, 40% of them privately financed. Herman Hertzberger's ensemble in "Stralau-Stadt," the farmstead-like construction in Stralau-Dorf by Brenner and Faskel, and a series of town villas, but also the modernization of the old glass-workers' houses on the street Alt-Stralau and the former palm oil silo on the bay, already convey the impression of a well-advanced process of transformation which, though writing a new chapter, still preserves the testimony of history.

The urban landscape at Rummelsburger Bucht represents the transition between the urban and the rural Spree. In its natural course from east to west, the city Spree travels 16.5 km to Charlottenburg palace, accompanied by an incomparably varied, partly fallow, partly underused or misused, partly visionary riverbank landscape. From the Slavic fortress village of Köpenick to the Askanian fort of Spandau, the water city of Berlin unfolds, with the Spree as its aorta, 200 km of navigable rivers and canals, more than 600 km of shoreline, and 50 lakes — a waterworld that to a large extent is still terra incognita.

Architects	Gerhard Spangenberg, Berlin
	Reichel & Stauth, Braunschweig
	Schweger + Partner, Hamburg
Landscaping	Gustav Lange, Hamburg
Client	Allianz Grundstücksgesellschaft, Stuttgart
Project Developer	Unternehmensgruppe Roland Ernst
Address	Elsenstrasse/Hoffmannstrasse
	Berlin-Treptow

Christoph Tempel
In the Treptowers' Shadow

you might discover ...

Berlin is not Frankfurt. Whereas Frankfurt brings forth a new and spectacular skyscraper every year, Berlin—with few exceptions—sticks to its building height limit of 22 meters, called the "Traufhöhe." When a tower building does get constructed, it immediately attracts the attention of the skyscraper-inexperienced city dweller. Time to head out to Treptow, where the Treptowers are growing skyward, 31 stories and 125 meters high.

We take subway line 1, exit at the former terminal station Schlesisches Tor and walk east down Schlesische Strasse. Past Alvaro Siza's 1983 Bonjour Tristesse, past the Schaubühne's rehearsal rooms on Cuvrystrasse, past he painted waterfall directly opposite. Schlesische Strasse is an immensely busy street. People, cars, and trucks cram through the narrow portals of old commercial buildings that give no hint of the Spree River flowing beyond their five or six layers of courtyards.

Once over the Landwehrkanal things quiet down. Nothing points to the fact that here the Wall once screened East and West from each other. Here begins Treptow. The Treptowers slowly come into view, still blue-gray and far away, fairly large, but not as overpowering as expected. The site still seems far far away, and the idyll at the water's edge is enticing because it's so close. Fresh quark donuts, ten for five marks, and afterwards coffee at the riverbank on the wooden terrace of the former fishermen's club.

There is life around those donuts, they mark the entrance to the Treptow indoor flea market, where on weekends everything that's somehow usable is for sale. All kinds of faucets competing against oversized wrenches, five records for four marks, books at similar prices. The two large shed-roofed constructions were erected in 1915, at a time when, thanks to its good access to transportation lines, this part of Treptow grew to become a true industrial center. The halls' architecture recedes somewhat in face of the commotion, but merits a second glance in light of the slim steel supports. Bruno Buch built them for the Carl Beermann Machine Works; only ten years later General Berlin Omnibus company took over the lot and expanded the halls to their present form. To the left of a large gateway a sign identifies a small door as the entrance to the Arts Factory on Flutgraben. If the door is ajar, then don't miss the chance of seeing this great architecture by Alfred Warthmüller. The artists' working and living in the loft-like rooms and the unusual views of the Spree and the East Harbor are worth it, something that can't always be said for the art. With a bit of luck one can get up onto the roof, from here, the object of our desire, the Treptowers, draw closer and warn us to keep going.

Too bad that the present grounds of the transit authority have been cut in two; this means, back to Puschkinallee and through the smaller part of Schlesischer Busch to Eichenstrasse. The blue gas container

The Treptowers, decisively placed between river, road and rail

Photos:
Ragnar Knittel

Intersection: entrance to the Arena, left, the former bus depot; right the Twin Towers

Photo:
Christoph Tempel

On the near side of the
Spree River, service
centers and urban beach
life; on the far side, the
bustle of a city harbor.
Always present: the
Towers

Photos:
Michael Krone

at the corner of Eichenstrasse is too squat to pass for a tower. At present, Eichenstrasse is so dusty that both of the preserved 1870's villas there can hardly be seen. Eichenstrasse 1, endowed with the ruined charm of a slightly decayed bourgeois villa, stretches up its little tower as if trying to shake off its suave new neighbor which, though conformist, is a bit too close for comfort. The villa seems to be protecting itself from the modern buildings behind. We walk further through a kind of wasteland, with unlaid pipes and illegally parked cars. No more trees here. Our view spirals up along mirror-image shafts, the Twin Towers (architects: Kieferle and Partner, Stuttgart). One thought suddenly strikes us; isn't Treptow predestined for tower constructions— Treptow, Tower, Twin Towers, Treptowers...

Only as of late is it possible to go along Eichenstrasse all the way to the Spree. The Twin Towers complex lies along this new stetch of road from Hoffmann-strasse to the water. Two six-story

blocks, their white stucco and ribbons keeping them modern despite their fried and true natural stone (Rosa Beta) base, create a link to the two 60-meter high, sixteen-story twins. These, in turn, stand mirror-symmetrical atop a three-story, heavily fenes-trated substructure. A crown seems to top them off, or rather a diadem resting lightly on the tower's hair. According to the American-fifties-style brochure put out by the Roland Ernst cor-porate group, four more of these towers are still being planned.

We have passed the bus depot, home to the Arena, a well-known concert hall. Back a ways don't go over the rotting fence, as the gate calls for our attention. Its brick portal figures created by sculptor Arminius Hasemann give a sense of the respect the bus driver's profession once commanded. Two thick supports each carry one of the uniformed figures, with their peaked cap, protective goggles and heavy gloves. On the left side, a cowboy has since begun riding for ciga-rettes. On the right pillar appears

a stone bear from Berlin's coat of arms, coverd by a slightly cracked sign for the Arena. In front, the ever opend red and white barrier and an evergreen streetlight.

Until half a year ago, streetball players and skateboarders would gather at the water front. The afternoon dancers enjoyed international food and drink and above all black music. Remains of an urban beach life still exist although the place is deserted now, with the service-sector twins staring down like extraterrestrial gate-crashers. Fights over rents and neighborhood intrigues forced the Yaam club into a new domicile, also at the water and not all that far away. But the charm of the original is gone.

The bus terminal built in 1927 by Franz Ahrens spans 70 meters without using pillars; it is considered an outstanding engineering achievement and can still be experienced in its full grandeur during special events. Last summer it was possible to party hard on the roof and watch the Treptowers grow. Now we are in their shadow.

Actually, why the plural? Treptowers? All we ever see is one finger pointing blue-gray toward the sky. That redoubling which appears logical in the name Twin Towers is most confusing in the Treptowers. The impression almost arises that this is a case of pluralis majestatis and that the currently tallest office building in Berlin intends to hold court between Elsenstrasse, Hoffmannstrasse, and the Spree.

The complex consists of three parts, a comb-like building with three "teeth" (Schweger + Partner, Berlin and Hamburg), the Tower (Gerhard Spangenberg, Berlin), and two historical constructions at the corner of Hoffmann- and Elsenstrasse, now connected by a new strip (Reichel & Strauth, Braunschweig). From here, the tower seems almost forced; but from the Elsen Bridge it seems much taller and slimmer, almost gallant.

But now it's time to finally gain some skyscraper experience and see all of Berlin, a rather unfamiliar view as the city has no real elevations of its own. The

little exterior lift that so prominently bloats the slim profile in our photo no longer exists. The ride was, in any case, something for construction workers well used to heights.

Unfortunately, nobody who isn't a tenant of the Allianz Insurance Company will ever get to enjoy the view from 125 meters. There will be neither a sightseeing platform nor a restaurant nor a cafe. But only from the top can the Treptowers' position within the city be realized, as one's glance travels from the much lower Twin Towers to the East Harbor on the far bank of the Spree, to the striking Oberbaum Bridge to the west and doesn't rest until it finds a similarly airy elevation at Alexanderplatz. The view to the south reveals the district's green heart, Treptower Park with its two tree-lined fingers, Puschkinallee and the street Am Treptower Park, which seem to bear the greenery toward tree-starved Kreuzberg.

The Treptowers are excellently linked to communications of all kinds. The commuter rail-

road awaits guests at the Treptower Park station right in front of the building. Elsenstrasse, one of the city's main arteries leading east, runs right past the grounds, and Treptow Harbor makes the Spree accessible. Suddenly, from above, eleven courtyards filled with greenery open up before one's eyes, completely unexpectedly (planning: Gustav Lange, Hamburg).

The main entrance to the Treptowers is from Elsenstrasse, in a brick house originally built in 1927/28 for the AEG. After the war, the building became the collective "Elektro-Apparatewerke Friedrich Ebert" (EAW), one of Treptow's biggest employers. Allianz Insurance is to move its new headquarters for the eastern German states here, and as of Spring 1998 will employ 2,500 people on 85,000 square meters, half the Treptowers' total floor space. The building on Elsenstrasse will become a cafeteria and training center; the lower buildings have also found use, while the tower is to let. The second one of the historical

Lush greenery; villas and front yards bordering Puschkinallee

Photos:
Ragnar Knittel

buildings marks the southern end of the complex. With its four stories it leads up to the surrounding apartment buildings. For the moment, however, this area is still too much of a construction site to call it a street. Directly adjacent to a major construction project, the grounds are drafty, dusty, and full of trucks.

The EAW collective has vanished, but its social facilities still exist. Between Elsenstrasse, Hoffmannstrasse, and Puschkinallee one can find two retirement homes, a clinic, and four daycare centers. The absolutely prime location between Puschkinallee and Am Treptower Park is occupied by a retirement home and a large daycare center.

No path leading from the villa gardens to Puschkinallee, so it's back to busy Elsenstrasse and, just a stone's throw further, to the six-lane intersection with Puschkinallee. The green of the trees lights up like in France. The whole area was dotted with villas-for-rent at the turn of the century. Many employees of the industrial area toward the Spree

lived here. The crass disparities and wild mixture here are nothing new; tranquil life, gardens, trees, versus huge blocks, highrises, and industry. Yet the service-sector stronghold Treptowers come across as very restrained. Only now and then does the tower peek through the leaves of the trees.

Trees in rows of four line border Puschkinallee. Every fifth tree has a green number, as if Treptow's parks department wanted to make sure none get lost. Almost all the villas are protected landmarks; the area is protected as an ensemble, and rightly so. There is no street in Berlin that exhibits such a southern flair. The buildings contribute less to this impression than the green roof that covers the complete breadth of the street. The five newly-built villas that recall a historical original from 1890 (architects: Schuh und Hurmer, Munich), of yellow brick with ornamental red stripes, and a zinc colored receding tent-roof all fit most pleasantly into the ensemble.

The Park House is next door, in a pre-automobile sense a cultural house complete with cafe in park-like surroundings. Once again we stand at the fork between Puschkinallee and the Am Treptower Park street. The blue gas tower disgracefully neglected before now signals the end of our road.

13

Architects	Joppien Dietz Architekten, Berlin
	Weidleplan Consulting GmbH Berlin
Project Architect	Jörg Joppien
Structural Design	BGS, Berlin
Landscaping	Landschaft Planen & Bauen, Berlin
Client	OSB Sportstättenbauten GmbH, Berlin
Address	Am Falkplatz, Berlin-Prenzlauer Berg

Nils Ballhausen
The People's Sport, etc.

Max Schmeling Hall in Berlin-Prenzlauer Berg

The Europewide competition held in 1992 called for a judo and boxing hall. In order to box, one needs, according to international regulations, 36 square meters of net floor area. Max Schmeling Hall offers 21,360. A difference of 21,324 square meters remains to be explained.

House or lunar capsule — Robert Venturi contrasted the two thirty years ago to demonstrate the "tension between the means and the ends of a program." Whereas the spaceship has but one simple goal — a moon landing — which it attempts to reach by highly complicated means, the house must fulfill a much more complex program with elementary technical methods. Seen this way, sports halls have a lot in common with spaceships. Their goal: protection from the elements for the athletes and spectators.

Max Schmeling Hall takes its place among the playing fields of Friedrich Ludwig Jahn Sports Park along with areas for soccer, tennis, and track and field. Max Schmeling has become Daddy Jahn's good neighbor. The sports park, Falkplatz north of the hall, and the Wall Park, currently under construction parallel to the hall, join to create an interwoven green island cut out of the dense sea of late 19th century apartment buildings. Up until 1918 the Second Infantry Brigade trained here on their parade ground "To the Lone Poplar." In the 1920's the first sports grounds were officially opened and in 1951, on the occasion of the World Youth Games, Jahn Stadium was dedicated to the people. The embankments of its stands were constructed of the ubiquitous rubble left over from the war and, as long as the Wall stood, proved to be advantageous to the marksmen of the border guard.

1988 the Eastern Capital and the Western Half City decided to submit a joint application to host the Olympic Games in the year 2000. Sometime afterwards the Wall fell and not much later hopes for the games had to be abandoned. Nevertheless, Berlin decided to continue with plans for two sports halls: a new bicycle track on Landsberger Allee and a new sports hall in Jahn Park.

The winner of the competition for the new bike track was the French star architect Dominique Perrault, for Max Schmeling Hall the winners were Anett-Maud Joppien, Jörg Joppien and Albert Dietz; an architectural team whose oeuvre complet, as they like to point out, consisted at that point of one kiosk.

The architects moved the building westward, away from the official site on Schönhauser Allee, and burrowed their sports hall into the ground on a line with Jahn Stadium. The design has a gleam of something akin to a bad conscience about it. No glorious solitaire was set here. The architects withdrew radically in face of the scarce green areas, hid the volume of their building under grass and fled to the outermost corner of the grounds — were they determined to build at all? They discussed their work with the neighboring residents again and again and surely more than every experienced architect would have done. The design itself, more-

over, always contained an element of cautiousness. The last image evoked, one of a building which functions as a green bridge to help unite East and West, appears touching and yet plausible. The green roof of the hall creates a transition to Wall Park, which runs parallel to it (design: Gustav Lange) and which was based on an idea resulting from a citizens' initiative.

The surrounding housing area behind the border installations was quiet for a long time, as if nonexistant. "If you laid yourself down on the street here, you would've frozen to death before a car came by to run you over," says the majordomo who ought to know. Currently, megaevents create traffic snarls of confused drivers who only slowly come to realize that there is no visitors' parking here and never will be. The new sports arenas were purposely built near subway and city rapid-line stations.

The spectators who nevertheless reach their goal experience the main facade of Max Schmeling Hall on Falkplatz as a glass-clad section. Its gentle curve traces the contour of the hill, with the striking roof at mid-field countering the movement. If one looks closely, one recognizes the three nave-like parts of the whole: the middle is filled with the arena for large sports and other events, the western part contains two neighboring triple gymnasiums, and in the eastern part another gymnasium and a ballroom is located. When the actors show off their warm-up program, the wait in line at the ticket office goes that much faster.

Max Schmeling Hall goes underground. The green slopes of the hall can be walked over and lead to the bleacher entrances. Between the slabs are light courts or special entrances for athletes and the media.
The ALBA basketball team on the field

Photos:
Friedrich Busam (1)
Erik-Jan Ouwerkerk (2)

Main entrance as a glass
section; entry platform
in the evening.
Nearby: a densely
built-up quarter of the
Gründer era.
Stairwell layer at the end
of the entrance hall

Despite the transparency of the facade, the playing field is not visible from outside, thanks to the
torturingly adroit placement of a concrete parapet
wall which, to top things off, is so low that one
begins to doubt one's adulthood. No hopping up
and down or craning of the neck obliterates the
fact that the playing field is five meters below the
entrance level.

Via metal doors fit into the facade's grid, one
passes through the glass curtain, finds oneself
suddenly in the main space of the building and
loses the important end of the ticket stub but never
one's direction: entrance behind, bleachers on
three sides, playing field below. A spacious walkway, as high as the building itself, leads by snack
bars and guides the spectators to their seats; 4,000
to the lower stands, 3,500 to the upper stands via
a separate layer of stairwells. That these are hardly
the "cheap" seats is made clear by the media
cabins, which are also located on this gallery level.
Narrow stairs lead to yet loftier heights, to a circular passage along the skylights. Here it's standing
room only as this is the "peanut gallery." The
spectators relax against the steel railing, plastic
cup in hand. The playing field is dizzyingly far
below them. The grass of the green carpet outside,
sloping away behind them, remains reassuringly
within reach. Exciting perspectives open up to the
spectator at the ends of the stands. The two suspended platforms have been cut off vertically here.
Instead of hairpin curves, which would have spa-
tially made the construction appear disconcerting,

The playing field. The "supported stone cushions". The gaps between the bleachers. The room-high walkway

Photos: Jörg Joppien (1)
Friedrich Busam (2)
Erik-Jan Ouwerkerk (2)

the fissure has created impressive crevices into which, hopefully, only glances will fall. Here the bulbous profile of the upper stands is visible. The curvaceous concrete proclaims neither force nor severity but rather comfort in the form of supported stone cushions.

The only element floating over the uppermost gallery is the roof. The large rectangular skylight renders the roof construction partially visible: a school of fourteen fishbelly trusses connected to form a metal-clad plate which "swims" on fixed columns. The trusses' flexible elastomer supports allow for changes in length due to temperature fluctuations. The facade connections need take up only minimal forces and the supports can remain slender. The roof appears to only graze the building, an independent, inflated, aerodynamic body.

School teams also enter the hall from Falk-platz, although in this case they use the two side entrances. Under the lateral grass slopes are hidden dividable auxiliary halls, in which physical education is held without a lot of audience. An important basic idea of the original competition for Olympia 2000 was that after the Olympic games the sports hall should be suitable for everyday school and community events without expensive renovations. The resulting concept, in which, very simply, the flanking auxiliary halls can be used as foyers for media and spectators, didn't need to be changed even after the Olympic Committee rejected Berlin's petition for the games in September of 1993. These big boxes allow for everything.

Physical education. Two triple sports halls lie in the western section of the building; one in the eastern section, next to the ballroom.
For large events, the auxiliary sports halls can —and that is the amazingly simple part of the design concept— be made into foyers for the media and the public.

ALBA-Berlin against Tatami-Rhöndorf

All photos:
Erik-Jan Ouwerkerk

Long passageways lead to the dressing rooms through which classes are led in shifts past the inserted egg-shaped teachers' cabins and into the gymnasiums. Daylight falls onto the multicolor lines of the parquet through the curved roof with its laterally running ribs. The glazed wall of the entrance facade throws the balance of light off a bit. Different light zones emerge, near the window or deep in the interior of the hall, and when playing in the undivided gymnasium one may be blinded by the daylight.

The neighboring ballroom, on the other hand, contemplative, almost festive, of concrete and parquet, has that certain intimacy which is to be expected below ground. For a space in which no balls are to fly, the walls are almost majestically high. They reach up to the calves of the VIPs who, in the lounge diagonally above, recover from watching the games, as a lofty strip window discloses.

All prominent guests enter the building through a special entrance in the eastern slope. There their ways part: the spectators move upward to the champagne reception and the athletes go down into the bare labyrinth of raw concrete and neon lights. Bright colors mark dressing rooms, warm-up rooms, saunas and judges' rooms.

The representatives of the press have their own entrance a few meters farther on. A remaining space which resulted over the slope of the underground parking garage's ramp was made into an interview room. The inclined wall which braces itself against the earth and—next door Jahn Stadi-

um exerts its force too—creates a light slit in the ceiling making obvious that one is in the outermost corner of the building. Up to a hundred journalists sit here in tiers as if in a university lecture hall and listen to what the main actors have to say about the game.

Victory and defeat in sports is attributed usually to the trainer, sometimes to the athletes, and never to the arena. Max Schmeling Hall received nothing but praise after the first victories of the basketball team which completed its home season here in 1996/97. The successful team not only advertises for the waste disposal firm ALBA but also for the hall, the client, the architects, the district, and the city. In order to equip a successful team, it seems, one doesn't just need the right shoes but also a new sports hall. The international format, the density, the closeness, the noise of the spectators all fire one on. The excitement of novelty beckons like a meadow covered with newly fallen snow. The hall still has to return the athletes' compliments. Max Schmeling Hall is a social event whose outcome, as is usual in the world of sports, is uncertain. The first few minutes of the game, at any rate, couldn't have been better.

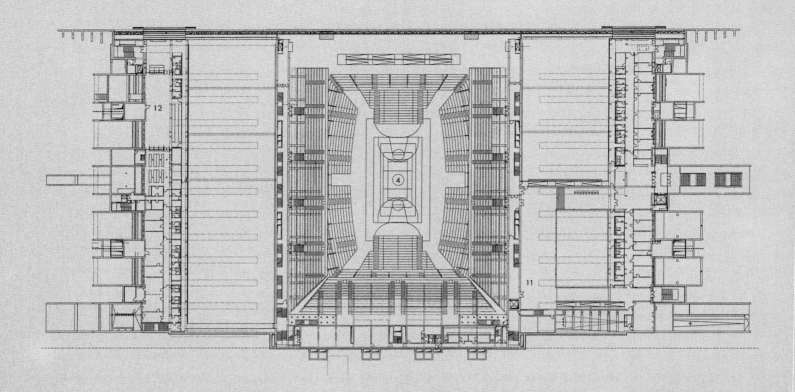

**Ground floor plan, upper
floor plan and section,
all to a scale of 1:1250**

 1 public entrance
 2 media entrance
 3 athletes' and VIP
   entrance
 4 arena
 5 foyer
 6 triple sports halls
 7 teachers' cabins
 8 changing rooms
 9 ballroom
10 interview room
11 media lounge
12 restaurant (planned)

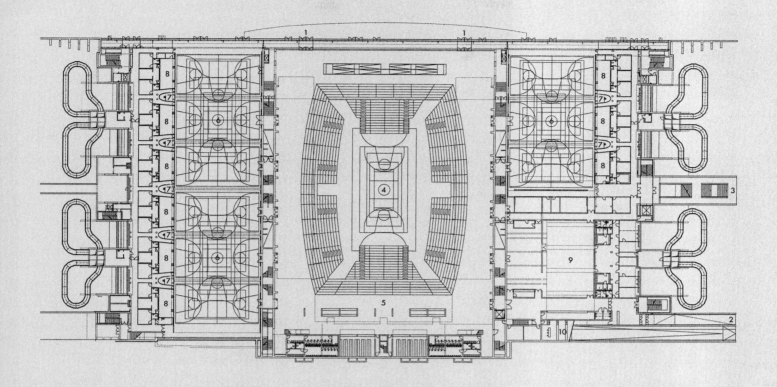

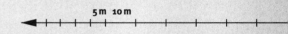

5 m 10 m

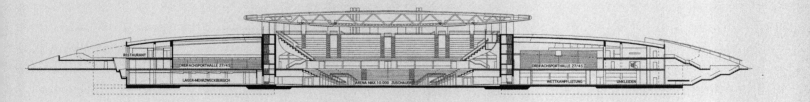

RESTAURANT
DREIFACHSPORTHALLE 27/45
LAGER-MEHRZWECKBEREICH
ARENA MAX. 10.000 ZUSCHAUER
DREIFACHSPORTHALLE 27/45
WETTKAMPFLEITUNG
UMKLEIDEN

Architects	Claude Vasconi, Dagmar Groß, Paris
Architect of Preservation	Jürgen Lampeitl, Berlin
Structural Design	Polónyí & Fink, Berlin
Urban Design	Claude Vasconi, Paris
Landscaping	Seebauer, Wefers & Partner
Client	Herlitz Falkenhöh AG, Berlin
Address	Berliner Strasse, Berlin-Tegel

Paula Winter
Legible Industrial History

Borsig Tower Commercial Park

All photos:
Erik-Jan Ouwerkerk

The delicate steel construction of the historical works has been cleared aside and awaits positioning in the new building. Three brick gables are still in place, two have been moved. They stand waiting.

The hundred years of the Borsig Works' history would have come to a close had one merely reconstructed the kettle forge and the lathe and assembly complex. Even restorations have something irrevocable about them despite their not signifying the finality of demolition. Restorations acknowledge the mark of time.

In the emerging "Borsig Tower Commercial Park" the original frame construction is being aligned into nave-like halls into which the new shopping center will move in 1998. The architect, or rather the cooperation between architect and historical preservationist, is to be credited with the continuation of a history. The design extends the viability of the works; the planned spatial structure includes a temporal structure. This temporal structure encompasses the short span of time which is photographically documented here: the supporting trusses exposed, the slender steel elements stacked into piles and the brick gables individually visible, as if someone wished to explain the composition of the works to a visitor.

The individual supporting trusses (a total of 130 lined up every 6 meters in the longitudinal axis), having been freed from their crane rails, show their many different, artistically layered steel profiles. Each of the rectangular supports is composed of four U-shaped columns joined on their long sides by a triangulated framework and on their short sides by metal plates. The amazingly slender roof trusses (joined U-beams as top and bottom chord and connected L-beams as web members) continue, for a while, their 18 meter stretch across the emptied space below. Then they are moved aside, cleaned, stacked into a compact bundle. The gables with their northern German brick gothic style, which the official master builders of Berlin, Reimer and Körte, erected in front of their sparse steel construction, were always mighty pieces of theatrical scenery from elsewhere and so they appear, now more than ever.

In literature there exist stories which take place within other stories; one speaks of framework stories and subplots. And exactly that is occurring here. The old industrial halls 2, 3, 4, 8, and 9 are being imbedded into the new structure of the shopping center. The glass-roofed interior corridor runs through hall 3. The furrow of a former ditch has been filled with soil and made densely verdant. The mall is organized along this green axis. The two reconstructed industrial halls to the right and left will later shelter approx. 120 shops each. An upper floor is to be suspended into this space. The resulting floor-to-ceiling height of the ground floor is 5 meters, of the upper floor 4.5 meters. The commercial "street" under the glass roof takes advantage of the whole of the hall's height. The old brick fronts are set asymmetricaly into the south facade, its solid expanse torn open by a wide glass

The Borsig Tower erected
1924, was Berlin's first
highrise. Now restored
and put back into use.
The long nave before the
deconstruction

Process of careful
deconstruction: the steel
columns and roof trusses
have been taken apart,
the rust removed, and
lain aside

The gothic style brick
gables, designed 1898
by Reimer and Körte,
will become part of the
new shopping center's
south facade

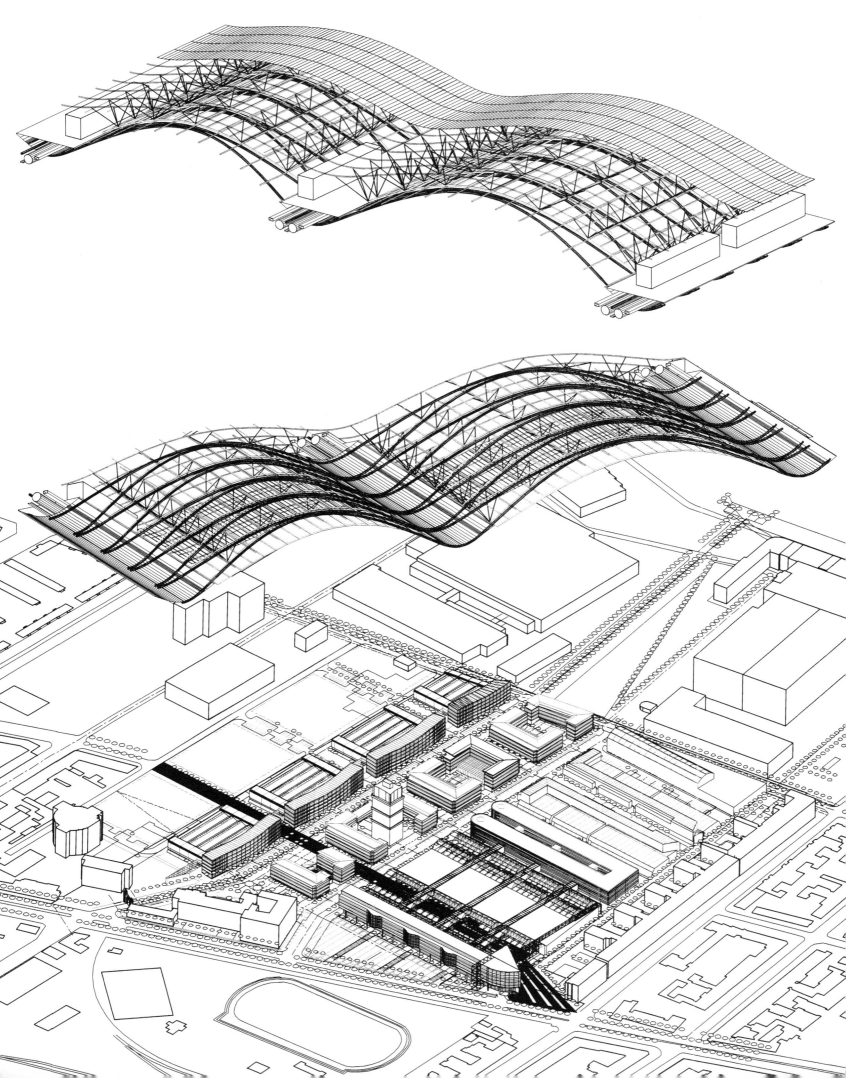

The framework,
composed of extremely
slender trusses and
columns, represented
highest technical
standards at its time

The new roof traces
the rounded brick gables
of the old halls. The roof
consists of two layers:
an inner membrane,
glazed or opaque, and an
outer membrane with
exterior sun protection

Isometric view of the
commercial park.
Claude Vasconi won the
urban design compete-
tion in 1994. The new
shopping center
appears east of the
Borsig Tower. Next to it,
to the north, the
Phoenix Technology
Center, which opened
this summer. A hotel
and office complex will
occupy the central area

The preservation of the historic framework is not just an act of taking care of a monument; indeed, its proportionality and spatial qualities set standards for the new construction

window. The new roof, independent of and almost floating over the halls below, traces the rounded gables in a softly flattened wave. The roof consists of a double membrane: the actual boundary of the space below (glazed or opaque) and an outer membrane with exterior sun protection. The old and new spaces in the hall, framework story and subplot, flow together here.

In order to reuse a historical structure one has to overcome several obstacles: the quality of the substance, a possible increase in loads, and fire protection codes. The columns and truss beams proved to be in good shape. No new loads resulted from the chosen roof design, but the addition of suspended floors made it necessary to reinforce the existing structure. The solution appears surprisingly simple and appropriate: small solid steel square columns joined so as to prevent shear forces, strengthen the original profiles. Fire protection requirements were satisfied in the roof (F 30) through a painted-on coating. In the columns (F 90) a combination of measures was used: the old structure was completely relieved of its bearing function, the section (or rather: the sturdy elevation) of the new solid steel cores provide fire resistance and in addition, the space between old and new supports was filled in with a fire-protective mortar.

Adolf Behne wrote in 1927 that, "Imagination has nothing to do with the rarity value of the elements [of a structure] but rather with the combination, assignment, and connection of the elements into a discovered, invented, enhanced result.

Imagination which is fruitful is associated with the harshest reality." Now that Claude Vasconi's isometric drawings have come along portraying the same lightness as the dissected serial parts of the bearing structure, one is tempted to expect a result in the sense of Behne's words.

One would like best to discover a relation or equality between the perfected, pared-down construction of the historical halls, a construction which corresponded to the newest industrial standards at the time of its erection, and Vasconi's passion for modern technical detail. The assertion that the historical preservationist and the structural engineer demonstrated talent and imagination when they put their finger in this pie comes naturally.

Construction for the shopping center with aprox. 22,000 sq. m of sales area began in the Fall of 1996. The official laying of the foundation stone, a gesture meant to endear a new building to the public's heart, followed in August of 1997 and the opening is planned for the beginning of 1999. The core building with the old works and new sales areas will be joined, along its flanks, by two new structures, an office building and a parking garage. The office building with its striped facade will stretch along Berliner Strasse. The parking garage on the west side, whose height and massing will correspond to those of the surrounding buildings, is to be wrapped in greenery. The three-part complex will make up approx. a quarter of the 40,000 sq. m large "Borsig Tower Commercial Park,"

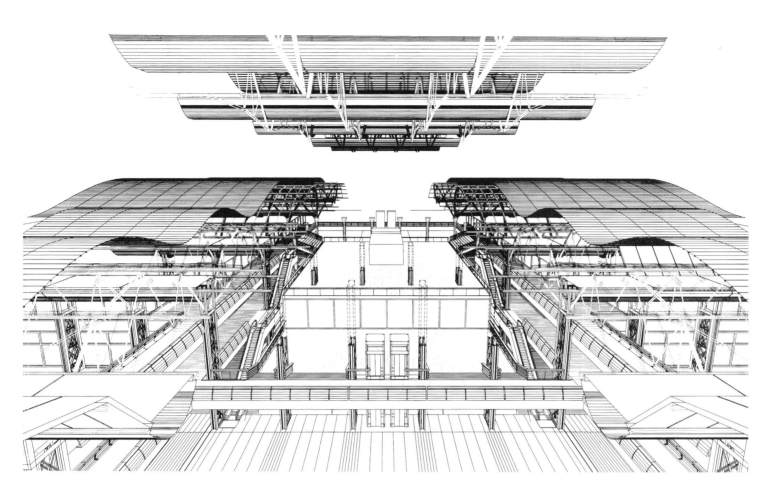

a project which in parts is already underway and for whose overall urban design Claude Vasconi placed first in a 1994 competition. The Phoenix Technology Center on the neighboring plot has already been opened (architects: Walter Rolfes and Partners, Berlin) and the housing which will form the northern border of the site is for the most part finished (architect: Norbert Stocker). To follow are office buildings and a hotel in the central area of the site around the Borsig Tower (urban design: Axel Schultes/Deubzer König, Berlin) and a commercial and innovation park (architect: Walter Rolfes and Partner) which was begun in May. Areas to the south have been reserved for industrial use.

The Borsig site is surrounded by two residential areas, Alt-Tegel to the north and housing complexes around Bernauer Strasse to the south. The Borsig complex can be reached on foot from both areas. Interior streets and green paths will link the Borsig Tower Commercial Park to the surrounding urban areas, which in turn stretch westwards to Tegel Lake. The main entrance to the Borsig complex will still be from Berliner Strasse which borders the approx. 40-acres large site to the east.

The Borsig Tower, symbol and focal point of the complex, was in 1922–24 the first highrise to be built in Berlin and stands restored since mid-1995. Here, amidst the construction site, the client resides.

Axonometry of the double-layered roof. The floating roof spans the new and the historic halls and thus constructs a unified composition

Memo on the 350th Birthday of Unter den Linden

Visual Moments and Quotations

Photos:
Akinbode Akinbiyi

Heinrich Heine, 1822 ... But I can see that you are no longer listening to my story and instead are gazing astonished at the linden trees. Yes indeed, those are the famous lindens, of which you've heard so much. Chills run down my spine when I think that perhaps Lessing stood on this spot; so many of the great men that lived in Berlin loved to stroll under these trees. Here walked Frederick the Great, imagine, here he strolled! But isn't the present just as glorious? Look at the beautiful ladies! Such figures! I wax poetic! ... What a lot of decorated gentlemen! What an abundance of medals! When one is measured for a coat, the tailor asks, "With or without a notch (for the medals)?" But wait! Do you see the building on the corner of Charlottenstrasse? That's the Café Royal! Please, let's stop in there, I can't go by without looking in for a moment. You don't want to? Well, on the way back you must come in with me ... Now have a look to the left and the right. That is the great Friedrichstrasse. Observing it, you can visualize the idea of infinity. But let's not stand here too long; here you can catch a cold. There's a terrible draft between the Hallesches and the Oranienburger Tor ... Here to the right you can see something new: boulevards are being built to connect Wilhelmstrasse with Luisenstrasse. And here we should pause for a moment and have a long look at the Brandenburg Gate with the Victory standing on top. The gate was designed by Langhans after the Propylaeum in Athens and consists of a colonnade with twelve great Doric columns. The goddess up there should be sufficiently familiar from recent history. The good woman has suffered her fate as well ... Now let's turn around, I've worked up an appetite and am longing for the Café Royal. Shall we drive? The hackney-carriages are right here at the gate. Quickly, coachman! How Unter den Linden surges! Look at all the people milling around, not knowing where they will dine today! Have you grasped the idea of dinner, my dear man? If you've grasped this, you've grasped all the doings of men...

Christa Wolf, 1969 I always enjoyed walking along Unter den Linden, and, as you know, my best walks were taken alone. Recently, after I'd avoided the street for some time, it appeared to me in a dream. Now I can finally tell you the story.

The street's fame never really bothered me; not while I was awake and certainly not while asleep. I realize that that was due to its fate as an east-west axis. Unter den Linden and the street that appeared to me in my dream have nothing to do with each other. One is abused in my absence, by newspaper pictures and tourist snapshots; the other stays pure, ready and waiting for me, even over longer periods of time. I admit that the two could be confused with each other at a superficial level. Even I make that mistake: when I cross my street and don't recognize it ... Strange characters crossed my way in the rapidly dissipating crowd after the play's end. Not all were christened with Spree water and had grown up under pines. I remember an Indian with a ruby-red stone on a snow-white turban, and slender black people who moved as if they were dancing, and above all one droll couple which emerged from the lively flow and, tightly entwined, headed for the statue of Alexander von Humboldt, which they—the boy and girl both—looked up at silently and attentively ... They were pleased at my smile, said something in their soft, singing language—praise, I believe, which could have as well been meant for me as for Alexander von Humboldt—and moved away on pliant, flat sandals. I generously placed my street at their disposal, since they had come from so far away to see it. I liked the fact that even queer foreign birds could find their feed here. You see, I was not far from liking everything that came my way.

Arthur Eloesser, 1911 Last Sunday, as it suddenly turned spring, I was strolling down our revered street Unter den Linden, some obligation or other having led me to the city center, and found her odious and empty, abandoned and alone in splendid isolation. On the broad way down to the Brandenburg Gate hardly a flaneur could be seen, let alone poets, for despite her historical dignity, she really did once have a poetic touch. E.T.A. Hoffmann peopled her with nighttime visions, in the days when oil lamps still flickered, and Heine met beautiful children here, who were not supposed to greet him openly. Only the police still seem to insist on their old rank by holding up traffic on the only lively corner of Friedrichstrasse, which soon creates an impression of chaos. But it is only rushed through-traffic; Berliner's no longer stroll along Unter den Linden. That used to be different. The true Berliner started off at his native Alexanderplatz, and paid a visit to the most elegant street of all in his Sunday best. Working citizens lived between Alexanderplatz and Kurfürsten Bridge, and if one reached a rather tightly predetermined status, he was allowed to move to Oranienburger Strasse. The center was still the center, whereas today's unshapen expanse allows one to recognize neither the city's head nor heart.

Alfred Andersch, 1962 During my strolls through Rome, which I often use now to look at apartments, I see myself now and again walking along Friedrichstrasse, on a cold and dry October day, I was at the theater box office and from the Weidendamm Bridge, looked onto the smoldering skin of the Spree as it lay before me in the cold morning; and now I stand at the corner of Friedrichstrasse and Unter den Linden and view the wide, empty, gray-blue prospect with its sparse lines of pedestrians on the sidewalks and its few cars on the road. Even the sky here looks emptier and harder than the sky on the other side of the Brandenburg Gate ... It's crazy, but in the center of Berlin, in whose packed life and action I often walked as a child, I'm a solitary, strange, straying figure. I enter Hedwig Cathedral, its interior sparklingly and tastefully restored, and some people are actually sitting here praying, mass is being read at one of the side altars.

Outside again the sparse loneliness of the square, not a soul at Gendarmenmarkt, not one car, and these are the early hours of a working day. The dome-topped towers of the French and German Cathedrals loom over the ruins of their churches and the steps of the Schauspielhaus's majestic flight of stairs have burst. Here, in this emptiness, in this silence, I should like to live, more so than on Kirchstrasse in Moabit.

Chronology

of Building Events from January to December 1997

"Anything but objectivity," wrote Billy Wilder in 1927. "It disquiets the heart and makes the character irresolute and unbalanced." Let's just leave it at that for now. Objectively speaking, the year 1997 splits into both a decisive and an indecisive part. The speed of construction has most decidedly remained undiminished, and the ribbons of the topping-out garlands flutter decisively over the city; meanwhile, those who previously didn't care for decisions at all have firmly made up their minds. The ministries are progressing, the state representatives appear on the shore, and the buildings of the federal government are pushing their way up to roof height. 150 embassies will eventually move to the Spree, but since they generally need offices as well as a residence, it's going to take a while. Macedonia, on the other hand, is already there.

What is still undecided are the so-called "major themes" in Berlin. Who wants to predict the future of the Schlossplatz? Everyone, of course — which was the rationale behind the famous six-part open forum "Schloss — Palace — House Fatherland." The "Inner City Master Plan" is taking small steps to shape the urban idea and image of both Berlin's centers; as far as possible, these steps have been noted. In the minds of the city's inhabitants, the controversy surrounding the Holocaust memorial merges with the Senate's indecisive position on the role of the Jewish Museum, which, though as good as finished, cannot and will not be opened before 1999.

Meanwhile, the politicians have most decidedly gotten around. This year's chronology had a hard time keeping track of all the trees they planted, all the cornerstones they laid, all the celebrations they opened, all the appearances they made.

A chronology cannot place emphasis; it has no headlines. Still, mood plays a role. If there are too many retrospectives, anniversaries, or old names, the impression may arise that the redefinition of Berlin — the most undecided of the undecidable — is being attempted via its glorious past.

But the crux of the chronology remains: since it occurs only one day earlier, a significant event like the simplification of the city building code appears directly above the "Dove galantine with autumn salad and truffle" served by chef Rolf Schmidt in the first display of Berlin gastronomy.

This time, the texts that comment on current events are drawn from the newspapers; they reflect the mood more directly than last year's literary delicacies. Of course the camel race hardly has the objective significance we have attributed to it here, but on the other hand even Alfred Kerr gushed about camels in the capital city in 1895.

Every Berliner knows that the art dealers are migrating from Charlottenburg to Mitte, and the chronology simply provides another confirmation of which way the wind is blowing. On June 26th, we noted a nocturnal resolution by the government coalition in favor of reducing Berlin's 23 districts to a total of 12. As of yet, the matter is still undecided ...
The editors

January 1997

The urban design theme of the year is the Berlin master plan commissioned by City Development Senator Peter Strieder and former Senate Building Director Hans Stimmann and introduced in November 1996 (cf. BBA '96, 11.29.1996)—"Planwerk Innenstadt Berlin"—which is supposed to offer guidelines for getting the disparate centers in the city's West and East heading on their way to future development. Distributed throughout the upcoming year are a diverse set of events meant to facilitate discussion among the Senate, the district governments, investors, architects, and the public. In shorthand: The guidelines for building density and mixture of uses, for setback of spaces for private auto traffic, for increase of residential density in the central city, as well as for resumption of the city's historic outline all partly collide with the sectoral development plans for

January 1997

More and more Chinese are discovering Berlin, according to a report from Berlin Tourism Marketing GmbH (BTM), which in 1996 (the Year of the Rat) started counting visitors from the Empire of the Middle. Following its initial tally of 15,849, BTM certified a 124 per cent rise in Chinese tourists' interest in Berlin.

1.8.1997

Address: Am Schlossplatz 1. After much hesitation (and maybe owing to the lovely address), the Federal Chancellor selects the Staatsrat (former GDR executive council) building (architects: Roland Korn and Hans-Erich Bogatzky, 1962–1964) for the provisional site of his Berlin office for the time between the Bundestag's move (1999) and the completion of the new Chancellory building along the Spreebogen (expected to be finished by April 2000). He did not want to retard the move from Bonn to Berlin, the Chancellor said. In the Staatsrat building, he will be presented with the following objects (among others): the Eosander

Berlin—1918 *Ben Hecht*

This little man was obviously Karl Liebknecht. I had heard of him only an hour ago (although among politically-minded folk he was world famous) but I watched him with excitement. He was my first glimpse of Brutus, Robespierre, Garibaldi, Bolivar, Washington—a leader of revolution, a stormer of kings' palaces…

I hurried on after Liebknecht and his marines, guided by Liebknecht's voice. He was making a speech.

I arrived in a large bedroom. The tall marines stood lining its walls. Their carbines were grounded, their faces raised in stiff attention. Liebknecht's sharp voice was crying out strange phrases in an emperor's bedroom. I recognized some of them—"freedom for the proletariat has come—workingmen are the new dynasty—"

The speech done, nobody moved or made a sound. Liebknecht started undressing himself. There was a fierce, lyric look in his black eyes. Liebknecht, the little workingman with a gift of gab, was undressing himself in the bedroom of a Hohenzollern emperor—and about to lie down in an emperor's bed!

A several minutes, Liebknecht stood barefoot in a suit of long winter underwear. Some of its buttons were missing and the flap seat was baggy from too much laundering. He picked up his bulging brief case and four large books. With these under his arms, he approached the Kaiser's bed. Someone turned off the ceiling lights. A lamp was left burning on the spindly-legged bedside table. The large room became shadowed. The white snow falling was like a face in all the windows.

the districts of Charlottenburg, Tiergarten, and Mitte. Flashpoints in the East: the street line on Leipziger Strasse, Mühlendamm, and Grunerstrasse, a low building structure bordering Fischerinsel, a loose set of buildings on the Marx-Engels-Forum, the extension of Landsberger Allee through to Alexanderplatz, as well as greater density for Karl-Marx-Allee. Flashpoints in the West: Narrowing Strasse an der Urania and Lützowstrasse, a redesign for Hardenbergplatz, extending Hertzallee through to Ernst-Reuter-Platz, and greater density for the Hansaviertel. Planners for City-East: Dieter Hoffmann-Axthelm and Bernd Albers. Planners for City-West: Fritz Neumeyer and Manfred Ortner.

1.1.1997

Berlin Gasworks (Berliner Gaswerke, GASAG) celebrates the 150th anniversary of the firm's establishment. The exhibit specially conceived for the occasion, "Fire and Flame for Berlin," will be on display through May in the Museum for Transportation and Technology.

1.7.1997

"The first million is always the hardest." This platitude's truth is demonstrated in the Info-Box. While it took ten months for the promoters to get their first million visitors, the magic number two million was reached already half a year later. To be continued.

portal of 1713, from whose balcony Karl Liebknecht proclaimed the socialist republic in 1918, the history of the German workers' movement as a glass painting in the major landing, the diplomatic hall in the east wing with doves and ears of grain, and much more. In light of its projected occupancy by the Chancellor and later use by the Federal Building Ministry, the entire building (designated for landmark protection) now appears to have been saved from what had once seemed like certain destruction after the fall of the Berlin Wall.

The marines had stiffened. They stood watching the little man in the homely suit of long underwear approach the royal bed, and I felt that a queer sort of battle was going on—one of which I had never yet read in the histories of revolutions. Things in the shadows were giving battle to the hundred ribbon-capped marines standing against the walls. I could almost see the enemy—a line of kings from the bearded Barbarossa to the gimpy-armed earth shaker, Wilhelm; Black Eagles and Court Balls, and the gonfalons of ghostly guardsmen. Not only the walls and furniture were breathing these phantoms into existence but they came even more vividly out of the stiffened faces of the revolution's shock troops—the mutineers of the Royal German Fleet.

Liebknecht, the People's Leader, placed his bulging brief case and four reference books on the small bedside table and crawled in between the the cold royal sheets. The room had become heavily silent. I heard the royal bedsprings creak as Liebknecht stretched out his legs. Then, as he turned to reach for a book, there was a sudden sharp noise. The spindly-legged bedside table, an antique, had collapsed under the unaccustomed weight of revolutionary literature. The lamp hit the floor and one of its bulbs exploded. And the Soldiers of the Revolution fled. To a man, the hundred marines rushed in half panic out of the bedroom, routed by more ghosts than I had been able to imagine.

I began my first cable to the Daily News syndicate of seventy American newspapers with the information—"Kaiser Wilhelm returned to Berlin last night—"

1.9.1997

Construction start for the new hospice for AIDS patients in Reichenberger Strasse, Kreuzberg. Architect: Michael Julius Zielinski, Berlin. Supporting the planned six-story house with 16 apartments, common rooms, and guest quarters is the organization "zuhause im Kiez" ("At Home in the Neighborhood"), which needs to raise an extra DM 2 mill. to supplement the DM 4.3 mill. approved from public housing funds. Since 1989 the "ziK" organization has found room and board for 1,000 people infected with the virus.

1.12.1997

Ignaz Bubis, Chairman of the Central Council of Jews in Germany, turns 70. At a dinner celebrating the occasion in Schloss Bellevue, President Roman Herzog characterizes Bubis as, "the very model of what we imagine a democratic citizen to be," and thanks him for the contribution he has made, as a "German of Jewish faith," to Germany's welfare and reputation.

1.15.1997

Presentation of the future party headquarters for Bündnis 90/Die Grünen (Alliance 90/The Greens) on the Platz vor dem Neuen Tor. The old five-story building is just minutes away from the Chancellory and is embedded in two adjoining new buildings by J.P. Kleihues. It can be expected that renovation of the 2,000 sq. m. will proceed according to ecological criteria. Architect: Walter Sauermilch; estimated moving date: autumn 1999.

1.10.1997

"Victoria & Albert, Vicky & and the Kaiser: A Chapter in Anglo-German Family History," exhibit in the Deutsches Historisches Museum. Through March 25th.

1.13.1997

The Berlin housing construction company GEHAG hands over to the Akademie der Künste (Academy of the Arts) on permanent loan a bundle of 450 drawings, sketches, and models from the early work of Bruno Taut (1880–1938), in addition to fifty watercolors, drawings, and a sketchbook belonging to his brother Max Taut (1884–1967), the first director of its architectural division following the Academy's re-establishment in the Western sector of Berlin.

1.15.1997

Ten thousand people come to Friedrichshain to commemorate the murder of Rosa Luxemburg and Karl Liebknecht on the 78th anniversary of this event.

Rosa and Karl *Lothar Heinke*

They're selling red carnations already in the subway station at Magdalenenstrasse: "a mark fifty for Karl and Rosa." The closer the early risers get to the memorial at Friedrichsfelde with the graves of the labor leaders murdered 78 years ago, the louder and more cacophonous the pleas and cries become: "Hot tea, prepared by a friend of the Free German Youth," or "Support the solidarity campaign 'A Notebook and Pencil for Every Cuban Schoolchild.'" Here, the "blue-shirts" march "back to the future;" over there, a "Solidarity Committee for the Victims of Political Persecution" solicits greetings for "prisoners" like ex-defense minister Kessler or the "Scouts for Peace." They give current addresses for these "victims of the justice of revenge" — "send solidarity greetings!" — and for the judges — "send protests!" For 50 Pfennig you can buy a "Manifesto of the National Committee for a Free GDR," in which the peoples of the world are invited to support the fight for independence of occupied East Germany ("West German occupation get out!"). For the Bolshevist Youth, it's either "Socialism or Barbarism;" the German Communist Party lives (with Ernst Busch and hot mulled wine); a "Socialist Alternative" warns the PDS party: "The course is set straight for social democracy." While agitators from every German state met in front of the cemetery, around the porphyry gravestones tens of thousands quietly commemorated Rosa Luxemburg, Karl Liebknecht, and other socialist leaders. The graves were adorned with wreaths placed there in the early morning by the PDS, covered over with countless flowers. Organizers saw to it that banners and slogans were left at the door. All were united around Karl and Rosa, the Enemy from within was nowhere to be seen. No policemen either — or rather, only one. Police Chief Hagen Saberschinsky himself kept an eye on the leftists — in plain-clothes.

A Whiff of Monarchy *Mathias Remmele*

Where would the German Historical Museum (DHM) be without the Chancellor and his penchant for history? It might not even exist! In 1987, at Kohl's instigation, the museum was given to Berlin as a, "gift from the federal government," to celebrate the city's 750th anniversary... The plans for the new DHM were already well advanced when the Wall came down and the old Zeughaus fell to the DHM. The dream of a new building was over—for the time being. But the museum-makers and the new lords of the Zeughaus soon had an idea. Their building, they said, was much too small. German history needs space, and so it would be quite unthinkable to accommodate both the permanent collection and the temporary exhibitions together in the Zeughaus. For the changing exhibitions, an annex was needed.

The Chancellor was easily persuaded of the DHM's urgent need for space, and quickly recognized the chance to portray himself as the builder of a new historical museum after all. And since, as everyone knows, he is an indisputable authority in the field of art and architecture, and since he has taken a special interest in the reconstruction of the capital city, and since there have now been so many competitions in Berlin that have produced doubtful results, and since Kohl didn't want to play second fiddle to his friend Mitterand (who is also an inspired patron of architecture)—for all these compelling reasons, Herr Kohl made a bold and solitary decision regarding the DHM. He invited the "world-famous" American architect Ieoh Ming Pei to Bonn for talks and asked the master if he could imagine becoming "artistically involved" in the German capital, or in other words, if he would like to design the annex for the DHM. Who could have resisted?...

1.16.1997

With the exhibit "Construction Site: Czech Republic" (through March 2nd), the Academy of the Arts takes a third look at building going on east of Berlin; 1994 "Construction Site: Poland"; 1995 "Construction Site: Moscow".

1.17.1997

The German Historical Museum (Deutsches Historisches Museum, DHM) and architect Ieoh Ming Pei request a benevolent evaluation of the annex building for the DHM's home (at the Zeughaus in Berlin). Nobody can really revoke the Chancellor's positive assessment, and so the new building costing 100 million marks gets favored from the political angle. To be sure, there are complaints about the "whiff of monarchy" that clings to the commission undertaken without a competition, but there is

1.16.1997

Art assignment: In the casino of the Berlin Parliament in the former Prussian Landtag building, the triptych "The Opening of the Berlin Wall" by the West Berlin painter Matthias Koeppel is ceremoniously unveiled. A year's work, endowed with DM 300,000, resulted in the 30 sq. m large mural, on the left wing of which the Wall's opening on November 9th, 1989 is depicted. The centerpiece portrays people occupying the Wall in front of the Brandenburg Gate, and the right wing the start of demolition of the Wall at Potsdamer Platz. In addition to the triptych's decidedly Western perspective on these events, it is especially conspicuous how Berlin's Red-Green government of the time is only represented on the margins (and then only in the person of Berlin mayor Walter Momper), whereas the current governing officials who commissioned this work are set in the right light.

also recognition for the potential in the annex nicknamed the "show house." Five models of the new building have been prepared for an exhibit open to the public; later, two of these are to be on display in the foyer of the Zeughaus.

1.20.1997

Jan Karski comes to Berlin to deliver a lecture on the occasion of the 55th anniversary of the Wannsee Conference. Active during the war as a courier between the Polish underground and the government-in-exile, he succeeded, with the help of members of the Jewish resistance, in being smuggled into the Warsaw Ghetto, and later into the Izbica Lubelska concentration camp. In 1943 he reported to President Roosevelt at length on his experiences. Filmmaker Claude Lanzmann was able to win Karski for his documentary "Shoah" in the late 1970s. The 82-year-old authority on Eastern Europe has never again set foot on German soil.

1.23.1997

At Landsberger Allee, the starting shot is sounded for the 86th Berlin Six-Day Race, with which the new Velodrom will be opened (architect: Dominique Perrault, cf. BBA '96). Following a lapse of seven years, this takes up a tradition whose origins go back to the year 1909 in the exhibition halls at the Zoo. Additional venues were the Sportpalast in the western and the Werner-Seelenbinder Halle in the eastern part of the city, as well as the Deutschlandhalle (following the razing of the Sportpalast).

Drowsily rolling from the bunk
Asleep at the wheel!
Rubbing the temples
Just dreaming of seas, gulls, buoys!
Salty!—
The neck stretches
Entering the eternal circuit
Running running overheating
Circling the course of time
In a race against the clock
Round and round the cyclist's chain
And second by second the second hand goes
Further—
On—
Go!
And they're off and running running
Rounding off
The seconds! Action!
Then the music! Music music victory victory!
"Where to rest"
With a drumbeat
365 days
The pneumatic heart pumps
Full of misery full of pain
The circulation of blood!
Circulation;
Always the gentleman in tails...
Circulate! Run!
Stop!
The second day.
Walter Mehring

End of January 1997

The concept of a "German National Theater" and its title shock the public in Berlin. Berlin's Senator for Cultural Affairs, Peter Radunski, recommends consolidating under a single General Director the four big houses in the Mitte district (Staatsoper, Komische Oper, Schauspielhaus, and Deutsches Theater) and then laying them at the feet of the federal government. For pecuniary reasons, naturally; for Berlin's cultural budget is small. As a reconciliatory gesture, an alternative name is suggested: "Foundation for Capital City Culture."

1.26.1997

100 years ago, the Jewish photographer Erwin Blumenfeld was born in Berlin. The photographer, who aimed "to distill the unreal from the real," started out as a fashion illustrator, formed friendships with the Dadaists, and became a big admirer of George Grosz. In 1919 he went into exile in Holland, later in France, and in 1941 in America. In 1962 he returned once more to Berlin. On July 4th, 1969 Erwin Blumenfeld died in Rome.

1.23.1997

Through March 23rd, the "Hidden Museum" at Schlüterstrasse 70 shows works by the Jewish photographer Lotte Jacobi. In addition to her well-known pictures from the Berlin of the Weimar Republic, there are photos from her time in the United States, where she was forced to emigrate in 1935.

My Dearest Mathilde *Heinz Knobloch*

One day in December 1913, Rosa Luxemburg came to her apartment to announce an article for the Sozialdemokratische Korrespondenz.

It was their first meeting. In Mathilde's words, "When Rosa Luxemburg came to see me for the first time... she immediately made a deep impression on me. Her large, shining eyes that seemed to understand everything, her modesty and goodness, her almost child-like delight in everything beautiful, made my heart beat faster for her. Admiringly, I looked up to her, an intellectual giant in almost shabby clothes."...

Mathilde Jacob's five-year association with Rosa Luxemburg— from the end of 1913 to January 1919—was the high point of her life. Conversely, in view of all that Mathilde did and was able to do for her closest friend during this time, one could maintain that without her, Rosa Luxemburg could never have survived her years of imprisonment during the war—not psychologically, and most certainly not as productively. The excerpts from the 153 surviving letters from Rosa to Mathilde should be read with this in mind; 148 of them were written from prison.

1.25.1997

At the Brandenburg Gate, now open only to buses and taxis, the Berlin Transit Authority (Berliner Verkehrs Betriebe— BVG) presents the latest additions to its fleet of buses. Officially designated as buses with "feel-good quality," and equipped with air conditioning, no longer breakable windows, and "stoop" technology (allowing problem-free access even by baby carriages and wheelchairs), they are supposed to provide greater public comfort for passenger transportation.

1.27.1997

For the second time in its postwar history, Germany officially commemorates the victims of National Socialism on the day of liberation from Auschwitz. In contrast to the Bundestag, the Berlin Parliament does not hold a memorial session of its own and instead joins two Jewish Community events taking place at the Centrum Judaicum. The declaration made by parliamentary president Herwig Haase in the Parliament's name—in which he calls for a commemoration of all victims, including "those who were perpetrators earlier or became perpetrators later"—receives indignant opposition from the public.
Artist Horst Hoheisel projects a photo of the opening gate at the concentration camp Auschwitz-Birkenau, sporting the contemptuous sentence "Arbeit macht frei" ("Work liberates"), onto the Brandenburg Gate at night.

1.27.1997

Streets, squares, and their names I.
The Tiergarten district honors Mathilde Jacob, secretary, confidante, and friend of Rosa Luxemburg. As of today, the square in front of the district town hall bears her name, and a memorial plaque commemorates this Jewish woman, murdered 1943 in the Theresienstadt concentration camp, who lived and worked for years in Tiergarten.

Understandably, only two of Mathilde's letters to Rosa have survived. But there is also an account written by Mathilde Jacob, presumably in 1929. It comprises 135 pages and is preserved as an unpublished manuscript in an archive in California. Mathilde called this memoir "Rosa Luxemburg and her Friends, 1914–1919." The account begins with the first meeting of the two women and ends with the events after Rosa's death. Clearly Mathilde didn't consider her own life important enough to relate at least a few of its stations, a fact we later readers regret. But how could Mathilde have known her own fate and that of her family?...

The words "My dearest Mathilde" appear for the first time in a letter from Christmas 1916. Mathilde had sent a gift: fresh flowers and a cake her mother had baked. Sonja Liebknecht sent a small Christmas tree. "I am absolutely delighted, the room shines and has a festive appearance. The poor prisoner who cleans here said today, 'When you see that, it makes your heart laugh in your body.' And she is exactly right. My heart really does laugh when I see this splendor. But of course I am crushed by the foolish luxury you are pursuing on my account."

Rosa has no patience for writing. "I want to talk to you." And at the end: "Unfortunately, we won't be able to see each other for the feast. But I will celebrate it whenever you are here. Once more, a kiss from your R."

2.4.1997

On the occasion of the 350th anniversary of Unter den Linden the Kunstforum (Art Forum) in the Grundkreditbank presents an exhibition on Berlin's grand boulevard through April 27th, 1997. Along with the linden scroll registering all the buildings from the years 1819/20, views by Schinkel, Eduard Gaertner, and Adolph Menzel are exhibited. The real day for celebrating this great occasion is actually April 16th, 1947, when the Prussian Elector Friedrich Wilhelm decreed the "Planting of Nut and Linden Trees to Prepare a Gallery from the Hundebrücke to the Thiergarten." A supplementary show of photographs from the period between 1855 and 1928 is on display at the Stadtmuseum in the Knoblauchhaus.

1.29.1997

Change in needs: For two years, an uncontested design by architects JSK Perkins and Will, Frankfurt/Berlin has been under consideration for the expansion of the Papestrasse train station. It calls for an ICE center with six north-south and four east-west platforms as well as a tourism center, which would make it the second-largest train station in Berlin after Lehrter Zentralbahnhof. It is by now obvious that the usage concept (a 230-bed hotel, a 30,000 sq. m shopping mall, and parking space for 3,500 cars) is unrealistic. New decisions are expected.

February 1997

Sony commissions 56 elevators and 12 escalators from the Berlin company Otis for its project on Potsdamer Platz. Some are custom models called for by architect Helmut Jahn. It is the biggest contract in Otis' history.

2.3.1997

45th anniversary of the cornerstone-laying for Karl-Marx-Allee. The boulevard was supposed to "orient itself toward the model of the Soviet Union, toward socialism in substance, and in form basing itself on national traditions." After a design by Hermann Henselmann, a long major thoroughfare 1.7 kilometers long and 90 meters wide was built, with gateways at Frankfurter Tor and Strausberger Platz. The 7–9-story residential blocks were clad in Meissen ceramics and given luxurious interior decorations.

2.4.1997

At 3:20 p.m., Helmut Kohl breaks the ground with the ceremonial first spadeful of earth for the future Chancellor's Office on the Spree Bend. The design by Axel Schultes and Charlotte Frank,

2.4.1997

Conclusion of renovations of the hundred year old Lutherkirche in Spandau. In the church interior, which once offered room for 1,600 visitors, four floors with a total of 9 residences were installed. The downsized vestry now holds 300 visitors to the church. Architects: Dieter Ketterer & Partners. Cost: DM 8 mill.

1.30.1997

The nonpartisan senior steering committee of the Bundestag announces its decision: culinarily speaking, there won't be any Berlin Republic, but a Munich Republic instead. The roof garden restaurant of the Bundestag will be managed by Munich chef Michael Käfer. It will be, according to Käfer, a "café-restaurant with dishes in a bistro-and-brasserie style."

End of January 1997

At Alexanderplatz subway station, a change in decor. The new exhibit on the walls along the platform for the Number 2 Line is called "privat" ("private"). Thirty large-sized pictures were selected from an anonymous competition in which 906 Berlin artists from 33 countries participated.

2.1.1997

Heiner Carow, the movie director for Defa (the East German film production company) dies at the age of sixty-seven in Berlin. His best-known film, "The Legend of Paul and Paula," elevated him in both East and West to cult status as a director. Other films were: "Icarus," "Till Death Do You Part," "The Russians Are Coming," as well as the first gay Defa movie, "Coming Out," for which he received a Silver Bear at the 1990 Berlin Film Festival.

The present owner, DePfa Immobilien, renovated the first few blocks in accordance with landmark preservation laws, and the repairs are continuing, even if at reduced expense ever since public funds were cut.

3.2.1997

On February 2nd, 1947, two years before the founding of the GDR, actor and singer Ernst Busch receives a license from the Soviet Military Administration to open Germany's first postwar record company. "Lied der Zeit GmbH" becomes "VEB Deutsche Schallplatte" in 1955. Its pop music "Amiga" label, which was taken over by BMG Ariola in 1994, is where all East German rock bands, from Silly to the Puhdys, publish their work.

reworked several times since it it won the design competition in 1992, foresees a 36-meter high cube, the so-called Chancellor Building, encased on two sides by parallel five-story administrative tracts for a total of 310 office units. The administrative tracts are grouped around several wintergardens serving as thermal buffer zones within an overall ecological concept. The facade of the so-called Ehrenhof, corrugated, freestanding concrete walls in front of a large glass facade, is intended to symbolize the office's openness and proximity to the people. Costs run at about DM 400 mill., with a useable space of 19,000 sq. m. Dedication is planned for late 1999 or early 2000. Should the parliament manage to keep to its scheduled mid-1999 move into the rebuilt Reichstag, the Chancellor will reside in the Staatsratsgebäude.

2.5.1997

Fiftieth anniversary of the death of Hans Fallada (Rudolf Ditzen), the author for the "little guy" ("Peasants, Bosses, and Bombs," "Whoever Feeds Once from the Tin Bowl," "A Wolf Among Wolves," "Little Man, What Now?"). Less well known are the pieces he contributed in early Thirties to the "Vossische Zeitung," "Querschnitt," and "Die Literatur." Fallada spent his childhood in Berlin, returned there in 1930 for three years, and then again in 1945 in order to serve the new era after the wishes of his friend Johannes R. Becher. He writes for the "Tägliche Rundschau," the newspaper for the Soviet occupying power, and in four weeks commits his novel "Everyone Dies Just for Himself" to paper. In 1947 he dies in a small house in Pankow; the street leading there is named after him.

2.6.1997

After stops at the Musée d'Orsay in Paris and the National Gallery in Washington, it is now time for the Staatliche Museen im Alten Museum to open the grand retrospective "Adolph Menzel, 1815–1905. The Labyrinth of Reality." The Parisian title was "The Neurosis of Truth." At last, works from the collections of both the Alte (Eastern) and Neue (Western) Nationalgalerie are on display together. The first major Menzel exhibit of the Berliner Nationalgalerie, with close to 7,000 items catalogued, took place in 1905, shortly after Menzel's death.

2.6.1997

Grand opening of the "Plaza Marzahn" in Mehrower Allee 20. The shopping center (with 110 publicly-financed apartment units) cost about dm 80 mill. Developer: Investorengruppe Gädecke und Landsberg. Architects: Baasner, Möller und Langwald, Berlin.

2.10.1997

The art scene and art galleries leave their traditional locations in Charlottenburg, Kreuzberg and Wilmersdorf to settle in Berlin-Mitte. Pars pro toto: the gallery owner Bodo Niemann (photographic art and the like) moves out of Charlottenburg, Knesebeckstrasse, into the Hackesche Höfe.

2.15.1997

"Musehnsucht" ("Museyearning"): 25,000 visitors are counted during the long night of the museums on the streets of Berlin. Building fans enjoy feasting on the architectural models in the Werkbund Archive. Confectioner Wilfried Sobotta used biscuit, butter cream and marzipan to remodell K.F. Schinkel's Bauakademie.

2.19.1997

Topping-out ceremony for the fire brigade coordinating center in Berlin-Siemensstadt. Following the completion of this building early in 1998 and a testing phase, as of 1999 this central office is supposed to steer and coordinate fire brigade deployments in Berlin and Brandenburg, thereby shortening deployment times by up to three minutes. Architects: Fissler/Ernst, Berlin. Total cost: DM 80 mill., of which DM 50 mill. goes toward computer-run technology.

2.21.1997

Streets, squares, and their names II. In the shadow of the Olympic Stadium and Le Corbusier's Unité d'habitation, a small ceremony witnesses the renaming of Reichssportfeldstrasse into Flatowallee. With this renaming, the district of Charlottenburg honors the Jewish athletes Alfred and Gustav-Felix Flatow, each of whom won gold medals at the 1896 Olympic Games in Athens. Both were murdered in the Theresienstadt concentration camp. On the very next day, the name Flatow had been crossed out on the new signs by persons un-known.

2.21.1997

Topping-out ceremony for the Heinrich-Heine-Forum—a mixed commercial and housing project of HANSEATICA. 156 residences and 38 luxury apartments in a boarding house are planned. The u-shaped construction across from the Engelbecken on Heinrich-Heine-Platz 8–12 has incorporated into the project a riding and drill hall (based on model designs by K.F. Schinkel) designed by Karl Hampel in 1929/30, including a 6,700 sq. m large shopping arcade. Architect: Karl-Heinz Cammann, Berlin. Construction cost: DM 140 mill.

February

2.5.1997

One day before the topping-out ceremony for the Dresdner Bank on Pariser Platz (Architects: v. Gerkan, Marg, & Partners), a 800-ton crane lifts the final component of a flat steel dome onto a building shell that is thereby completed on schedule. The steel construction, weighing 35 tons and 29 m in diameter, was pieced together on the neighboring property. Business will get started in the new executive office of the Dresdner Bank (construction cost: DM 150 mill.) in November.

2.6.1997

Opening of the retrospective for Edward Kienholz and Nancy Reddig-Kienholz in the Berlinische Galerie (through March 31st). The exhibit displays works from 1954 through 1994, the "Environments" typical of both artists. From 1973 onward, when Edward Kienholz arrived in the city for the first time as a guest of the German Academic Exchange Program (DAAD), the couple has lived in Berlin. Edward Kienholz died in 1994.

2.10.1997

In the Toilet Dispute between the Berlin Sanitation Department (Berliner Stadtreinigung – BSR) and the district governments, a solution has been found. The BSR commits to maintaining 99 sanitary facilities, for which around DM five mill. will be raised annually. The major share for the remainder of the toilet quota, which comes to 210 for all of Berlin (85 fewer than before), is covered by a private firm under the slogan "Our job is making the cities of the world more beautiful."

2.19.1997

Conclusion of a contract on Potsdamer Platz: A joint building, around 20,000 sq. m large, is put up for the Filmhaus and the Deutsche Mediathek in the Sony-Center (architect: Helmut Jahn, Chicago). Those moving in as of 2001 include the German Cinematheque (Dt. Kinemathek), with a film museum and the Marlene Dietrich Collection, the repertory movie theater Arsenal, and the German Film and Television Academy. The Deutsche Mediathek, a library for television and radio, will be newly installed. Also to be included in the Sony-Center will be an underground cinematic multiplex with 8 halls and the three-dimensional superscreen cinema Imax 3 D. Symbolic gift of the city to the investor: A suitcase for shoes owned by Marlene Dietrich (who never felt at home anywhere unless she had packed 31 pairs of shoes) and a pair of pink slippers ribboned with her personal label.

2.24.1997

Symbolic groundbreaking for the new parliamentary building in the Dorotheenblöcke east of the Reichstag. The model shows eight blocks lined up close to each other, each observing the "Berliner Traufhöhe" (the traditional eaves height) and with quadrangular interior courtyards linked by two above-ground and one underground passageway. There are five participating architectural firms: Busmann and Haberer, Cologne; Pi de Bruijn, Amsterdam; von Gerkan, Marg & Partners, Hamburg; Schweger & Partners, Hamburg; as well as Thomas van den Valentyn, Cologne. Three old landmark-protected buildings are integrated into the complex on both sides of the Dorotheenstrasse: the Reichspräsidentenpalais (Imperial Presidential Palace) of 1904, in which the German Parliamentary

2.24.1997

The art collectors Erika and Rolf Hoffmann and their pictures move into the house on Sophienstrasse 20/21 in the Mitte district. Berlin gains something intended for Dresden: The painter Frank Stella was supposed to build the art museum in Dresden, according to the collectors' wishes, but the authorities rebuffed them. In Berlin, the former shirt manufacturers opted for an old sewing machine factory made of brick. The renovation and addition of a story to the building were carried out by the architectural cooperative Becker, Gewers, Kühn & Kühn.

2.27.1997

Premiere of the musical "Space Dream" in Hangar II of Tempelhof Airport. For about 8 million marks, the airplane hall was transformed into a permanent musical theater with 1,438 seats. Inventor, author, and composer of the musical: Harry Schärer, Baden/ Switzerland.

2.28.1997

Address: Jägerstrasse 54/55. In 1790, as a 19-year-old, Rahel Levin (later Rahel Varnhagen van Ense) opened her first literary salon here. Today a plaque is affixed to the house commemorating "the cleverest woman in the universe" (Heinrich Heine), who hosted Ludwig Tieck, Franz Grillparzer, Adalbert von Chamisso, the Humboldt brothers, Friedrich Schleiermacher, and Jean Paul, and where Count Pückler drove by with a team of four stags.

3.3.1997

A delegation of architects, entrepeneurs, and politicians with Undersecretary Wolfgang Branoner of the CDU at its head sets out on a compelling business trip. Today they are to present plans in Moscow for a "Berlin Haus". The eight-story office- and commercial building in a historicized de-luxe style is privately financed by the Berlin firms Görlich Unternehmen and Unternehmensgruppe Krebs GmbH & Co. The building will be a mere 800 meters distance from the Kremlin. Its purpose is clearlydefined: "An education and communication center, and basis for economic cooperation between Berlin and Moscow."

Society is to reside, the Chamber of Technology of 1914, and the house on Dorotheenstrasse 105. There will be 2,000 offices (Bonn standard: 18 sq. m) on approx. 53,000 sq. m of useable space. The Bundestag will, as (parliamentary president) Ms Süssmuth promises, keep "strictly to the stipulated cost framework" and not exceed DM 900 million. The buildings are supposed to be ready for occupancy by the end of 1999.

2.24.1997

With the award of the Golden Bear to Milos Forman, the director of "The People vs. Larry Flynt," the 47th "International Film Festival" in Berlin comes to an end after two weeks. Additional award-winners are the Taiwanese director Tsai Ming-liang for "He Liu—The River," as well as the actors Juliette Binoche for "The English Patient" and Leonardo DiCaprio for "Romeo and Juliette."

2.25.1997

Recollection of an historical absurdity: Fifty years ago today, on February 25th, 1947, the Allied Control Council decided on the dissolution of the state of Prussia, two years after the war's end. Without the state structure, which actually had long since ceased to be, its virtues were all the more able to hibernate better, cf. the Prussian Style.

2.28.1997

Berlin architect Daniel Gogel dies three weeks before his 70th birthday and a year after his long-time colleague Hermann Fehling (cf. BBA '96, 1.11.1996). Almost all the buildings of this architectural cooperative are hallmarks of the city, especially the Tiergarten Pavilion, which, built in 1957 as temporary architecture for Interbau, now celebrates its 40th anniversary and is routinely used by Berlin's city planning department to present public exhibits on city planning and architecture.

Three weeks ago, on February 7th, there entered into the house the restaurant VAU, an establishment ambitious enough to attempt reuniting culture with sociability. In the rooms fashioned by Meinhard von Gerkan, regular exhibits by well-known artists will be on view in addition to the opulent menus of chef Kolja Kleeberg.

End of February

After ninety years in Berlin, the bookseller Herder closes its doors. Its last domicile was the former Defaka department store on Tauentzienstrasse across from the Gedächtniskirche (Kaiser Wilhelm Memorial Church). After some major renovations, Herder's successor in the rooms it moved into just six years ago will be Munich bookstore Hugendubel.

3.1.1997

Reform in the fare structure for the Berlin Transit Authority (Berliner Verkehrsbetriebe—BVG) and its fare partners. Previously one could take a ride through the entire city and even into the environs of Brandenburg for the single fare of DM 3.90; now one has to think in terms of zones. The inner rapid transit (S-Bahn) ring forms the border for Zone A, the city limits Zone B, and the environs will become Zone C. Two zones cost DM 3.60, while the entire fare region remains DM 3.90. Except the 24-hour tickets, all other tickets will go up in price by 10%, which will provide the BVG with added revenues of 30 million marks annually.

3.2.1997

Premiere of the musical "Fame" in the Schiller Theater. Lots of celebrities.

3.3.1997

First evening in a series of events marking the 50-year history of the "Gruppe 47" (the "Group 47") in the Literarische Colloquium. With Peter Bichsel, Günter Grass, and Walter Höllerer. The group was founded in September 1947, its sustaining force was Hans Werner Richter, its statute was its letters, and the only ritual its annual meetings. It was the "salon" of postwar German literature. Among its award winners were: Günter Eich, 1950, Heinrich Böll, 1951, Ingeborg Bachmann, 1953, Günter Grass, 1958, Peter Bichsel, 1965. In 1968 the "Gruppe 47" wanted to get together in Prague, but Soviet tanks arrived ahead of them. It has not convened since then. The Ingeborg Bachmann Competition, which takes place annually in Klagenfurt/Austria, builds on the tradition of the "Gruppe 47," as does perhaps the "Literary Quartet" (the book review program on German television).

3.6.1997

Signed, sealed, delivered: In the presence, and through the cooperation, of Federal Environment Minister Angela Merkel, the last piece out of a total of 2,500 km of gas pipelines in the eastern part of Berlin (700 km of these cast iron) are sealed off. In 1993–95, 14 million cubic meters of gas seeped out of the ailing pipeline system and, among other things, damaged 26,000 trees lining the streets. Ms Merkel will stay until Sunday, March 9th, and use the marking of woodpecker trees to call for a nationwide initiative for the protection of trees with hollows.

3.7.1997

The Zentrum am Zoo, part of the 1957 Interbau exposition, is placed under landmark protection. This is the final ruling of the Berlin Superior Administrative Court after a 10-year legal battle between the Berlin Landmark Authority and the owner.

3.7.1997

BauNetz, Bauwelt's online architecture service, is honored both by the Industrie Forum Design in Hanover and the Design Zentrum Berlin with prizes for outstanding interface design.

3.7.1997

Opening of the 16th Berlin Music Biennale, which will present 22 debut performances (and a retrospective of compositions from the Seventies) with 56 composers from 20 countries. Through March 16th.

3.10.1997

On Monday at 6:30 a.m., under a sunny sky at Potsdamer Platz, a week of demonstrations for construction workers commences using the slogan "The government has left us out in the rain." 400,000 construction workers in Germany are unemployed; in Berlin and Brandenburg the number comes to 40,000. The week of demonstrations ends on March 15th with a protest march from the Brandenburg Gate ("Germany's premiere demonstration address") to the Gendarmenmarkt.

Protest Placement *Dorothee Wenner*

Last week Berlin became the capital of the construction workers' protest, which in view of the city's status as "largest construction site in Europe" is both logical and symbolic. Yet no other location could have made more clear how obsolete the traditional labor struggle has become. There was something poignant about it: men traveled in from far and near, men whose appearance showed that they were accustomed to heavy physical labor, or at least had been in the past. Such work leaves behind a certain weatherproofed exterior.

In actual fact, however, most of the demonstrators were still construction workers only in their own self-image; the majority of them were unemployed, on sick leave, or even on vacation. This puts them in a difficult position for negotiating with the people responsible for the sad state of the German building industry: strikes are no longer an effective medium of expression for people who are out of work.

It seemed almost grotesque when an activist shouted through a megaphone on Friday: "Everything stops when you say the word!" In fact, activity at construction sites over the course of the week was hardly interrupted at all, and even if building logistics were obstructed once or twice, on-site reserves of concrete were sufficient to keep on schedule.

For lack of personified opponents, the union leaders made an effort to at least stage the protests in a media-effective way. This strategy was reflected not only in the hearty "Good Morning!" aimed at early-morning television viewers, but also in the impressive outfitting of the demonstrators with red caps, raincoats, and flags. The latter were especially effective on Friday, when the demonstration parade split up for a while in favor of an unplanned, but all too tempting "excursion" to the construction site at the Reichstag… The avant-garde of the enraged workers stormed the main portal and

3.7.1997

The Lessing-Hochschule begins a new lecture series today on Berlin architecture. Architectural positions of Wilhelmine Berlin are presented in six weekly lectures. Selected topics include the historical center, national landmarks, Art Nouveau, and the Neue Sachlichkeit.

3.7.1997

The Swiss Weeks in Berlin (through March 23rd) provide the city with an exhibit of 81 drawings, especially of angels, from the late work of Paul Klee, in the Kupferstichkabinett (Engraving Collection) — on loan from the Bern Art Museum.

3.8.1997

Hartmut, but also a bit of Helmut, allows Berliners to sit outside in front of bars and cafés as of today. Hartmut designates the atmospheric high bringing sunshine and warmth — and which, together with the International Tourism Exchange opened by Helmut Kohl, moved Berlin's district governments to issue special permission for the outdoor season (usually starting at Easter) to open early. At the International Tourist Exchange, 97 representatives from 177 countries will be advertising through March 12th.

stood on the socle waving red flags: "Now we're on the move!" The television people were delighted, and the police let the demonstrators have their way for a while. It was as if a bunch of enthusiastic football players had found a lawn, but with no ball, only noisemakers to play with. And so they soon followed the union's call to continue the demonstration, where "people will see us" — and ran in the direction of the Brandenburger Tor.

While the stones flew around him, an activist with a skewered cabbage on his shoulder went on handing out Haribo Gummi-Bears from a concession tray. Then a union member explained that if German policemen are replaced with cheap immigrant labor, the construction union IG BAU will be happy to help maintain order at future police demonstrations in return for their cooperation during the past week.

"Went to the Reichstag once, threw three stones, no fire, no casualties, oh well!" a demonstrator from Mülheim summed up on his way back to the bus, along the Sony construction site. He cast a somewhat melancholy glance through the fence, where a pretty policewoman made sure that the "cheap immigrant labor" could continue their work unmolested.

The Deceiving of the Authorities *Jurek Becker*

... on the ground floor of an old tenement in Berlin is a small branch bank. One day one of the customers, a shady type with a criminal record, takes a look at the situation and comes to the conclusion that one could get a lot of money out of there with very little trouble. So he gets together with two others to plan the break-in... The only thing they don't know is where to put the money. None of them wants to keep it at home, since all three are known to the police... They mull it over some more, until a few days later one of the three arrives with a newspaper in his hand, beaming with delight. According to the paper, an urban expressway is being planned, exactly in the direction they need; completion is scheduled for such and such a day, on the occasion of some anniversary or another. They celebrate the news as a gift from heaven; no question but that they will wait for the new road, by which they can easily convey the money to their hideaway—after all, the bank isn't going anywhere.

Month after month passes, year after year—you know how hellishly slow things sometimes go around here. The anniversary approaches, but still the road entertains no thoughts of completion... And as if that weren't enough, one day one of them announces the dreadful news that the old building where their bank branch is located is going to be torn down in the course of urban renewal, in eight months. If the new expressway isn't finished by then, they can throw their carefully crafted plan out the window—a hopeless situation. What to do? In their desperation, they make a bold decision. They say to themselves, unless we act now, that expressway will never be finished. So they go to work in road construction.

Lola giggles for the first time.

... They set to work with a vengeance, in a race against the eight-month deadline. Now fortunately, we live in a country where good work receives recognition, and since no one knows their motives, they are inundated with awards. They receive bonuses, one of them becomes a brigadier, another an activist, yet another appears in the newspaper or TV news as a model roadbuilder... Just in time, the road is finished... Just in time, they rob the small bank, and just in time, they make it out of the city on the new expressway before the barricades are put up. In the summer-house, they count the stolen money. It is much less than they expected; they think their colossal effort deserves twice or three times as much.

"I like your story a lot," says Lola softly and, in an instant, demolishes my efforts to maintain distance. "But it gets thin toward the end. Nothing surprising happens anymore. They make a plan, carry it out, and everything works. It doesn't matter that in the end, the money is much less than they had hoped for. Don't you think?"
"Maybe," I say conciliatingly. "In any case, you're starting to get a much better handle on things."
"Let's assume they never break into the bank after all."
"Why not?"
"Don't laugh—they don't break in because the work in road construction has changed them, at least one or two of them. Work changes people, don't you agree? Wouldn't it be more surprising, and more logical, if they provided themselves the opportunity to break in, but suddenly didn't want to anymore? Instead of robbing the bank, they move on to build another road, because they think they can get more that way. They've tasted the blood of respectability. Doesn't it work that way?"
"You're a smart one," I say. "You make it sound so appetizing."
"Are you going to think about it?"
"And how."

3.11.1997

Opening of the small exhibit "how to live?" in the bauhaus-archive, with seven installments from the years 1927/1932. Table leaves, drawers, and pull-out tables demonstrate the bauhaus motto that design means, above all else, thinking practically.

3.12.1997

Decision in the Schinkel Competition. Theme: The International Aviation and Aerospace Exhibition 1998 in Schönefeld. A record number of participants: 480 works were submitted; there have not been this many submissions since the call went out for the first competition in 1952.

3.14.1997

The writer Jurek Becker dies of cancer at the age of 59. Jurek Becker was born in the Polish city of Lodz in 1937 and grew up in the Warsaw Ghetto. He survived the concentration camps Ravensbrück and Sachsenhausen. Many of his books grew out of his observations as a child, beginning with "Jacob the Liar," which made him world famous in 1969. He had to leave the GDR in 1977, and since then lived in West Berlin. Many of his novels were filmed, and he achieved great popularity with his television series "Liebling Kreuzberg."

3.17.1997

The Art Advisory Board (Kunstbeirat), consisting of six consultants and nine parliamentarians as well as Bundestag president Rita Süssmuth submits an (incomplete) list with the names of artists to receive commissions on the new government- and parliamentary quarter. Reichstag: Rosemarie Trockel, Gerhard Richter, Sigmar Polke, Anselm Kiefer, Ilya Kabakov, Bernhard Heisig, Georg Baselitz, Christian Boltanski, Günther Uecker. Dorotheen Blocks: Sij Armanani, Dani Karawan, the WES Group, Günther Förg, Jochen Gerz, Hans Haacke, Gerhard Merz. Alsen/Luisen Blocks: Ayse Erkmen, Gunda Förster, Katharina Fritsch, Ulrike Grossarth, Olaf Nicolai, Tobias Rehberger. A total of 30 million DM is to be spent.

1997 **March**

3.13.1997

Topping-out ceremony at the "Treptowers"—a 30-story highrise building with three 10-story segments—directly on the Spree in the Treptow district of Berlin. The building with its 165,000 sq. m of overall floorspace was erected in 660 days. Architects: Gerhard Spangenberg, Reichel & Stauth, Schweger & Partners. Developer: Allianz Grundstücks GmbH, which will also use half of the rooms. Project development: Roland Ernst Städtebau. Deadline for completion: early 1998.

3.14.1997

"Look into my wondering face"—an exhibit about the poet Else Lasker-Schüler in the Französische Dom on Gendarmenmarkt. Through April 27th.

3.15.1997

She would have turned 90 today. "Zarah Leander—Ich bin eine Stimme" ("I'm a Voice") is the title of a newly published book full of biographical, filmic, and photographic information. It was compiled by Paul Seiler, a.k.a. Paulchen, whose Schöneberg apartment contains absolutely incredible items on the topic.

3.18.1997

Egon Bahr, the cunning architect of "Ostpolitik" (the "Eastern policy" of detente), turns 75. A member of the Berlin SPD since 1956, Bahr accompanied the rise of Willy Brandt from Mayor of Berlin to Federal Chancellor, first as head of the Berlin Senate's Press and Information Office, later as director of the Planning Staff in the Foreign Office. His concept of "change through rapprochement" brought about the German-German Basic Treaty of 1972. After Brandt's resignation as Chancellor in 1974, Egon Bahr also withdrew from the executive branch and worked on helping to shape a Social Democratic "auxiliary foreign policy."

3.20.1997

As the twelfth award-winner since this honor was introduced in 1963, Wolfgang Kil receives the critic's prize of the Federation of German Architects (Bund Deutscher Architekten, BDA). He donates the DM 10,000 prize money (which would not have been unwelcome to a freelance journalist) to "Scheinschlag," the alternative city paper in the Mitte district, and justifies his decision by saying that he finds critical voices lacking in Berlin's architectural discussion. In his contribution to last year's Bauwelt Berlin Annual he describes a walk in time through the worlds of Treptow (in the East) and Kreuzberg (in the West of Berlin).

3.20/21.1997

"The virtual house" was absent. On this theme, Franz Schneider Brakel GmbH, the inventive doorhandle manufacturer, collects stars from architecture, philosophy, and art, including Peter Eisenman, Jean Nouvel, Toyo Ito, Eric Oger, and Rebecca Horn, in the Deutsches Architektur Zentrum (DAZ). Workshopping on the possibility "of making the virtual up-to-date for new approaches, through a creative process of remembering rather than by a permanent rendering of the possible." The designated prize of a "virtual golden doorhandle" was not awarded.

3.22.1997

"The Renaissance of the Railroad Stations." Opening of an exhibit in the former Dresdener Bahnhof near Gleisdreieck. On 1,500 sq. m the architecture of railroad stations, from 1900 to the present, is displayed. The exhibit was shown last year at the 6th Architecture Biennale in Venice and

3.27.1997

90 years ago today, KaDeWe (the "Department Store of the West") was opened. Built in 1906/07 by Johann Emil Schaudt for a company consisting of the firms A. Jandorf and M.J. Emden and Sons along with the Deutsche Bank. The plain facade and the name "Kaufhaus" instead of "Warenhaus" (the former emphasizing shopping, the latter stressing merchandise) was meant to entice the haute bourgeoisie. In 1926 KaDeWe was taken over by Hermann Tietz. The house was gutted by fire in 1943, was restored in 1950, installed its famous food department in 1956, expanded in 1977, and was enlarged one more time last year; it now encompasses 60,000 sq. m. retail space.

3.31.1997

The small- and medium-sized construction employers in Berlin and Brandenburg are the first regional association to leave the main Associations of the German Construction Industry.

March 1997

A bit further away from the political center of the capital city than the new party headquarters for Bündnis 90/Die Grünen (Alliance 90/The Greens —see January 15th,1997), the newly created "Heinrich Böll Foundation" (which is close to the Green party) sets up its main office in the middle of Berlin's new cultural center, in the Hackesche Höfe on Rosenthaler Strasse. Within a year, 125 people are supposed to find employment at this new location and, among other things, make "Green Memory," a collection of archival material on the history of the parties previously stored in Bonn, available to the public.

March 1997

As the second state following Bremen, Baden-Württemberg has opted for a competition placing its "Landesvertretung" (the office of the delegation representing the state in the Bundesrat, the German parliament's upper house) in

Critics' Prize: Wolfgang Kil

... Later I became a colleague of Gerhard Krenz, of all people. The same publisher that produced his Architektur der DDR also published a magazine called "Farbe und Raum" (Color and Space), a trade journal for house painters. They were looking for a new editor; on a whim, I applied and was hired. I actually knew nothing about color design and the technology of paint application, but it seemed that somehow colored walls must have something to do with architecture.

And what do you know, it worked: while all the political suspicion was directed exclusively at the "real" architectural journal, our readers were probably dismissed as a harmless marginal group. They left us alone, and so the three of us steered our colorful little boat ever closer to the main fairway. We used the theme of historic preservation to raise questions of urban renewal, and the new gable painting to address broader issues of urban design; the extravagant balcony draperies usual in the GDR were enough of an excuse to discuss the citizens' role in shaping the image of the city and their inclusion in its planning. I imagine the magazine's traditional readership was pretty upset, for they received less and less information on new anti-rust agents. Instead, we gained increasing popularity among architects, who liked the focus on aesthetic and urban-cultural debates.

This cat-and-mouse game of surreptitious themes lasted four happy, unmolested years. Then fatigue began to set in: in the West, postmodernism began to dip into the paint bucket in earnest, while on our side the gray began to spread—in every respect. The pretexts for our "colorful" themes became increasingly threadbare; so I quit.
Wolfgang Kil

conceived by the Hamburg architectural firm von Gerkan, Marg, and Partners. This firm is supplying the design for the Lehrter Stadtbahnhof, which will also be the high point of the exhibit.
Through May 19th.

3.22.1997

An agreeable decision: The large three-part table from which Günter Schabowski proclaimed the opening of the Wall is taken apart and will from now on be exhibited in parts in the Deutsches Historisches Museum (German Historical Museum) in Berlin and the Haus der Geschichte (House of History) in Bonn.

3.31.1997

As an Easter surprise, Krüger Belz architects offer flights along with their guided architecture tours. Customers can choose either a historic double-decker to fly over the new suburbs or a helicopter to look down on the eastern and western city centers.

March 1997

The uprooting of trees for the Tiergarten Tunnel—underway since May 1995 —is completed. 2,495 trees had to make way for the project. But the next generation is on its way. 3,900 saplings are planted throughout the neighboring districts within the S-Bahn ring.

the Diplomatic Quarter of Berlin's Tiergarten district. The property for the new building with 4,800 sq. m of useable space lies between Bendler-Block and Tiergartenstrasse, near the Gemäldegalerie (Painting Gallery) at the Kulturforum. First prize: Dietrich Bangert, Berlin.

March 1997

"Containerize," a traveling exhibit en miniature, traverses Berlin in construction containers. Current location: Rosenthaler Strasse in the Mitte district. First exhibit: "Structures." The futuristic architecture of the 20th century is alienated into design. All year long, eight different exhibits will be displayed at different sites.

Late March

Giorgio Grassi is pushed aside in the planning for the ABB grounds on Potsdamer Platz. After the usage concept had changed from office buildings to a conference hotel, the investor and the Berlin Planning Office requested a new architectural style, ergo new planners: T. van den Valentyn, Cologne, Deubzer/König, Berlin, Hilmer & Sattler, Munich, and another, as of yet unnamed architect.

4.1.1997

The Association of German Realty Agents (VDM) moves its headquarters from Königstein in Taunus to Reinickendorf in the immediate vicinity of the Real Estate Academy of the European Business School. 300 realtors in Berlin are members of the VDM; nationwide the association counts 2,800 members organized into 16 state associations.

4.6.1997

The poet Stefan Hermlin (born January 13th, 1915) dies. On April 28th, the Berliner Ensemble stages a reading called "Gedächtnis" ("Memory"). Christa and Gerhard Wolf are the speakers in the company of Günter Gaus, Klaus Wagenbach, Volker Braun, Günter Grass, and many other of his friends.

4.11.1997

Following the slogan "Bonn meets Berlin, Berlin meets Bonn," around 350 higher civil servants make their way from Bonn to Berlin. Bonn's Mayor Bärbel Dieckmann and her Berlin colleague Eberhard Diepgen exchange mascots from their respective cities' coats of arms (the Bonn lion and the Berlin bear). Motto: "Bonn and Berlin, a powerful team!" Three-day visitors' program at federal-government construction sites, in theaters, and in cabarets, along with "home parties" with Berliners playing host—the whole thing organized by a private agency calling itself "Werkstatt Deutschland" ("Workshop Germany").

4.12.1997

Official start for Berlin's newest means of inner-city transportation, the velotaxi. It looks like a bicycle with three wheels and a roof, but the technology, from brakes and shock absorbers to spokes, comes from motorcycles, and the covered passenger seat harks back to shipbuilding. Thus equipped to satisfy western driving-security demands, these 30 rickshaws travel along three constant routes through the inner city, from Wittenbergplatz to Adenauerplatz, from the

4.1.1997

The Berlin School for Technology and Economics offers a new course of study called "Technical Building Management," which teaches students the planning and servicing of electrotechnical systems as well as the marketing and administration of building space.

4.2.1997

"Construction Work by the Parliament and the Government on the Spree Bend" is the name of a touring exhibition which can be seen in the Berlin City Council Building beginning May 5th. With it, the federal government wants to shed light on the bewildering array of construction projects around the Reichstag, the Chancellor's Office, and the parliamentary buildings.

4.6.1997

The Jewish Community of Berlin honors 15 years of work by Berlin's Commissioner for Foreigners, Barbara John, by awarding her the Heinz Galinski Prize.

Stephan Hermlin, my friend, is dead. This century seems to be lost, for it is returning to its beginning, to a time before the betrayed revolutions and the World Wars, to a naive founding age; and now it is being abandoned by its traveling companions. It is as if a clean sweep were being made, and these years will accomplish it. Other generations will enter into the glistening waste. If they have any knowledge at all of the battles that were fought, the hopes that were buried, the atrocities that were committed, they owe it to the few candid witnesses who had the courage "to recognize a truth that spared almost nothing that was dear to them." What remains is the span between nothing and almost nothing, and that is much in a period of withdrawal from history, of the building of the wall at the end of the millennium.
Volker Braun, 4.28.1997

The age of miracles is past. Around the corners
The arc-lamp suns are sinking. The clocks
Are imprecise; they frighten us with their striking,
And in the twilight the cats are grey again.
The vesper sounds for peddlers and for heroes.
The heart falters like this verse, muted the cry.
The writing on the wall and the flight of birds say:
Youth is gone. The age of miracles is past.
Stephan Hermlin

Mid-April 1997

The exhibit "Party Commission: A New Germany"—devoted to propaganda from the former GDR, and on display in the German Historical Museum since December of last year—triggers East-West controversies. Owing to the enormous crush of visitors, the exhibit is extended through May 27th. The third guest-book is filled with messages of indignant rejection and enthusiastic approval. One visitor promises: "After the next revolution, there will be an exhibit about this exhibit."

Zoo to the Brandenburg Gate, and from the Brandenburg Gate to Alexanderplatz. The drivers are independent small businesspeople who can rent the vehicle from Velotaxi GmbH—the initiators of the idea—on a daily basis. Deviations from the itinerary are also offered.

4.11.1997

Europe's most modern assembly plant for rail vehicles in Lessingstrasse in Pankow is officially dedicated by ABB–Daimler-Benz Transportation (Germany) GmbH–Adtranz. Work has gradually been moving from Reinickendorf to the plant which was finished in May of last year where up to 100 rail vehicles, partial vehicles, and 60 double-decker buses can be built annually. The two-story construction of 15,000 sq. m is situated on the former Bergmann-Borsig grounds.

4.13.1997

Hardt-Waltherr Hämer, architect, Berliner by training, successful theater builder, and for many years a careful urban renewer ("IBA alt" and S.T.E.R.N.), turns 75.

4.15.1997

With little ceremony and in the dead of night (at 4:36 a.m.), the first rapid transit train in over 16 years is dispatched from the newly reopened Jungfernheide rapid transit station on its journey across the Süd-ring. The re-established

4.16.1997

The United States' largest all-service bank, Chase Manhattan, opens a branch office at Unter den Linden 12. The bank purportedly wants to participate in major projects like the Transrapid and Schönefeld Airport. Four employees at the moment.

4.17.1997

Cornerstone laying for the Innovation and Foundation Center on the Biomedical Research Campus in Berlin-Buch. For the time being, and through the autumn of 1998, there will be 2,500 sq. m of laboratory space. Biotechnology firms have already been applying for space. Over the next several years, a total of roughly DM 170 million will be invested in biomedical research in Berlin.

4.18.1997

The Supervisory Board of the project management for the Berlin-Branden-burg airport Schönefeld (PPS) awards 17 sectoral planning projects to 16 planning firms. The commission volume amounts to DM 15 million. Schedule: Summer 1997, preparation of the privatization contest; summer 1998, choice of investor or an investor consortium; late 1998, decision for a master plan, determination of the definite location of the future terminal; summer 1999, legal steps to constitute the planning act; 2002, planning act, legal revision, start of construction. Planned opening: 2007. Expected annual capacity 20 million passengers.

4.21.1997

After renovation and extension work lasting three years, the Deutsche Bank opens its new Berlin headquarters at Unter den Linden 13–15, and so returns to its previous home. On April 9th, 1870 Deutsche Bank had opened business on Französische Strasse. Under the direction of Fritz Novotny and Arthur Mähner, two historic buildings were connected via a glass-covered, 560 sq. m large courtyard and supplemented with a new building from Benedict Tonon. On the 13,000 sq. m of total useable space, there will be offices for

4.22.1997

Surviving his wife Renate by just a few weeks, Berlin painter Heinz Trökes (born August 15th,1913) dies. His last major exhibit took place in the winter of 1979/80 in Berlin's Akademie der Künste (Academy of the Arts). Following Alexander Camaro and Bernhard Heiliger, Berlin has now lost the last of those "Moderns" who were pioneers, dreamers, and poets in equal parts. Heinz Trökes drew what he dreamed; in 1983 he donated 31 of his sketchbooks to Berlin's Nationalgalerie, and he gave an additional 20 in 1995 to the Kupferstichkabinett (Engraving Collection).

April

2.5 km stretch of track, three completely renovated bridges, new signaling technology, and six new switches (construction cost: DM 70 million) bring Berlin's rapid transit ring a bit closer to completing the circuit by the end of 1999.

4.15.1997

Berlin's largest solar installation is dedicated. The 500 sq. m surface on the roof of the Ufa-Fabrik is meant to produce 37,000 kilowatt hours of electric power. A solar primer listing every sunny address in Berlin and Brandenburg will be issued in May; there are programs promoting solar installations sponsored by Bewag, the Investitionsbank Berlin, the Berlin City Senate B & SU and the Fraunhofer-Management Gesellschaft), and the Federal Office for the Economy.

4.16.1997

Tree Planting Day: For Unter den Linden's 350th birthday, City Development Senator Strieder plants a nine-meter high lime tree on the mid-promenade in front of the Prussian State Library. A bit later, in a stone's throw distance on the historic Schinkelplatz, more trees are planted with the assistance of another Senatorial department. Here Building Senator Klemann sets one of four plane trees into the soil of Berlin "at its approximate historical site." Two hours earlier, the very same Senator was single-handedly taking care that the last of a total of 423 trees (must apple from Normandy, "Brettnacher" trees from Brandenburg) would be planted on the the rooftop of the Velo-drome (architect: Dominique Perrault) in order to demonstrate the close ties between France and Germany.

4.18.1997

Topping-out ceremony for the house on Pariser Platz 1, south of the Brandenburg Gate. The planned completion date for the four-story building with 1,600 sq. m of useable space: December 1997. Developer and future user: Rheinische Hypothekenbank. The rooms are meant, above all, for show. The Commerzbank's contact office to the federal government, previously in Bonn, will also move here. Architect: Josef Paul Kleihues, Berlin. Construction cost DM 20 mill.

4.18.1997

Topping-out ceremony for the "Forum Köpenick", Bahnhofstrasse 33–38. Near S-Bahn station Köpenick arises a huge shopping center with 40,000 sq. m. shopping area and 1,100 parking spaces. Planned opening within six months. Architects: von Gerkan, Marg and Partners, Hamburg. Developer: Fundus Gruppe. Investment: approx. DM 454 mill.

top management in addition to the obligatory branch facilities. The building complex is also meant to serve as Deutsche Bank's showcase when Berlin becomes the working capital. A permanent exhibit with works from New York's Guggenheim Museum is planned for the ground floor. In the meantime, with more than 200 financial institutions, Berlin has become the second largest banking center in Germany—after Frankfurt am Main.

4.22.1997

The Berlin Outpost of the Netherlands Embassy is swayed by Dutch architect Rem Koolhaas' eloquent speech into letting him design its new embassy building. The complex is to emerge by 2001 on a 5,000 sq. m site on the Spree near the Mühlendamm Locks, and will consist of an office building, four apartment units, and an underground parking garage.

4.23.1997

Berlin architect Heinz Schudnagies dies at the age of 71 in southern France. Like Hermann Fehling and Daniel Gogel, he belonged to a group of architects whose principles and designs were read and seen as following in the footsteps of Scharoun, even though the unsurpassed lightness of their buildings dispels any thought of imitation.

4.24.1997

Topping-out ceremony on Badstrasse at the Gesundbrunnen rapid transit station between Badstrasse and Bellermannstrasse in the Wedding district: In the "Gesundbrunnen-Center" there will be 100 shops and 1,000 parking spaces on 25,000 sq. m of retail space. After it opens on September 30th, 1997, up to 40,000 visitors are expected daily, and 1,000 new jobs are expected. Developer: the ECE Projektmanagement GmbH, which is already running the Ring-Center, the Allee-Center, and the Stern-Center in Berlin. Architects: Jost Hering and Manfred Stanek, Hamburg. Construction cost: DM 300 mill.

4.24.1997

At the start of the Tempodrom season, Irene Moessinger (head of the Tempodrom) Arnulf Rating (chairman of the "Stiftung Neues Tempodrom" or "New Tempodrome Foundation"), and Frei Otto (architect) present revised plans for

4.26.1997

German President Roman Herzog gives a speech that shakes German souls in the Hotel Adlon. This is just what was intended by the "Partners for Berlin," who plan a prominent speech called the "Berlin Address" every year on this day, the anniversary of the "creation of a new City of Berlin out of the cities Charlottenburg, Köpenick, Lichtenberg, Neukölln, Schöneberg, Spandau, and Wilmersdorf, as well as 59 further municipalities and 27 estates" in 1920. The standard has been set, the name of next year's speaker is as yet unknown.

What is wrong with our country?
To put it plainly, it is the loss of economic dynamism, a social lethargy, and an unbelievable mental depression; those are the catchwords of the crisis. They form a ubiquitous triad, but in a minor key ... It is tremendously dangerous; for anxiety too easily gives rise to the desire to preserve the status quo at all costs. A society filled with fear becomes incapable of reform and the shaping of the future. Fear cripples the spirit of invention, the courage of independence, the hope of overcoming problems. Our German word Angst has already become a part of the American and French vocabulary as a symbol of our state of mind.
Roman Herzog, speech in Berlin, April 26th, 1997

4.29.1997

"Castle—Palace—House Fatherland" is the theme for a series of six events beginning today and dealing with the possible or avoidable reconstruction of the Berlin Schloss. 1st evening: "Score and Fantasy—On the Essence of the Original in Art," a discussion between musicians, sculptors and architects.

the Neue Tempodrom at the Anhalter Bahnhof station: "Ein Zelt, das hält" ("A tent that'll hold up") for DM 26 mill. The old Tempodrom has to make way for the Chancellory (cf. BBA '96, August 24th). Next to a large arena seating 3,000, and a small one seating 500, an open-air stage seating 800, plus a restaurant, a liquidrome is planned where "spherical tones" in pleasantly warm water will "create an oceanic feeling."

4.24.1997

Cornerstone laying for a new Japanese-German Center on Saargemünder Strasse 2. Its former home in the Tiergarten will become the Japanese Embassy again in March 1998. Architects for both renovation and the new building: RTW Claus Reichardt and Peter Billerbeck. Construction costs (which are funded by the Japanese): DM 12.5 mill.

4.26.1997

Topping-out ceremony for the "Stadtzentrum Hellersdorf" ("Hellersdorf City Center") on Stendaler Strasse. The plans of the Center based on the competition design by Brandt & Böttcher, 1990, envisions a rectangular square (120m by 120m), diagonal paths, and three highrise buildings as trademarks. There will be a total of 49,000 sq. m of retail space, 7,000 sq. m for other kinds of services, and 5,000 sq. m for restaurants. A shopping arcade, hotel, doctors' offices, and the "MARK(t) Brandenburg" for products from Brandenburg, not to mention the multiplex cinema "CineStar" and 140 residences, are to be finished by September of this year. The development corporation MEGA AG is representing five Berlin builders and carrying all processing and closing costs, according to the Public-Private-Partnership model. Several different Berlin architectural firms have taken part.

4.26.1997

As of today, the "Berlin Guestbook" (4.20 m high, 3.60 m wide—when open—and with a capacity of 1 mill. signatures) is displayed in the "Golden Pyramid" (18 m high, 24 m long on each side, and with a 200 person capacity) on the Schlossplatz. Like it or not, the city owes book, pyramid, and more to the indefatigable "Arbeitsgemeinschaft Schloss-Palast GbR mbH" ("The City Palace workgroup").

4.28.1997

The publishers Irene and Rolf Becker from Pullach, Bavaria, donate the 4.50 m high bronze, "Miracolo—L'idea di un' immagine," by Italian artist Marino Marini (1901–1980) to the Bundestag. The statue from 1969, a rearing horse, is meant to be set up directly on the Spree river in front of the Alsenblock. It can now be viewed at the Kulturforum on Matthäikirchplatz.

4.28.1997

Today construction work starts on the so-called Alsenblock and Luisenblock north of the Reichstag, in the Tiergarten and Mitte districts. Both of these buildings designed by Munich architect Stephan Braunfels lie west and south of the Spree and will be connected via a bridge (the "Spreesprung"). On 57,000 sq. m there will be 1,700 rooms for members of parliament, conference halls, the parliamentary library, administration, and a restaurant. The completion of the Alsenblock is planned for April 1st, 2000, while the Luisenblock is supposed to be ready for occupancy by the end of 2000. Estimated construction cost: DM 870 mill.

4.29.1997

Opening of the "Atrium," an office and business house on the corner of Friedrichstrasse and Leipziger Strasse. Dominating element: the 30 meter high entrance hall giving the house its name. Architects: von Gerkan, Marg, and Partners, Hamburg. Developer: Grundstücks-KG Kullmann & Co., construction costs: DM 250 mill.

April 1997

The Office of Müller, Knippschild, Wehberg, Berlin, wins first prize in the landscape competition for Luisenplatz in Potsdam. The 120x120 m square in front of that city's Brandenburg Gate forms the intersection of Potsdam's pedestrian shopping zone and the street leading to Sanssouci Park. A design- and lighting concept was demanded for the square, which is currently used as a parking lot.

4.29.1997

Berlin's municipal street-cleaning works—the BSR (Berliner Strassenreinigungsbetriebe)—has opened a second-hand store on Holzmarktstrasse in the Mitte district. They are selling by the cubic meter. There, for a bit of money, one may obtain treasures that the BSR collects daily in the form of household goods and electro-junk. The campaign's goal: halving the garbage dumps by the year 2000. Open daily except for Sunday, but closed on Monday like any good museum.

April 1997

"Pure Rixdorf Pleasure"—for the 100th birthday of the Kindl Banquet Halls, Bauwert-GmbH celebrates the prehistory of its Kindl Boulevard on Hermannstrasse in Neukölln with an exhibit and a book.

4.30.1997

"Lutter & Wegner" opens its new establishment on the corner of Charlottenstrasse and Taubenstrasse, close to its original site. In 1811 "Lutter & Wegner" was founded as a wine shop with an adjoining pub, soon occupied nightly by E.T.A. Hoffmann and Ludwig Devrient. The pub was destroyed in the Second World War. After the war, it moved to Schlüterstrasse.

5.4.1997

Sunday sports. 9 o'clock at Olympischer Platz: Start of the 25 kilometer race ("French Race") with more than 4,000 athletes from 34 nations. Victorious: the "Kenya Express" (first place for women, all 8 places among the men). 9:15 in front of the Deutschlandhalle: Warm-up for the Avus Race with Escort Pokal, Citroen Saxo Cup, Formel Opel, Deutscher Tourenwagen Challenge, and Formel Euro. Successful: the organizer ADAC (the German automobile club).

5.6.1997

"The Modern Epoch — Art in the 20th Century," exhibition opening by the Zeitgeist-Gesellschaft e.V. in the Martin-Gropius-Bau with 400 "Key Works of the Century." Controversial, and not just because of the cost (DM 16 mill.). Through July 27th.

April/May

5.1.1997

Max Liebermann in Berlin. On the occasion of the painter's 150th birthday, the Centrum Judaicum in Oranienburger Strasse reconstructs the small exhibit that the Jewish Museum in Berlin put together one year after Liebermann's death in 1936, since at this time no one else dared to honor the former President of the Academy of the Arts. Through August 3rd. Three days earlier, the Berlin art dealer Wolfgang Werner opened an exquisite little presentation. In this gallery, founded by Israel Ber Neumann, Max Liebermann had already been exhibited in 1927 and once more, during hard times, in 1935.

5.1.1997

Opening of the 34th Berlin Theater Meeting with Ödön von Horváth's "Casimir and Caroline." The press missed Peter Handke's "Preparations for Immortality," staged by Claus Peymann in Vienna, whom Berlin wants as director for the Berliner Ensemble.

5.1.1997

Wasmuth Booksellers & Second-Hand Bookshop and Ernst Wasmuth Publishers GmbH & Co, Berlin/Tübingen, celebrate 125 years in business. The shop at Hardenbergstrasse 9a was closed late last year because of excessive rent; a new location was found in Pfalzburger Strasse.

5.2. – 11.1997

The Landesbank Berlin has minted trial Euro coins in an edition of around 1.3 mill. pieces, with which the curious may test the future European currency's purchasing power during a "Europe Week" and "European Spring Festival" in front of the Rotes Rathaus (Berlin's City Hall). The coins (exchange rate: 1 Euro = 2 DM) were viewed more as collectibles than as negotiable currency.

5.2.1997

The Antiwar Museum in Müllerstrasse in Wedding celebrates its 15th anniversary. The institution is, however, much older. During the Twenties, Ernst Friedrich, grandfather of the current director, founded a museum to counteract the bellicose enthusiasm of youth at the time. He collected and exhibited objects and photographs that documented the horrors of war. 1933 the museum was destroyed by the Nazis and its director imprisoned. After his release he left Germany for good. His British grandson, Tommy Spree, re-established the Antiwar Museum in 1982 with the help of activists in the peace movement.

5.3.1997

Stating that, "Every human being has a name," young people recite for 26 hours without interruption the names of 55,696 Jews from Berlin who were deported and murdered by the National Socialists. This action by the group "Act and Unite" begins after the end of the Jewish Sabbath and lasts through Monday night. On Yom Ha Shoa, Jews around the world commemorate the more than six million victims of the Holocaust.

5.5.1997

With a symbolic groundbreaking by the ambassadors of Denmark, Finland, Iceland, Norway, and Sweden, construction work begins for a common Nordic embassy facility in the Klingelhöfer Dreieck in the Tiergarten district. The urban development design comes from the Viennese architectural firm of Alfred Beger and Tiina Parkkinen. The individual embassies were designed by different teams of architects (cf. BBA '96, 6.7.). This facility, which should be completed by early 1999, marks the beginning of the Diplomatic Quarter's re-establishment.

5.6.1997

The exhibit "The Other Moderns," the counterpart to the big Zeitgeist exhibit in the Martin-Gropius-Bau, opens in the "House of World Cultures," formerly the Kongresshalle. This perpetually endangered exhibition site is furthering the dialogue with unfamiliar cultures, and presents contemporary art from Asia, Africa, and Latin America, and not just their exotic history. Through July 27th.

5.6.1997

International Symposium "Berlin—Metropolis in Europe of the Future" at the Free University of Berlin. With Kurt Sontheimer, Ralf Dahrendorf, and many others. "The old questions, the old answers, there's nothing like them," (Samuel Beckett).

5.6.1997

After preparations lasting seven years, the cornerstone is laid for the shopping center "Schönhauser-Allee-Arcades." The center is a project of the Trigon-Unternehmensgruppe with the Essener Management für Immobilien-GmbH and the Bayerische Landesbank. By early 1999, customers will be able to shop in 90 stores on three floors with a total space of 30,000 sq. m.

5.9.1997

A decision has been reached on two first prizes in the landscape planning competition for the Government Quarter. Landscape planners Cornelia Müller/Jan Wehberg, Berlin, will design the square between the Reichstag and the Kongresshalle as well as Ebertplatz east of the Reichstag; Toni Weber/Lucius Saurer, Switzerland, win the northern part of the Spreebogen. Both designs will have to be revised. "The design for this open space proves that the Government Quarter is not closed off," promises Federal Building Minister Töpfer. 152 teams participated in the competition. The cost for the 87,5 acres large grounds is put at DM 54 mill.

5.10.1997

With a groundbreaking and shoveling campaign, Stadtbild e.V. ("City Image"—formerly "Historic Berlin Society") recalls the muddled discussion about remodeling the Lustgarten in front of the Altes Museum. The problem: The pavement on the square is protected as a designated landmark, and the competitive designs that face up to this stipulation (quite understandably) offer nothing but unsatisfactory solutions. The design by Hamburg landscape planner Gustav Lange, who received 1st prize in a second competition sponsored by the Senate Administration for Urban Development, proposes planting tubs that can be transported to and fro annually and seasonally. The "Alliance Foundation for the Protection of the Environment" now threatens to withdraw, since it cannot see any "lasting and durable improvement of the environment" in the design.

5.11.1997

Pina Bausch receives the Berlin Theater Prize of the Stiftung Preussische Seehandlung (Prussian Maritime Foundation). For the 10th time, the DM 30,000 honor is awarded for outstanding service on behalf of German theater. For 25 years, Pina Bausch has managed the Tanztheater Wuppertal (Wuppertal Dance Theater). Péter Esterházy gave the laudatio.

5.12.1997

As of today, unpublished works from the estate of Dietrich Bonhoeffer (1906–1945) are publicly accessible at the Berliner Staatsbibliothek. Dietrich Bonhoeffer, theologian of the Confessing Church and member of the resistance around Admiral Canaris, was hanged on April 9th, 1945.

5.14.1997

The "Mossehaus" on the corner of Zimmerstrasse, which achieved fame following its renovation by Erich Mendelsohn in the Twenties and which is now being restored à la Mendelsohn, today starts the "Mosse Lectures," an event sponsored by the German studies institutes at the Humboldt University, which reside here along with a printing office and a publishing house. George Lachmann-Mosse, historian and grandson of publisher Rudolf Mosse, begins the series with a lecture on "The Publicity of Culture".

5.14.1997

The Federal Printing Plant, which stopped being a government office in 1994 and became a federally owned corporation instead, moved into its new, modern building at Kommandantenstrasse 15 in Kreuzberg. Architect: Wolfgang Schuster, Berlin (BHHS & Partners). In addition to the offices and printing rooms the building encompasses, the complex also has the largest above-ground storage vault in Europe (high shelf warehouse with 11,000 sq. m capacity). Per year, bills valued at DM 20 to 30 billion will be printed here. Construction cost: DM 150 mill., about one day's production. The new building's cost is carried by the federal government.

Architects: RKW + Partner, Düsseldorf, Berlin, Frankfurt. Client: TRMF Grundstücksentwicklungsgesellschaft mbH + Co. Allee Arkaden KG, Berlin. Total investment: DM 250 mill.

5.8.1997

Thousands use the 8th of May—Liberation Day—as an occasion for viewing the exhibit "Remembrance of a War" in the German-Russian Museum in Berlin-Karlshorst. Over half the visitors are Russians.

5.9.1997

The 13th "Ostpro," merchandise trade fair for products from Germany's new eastern states, opens today in the exhibition center at the television tower (in Berlin-Mitte). Through May 11th.

May 1997

From this month on, Hauptbahnhof station will remain closed to long-distance and regional train traffic for one year due to necessary construction work on the tracks.

5.9.1997

In the atrium of the debis headquarters on the Potsdamer Platz construction site, Haydn's "Creation" is performed before roughly 1,000 visitors.

5.9.1997

25th Parliamentarian Soccer Tournament in the Köpenick stadium "Alte Försterei" ("Old Forestry"). Representative teams from Switzerland, Sweden, Finland, Austria, and Germany take part. The Bundestag team loses to the members of the Swiss Nationalrat 0:1.

We can go through the palace and we'll be in the Lustgarten in just a moment. "But where is the garden?" you ask. For heaven's sake, don't you see, that's the irony of it. It's a rectangular plaza enclosed by a double row of poplars. Now we're standing right in front of the cathedral; its exterior was refurbished quite recently. It received two new small towers on either side of the large one. The great tower, rounded at the top, is not bad. But the two small ones are a ridiculous sight. They look like birdcages. The story is told that last summer, the great philologist W. strolled through here with the visiting orientalist H. When the latter, pointing to the cathedral, asked, "What are those two cages doing up there?" the learned wag replied, "That's where we train parson birds."
Heinrich Heine, 1822

5.15.1997

From now on, the AEG company archive is part of the Deutsches Technikmuseum (German Technical Museum - DTM) in Kreuzberg. Housed in the postal package train station at Trebbiner Strasse are: the entire product line of AEG from 1883 on, the photo and film archive, and 4,000 meters of files, as well as the company's founding deed, signed by Emil Rathenau.

5.15.1997

Topping-out ceremony for the first building segment of the service and retail trade center "Storchenhof" in Hohenschönhausen, construction of which began in the summer of 1996. The building is expected to be finished this year. Plans include: Service, restaurants, shopping and leisure on a total of 16,000 sq. m (first and second building segments). Architects: Léon/Wohlhage, Berlin (decision from a 1993 competition); developer: Münchner Baugesellschaft mbH (MÜBAU), Berlin.

5.16.1997

"aufbau west—aufbau ost." The ideal industrial towns Wolfsburg and Eisenhüttenstadt, a much-discussed exhibit in the German Historical Museum. Through August 12th.

5.16.–18.1997

18th Volksuni (People's University), sponsored by the Humboldt University on Unter den Linden. Theme: "Globalization: Solidarity or Barbarism?" 1,800 come to listen. The Volksuni has been in existence since 1980.

5.17.1997

Opening of the exhibit "Goodbye to Berlin. A Hundred Years of the Gay Movement" in the Academy of the Arts. The exhibitors have put together 1,400 pieces from all over; the framework for the program was organized by Rosa von Praunheim. Through August 17th.

5.18.1997

For the second time, the "Carnival of Cultures" travels through the streets of Kreuzberg, a gigantic festival with 2,700 actors in self-made costumes, with no financial assistance from the Senate of Berlin. In tropical heat, 100,000 Berliners dance the samba, calypso, and hip-hop. 430,000 immigrants from around 180 countries live in Berlin.

5.20.1997

Under the motto, "Now residents can voice their misgivings," Building Senator Jürgen Klemann opens an exhibit in the Kongresshalle on Alexanderplatz where provisional construction plans for Alexanderplatz are up for discussion. The initial topic is the modified (i.e. reduced by a few highrises) design by architects Hans Kollhoff/Helga Timmermann, which was crowned by a jury in 1993. Originally, 13 highrise buildings, each 150m tall, were planned; that number has been reduced to 10. The share of housing was increased by 30 per cent, and a few residential buildings slated for demolition on Memhardtstrasse and Mollstrasse will remain standing. Once the plan is settled, the amount of floorspace around Alexanderplatz will more than double. No one is counting on a construction start before 2010. Exhibit through May 30th.

5.21.1997

Interior Minister Kanther symbolically takes possession of the new seat of the Interior Ministry on the former Bolle Grounds in the Tiergarten district. The move to Berlin for around 1,300 staff members is planned for July 1st, 1999. On 13th of March the Budget Committee, despite a veto by the SPD and the Greens, approved the federal government's bill to rent an available new building (architect: Jochen Bley), the so-called Freiberger office complex on the former Bolle grounds at Alt-Moabit in Tiergarten, for the Federal Interior Ministry. The contract with Munich pizza businessman Ernst Freiberger will run for over 30 years and cost the federal government DM 1.1 mill. monthly.

5.22.1997

France's Foreign Minister Hervé de Charette introduces a model and plans for the future French Embassy on Pariser Platz. The property is located on the northern side of the square. Its western neighbor is the new building for the Dresdner Bank. The competition tendered among seven French architects was decided on May 6th in favor of Christian de Portzamparc, known for his Cité de la Musique in the Parc de la Villette. With his design he proposes a sequence of differing building sections and courtyards, crowned by a "vertical garden". Property size: 1,800 sq. m, useable space 8,360 sq. m, estimated cost: Franc 150–175 mill. Planned construction start: 1999, planned completion: 2001.

May

5.16.1997

Until the year 2000, whoever has the good fortune to do so may climb aboard subway line number 2, and into the Berlin mineral water company Spreequell car, completely renovated for advertising purposes at a cost of around DM 880,000 (interior walls blue, benches and bar grips high-grade steel, legroom neon-lit). In the future, the BVG (Rapid Transit Authority) would only too gladly donate every tenth car in Berlin's subway fleet to the program "Move in AD" (meaning either "movement with advertising" or "making headway through advertising"— depending on your point of view).

5.17.1997

For his piece "One on the Kisser" (author: Rainer Hachfeld, director: Rüdiger Wandel), Volker Ludwig's Grips Theater receives the Friedrich Luft Prize (funded by the Berliner Morgenpost newspaper). An old rivalry (Morgenpost versus Grips) now seems over. A few days earlier, on April 29th, the Grips Theater was awarded the Gebrüder Grimm Prize for outstanding performances in the field of children and youth theater.

5.18.1997

With its victory against Telekom Basket Bonn in the fourth final game, Alba Berlin becomes German Basketball Champion of 1997.

5.19.1997

The first railway platform at the new Spandau train station on Klosterstrasse goes into operation. It replaces the station designated as Spandau Hbf. (Spandau Main Station) from 1911 to 1936 and afterwards as Berlin-Spandau in the Stresow neighborhood. A total of seven tracks are to lead through Spandau: two for the IC to Hamburg, two heading toward Hanover, two for the rapid transit line, and one freight train track. The railway station will be finished by the end of 1998, according to plans by Hamburg architects von Gerkan, Marg, and Partners. Construction cost: DM 120 mill.

5.21.1997

The second public event on "Castle—Palace— House Fatherland" questions the "Allegory of Patrimony." Guests from France, Warsaw, and Bucharest present their countries' attitudes toward their historical inheritence. Next event on June 18th.

5.21.1997

Topping-out ceremony for the House of the German Construction Industry on Kurfürstenstrasse in Schöneberg. Client: Association of the German Construction Industry. Architects: Schweger + Partner, Hamburg/Berlin.

5.22.1997

By tearing down two walls that served as barriers for the former GDR Interior Ministry, a 75 m long segment of Französische Strasse between Mauerstrasse and Glinkastrasse in the Mitte district is, at least symbolically, made accessible again. Paving the stretch with asphalt will be finished by the start of June.

5.22.–23.1997

An initial meeting of more than 30 planning teams is to push forward the preparation for a construction exhibition in 1999 called "Own Your Home". Six locations in Pankow and Weissensee were chosen for experimental designs which will be on exhibit beginning in September 1999: Buchholz-West, (northern section); Buchholz-West, (western and eastern section); Karower Damm; Karow-Teichberg; Buch V and Elisabethaue. The initiative was prompted by the Exodus of Berlin citizens to Brandenburg and consists of counteractive measures called "ownership-promotion and cost-effective apartment construction." The sites are made available partially by the State of Berlin, partially by participating construction firms. It will be the architects' task to find innovative solutions for constructions that save both space and money.

5.23.1997

Cornerstone laying for a housing colony between Töpchiner Weg and Drusenheimer Weg in Neukölln. In the so-called "Töpchiner Dreieck" ("Töpchiner Triangle") 48 row houses, 36 semi-detached houses, and an urban villa with 11 condominiums will be erected. Construction of these houses is made possible by a home ownership initiative by the state of Berlin, and much of the promotion is coming from the Investitionsbank Berlin.

5.23.1997

Berlin's Hertha has moved up. Into the 1st national soccer league. From now on, fortnightly in the Olympic Stadium. A brief retrospective: 1965 forced relegation, then a return and 2nd place in the league; since 1982 multiple demotions all the way down to the regional league, 1988 return to the 2nd league, 1990 1st league, back to the 2nd in 1991, and now up again.

5.24.1997

György Konrád, the Hungarian writer, becomes President of the Berlin-Brandenburg Academy of the Arts. His predecessor, Walter Jens, receives the title of honorary president.

5.25.1997

Topping-out ceremony for "Ring-Center II" on Frankfurter Allee with roughly 20,000 sq. m of shopping space. According to the owners, almost fully rented out to 40 stores. An opening in October is expected; "Ring-Center I" has been ready since 1995. Architects: HPP, Hentrich Petschnigg and Partners, Düsseldorf, and Manfred Stanek, Jost Hering, ECE, Hamburg. Investor: ECE Projektmanagement GmbH. Costs: DM 120 mill.

5.27.1997

Dedication of Argentina's Embassy in Dahlem (Auf dem Grad) by Argentine President Carlos Menem. Until their departure, Allied officers of the U.S. armed forces were quartered in the 2,919 sq. m large house built in 1930. The Embassy's property in the old Diplomatic Quarter in Tiergarten was exchanged for the new house.

5.30.1997

Opening of the Phönix Company Startup Center for Herlitz Falkenhöh AG on the Borsig grounds in Tegel. The Startup Center is the first building segment for the Industrial Park at Borsigturm. With 21 startup and 6 already inaugurated partner firms, the space is already 60% occupied. The Berlin Senate's business sponsorship program reduced the rental price to DM 12.80 per sq. m. Architect: Walter Rolfes, Berlin.

5.30.1997

The Chamber of Architects creates a series of lectures and visits with the title "Babylon Berlin. Architects—Planners—Landmark Preservation." The series intends to explore the tensions between preservation, restoration, and new construction of buildings. Today's focus is on the Spandauer Vorstadt in Berlin.

5.24.1997

Official opening of the "art'otel ermelerhaus" on Wallstrasse 70–83 in the Mitte district by Berlin investors Sylvia and Dirk Gädeke. The house with 109 rooms is furnished with 300 works by Georg Baselitz. The old section of the hotel consists of one of the very few Rococo buildings in Berlin not destroyed during the war. During the sixties traffic regulation displaced the house some hundred meters from its original site close to the Berlin Stadtschloss. Architects: Nalbach and Nalbach, Berlin.

5.24.1997

Peter Burk of Freiburg calls on all interested to attend the founding assembly of "Architects Beyond Borders" in the Architecture department at the TU Berlin.

The Accomplice *György Konrád*

What a sad, insignificant life, the national disease, ennui. How easily you grow old over the fact that nothing works, how easy it is to mendaciously exaggerate our petty vexations into global problems. We always have strategies! We seek the answer in world history: should we lie this morning or not? How many sentimental rationalizations for the sensible bounds of propriety. You spend a major portion of your time brooding over things that aren't worth brooding over, and yet it's so simple: the less often you have to take notice of it, the better the State. You take notice of your State like a low ceiling: when you stand up straight, you bash your head against it. You've made each other ill, like an oppressive lover who never allows you to forget him, because he is afraid that the moment he shuts his mouth he will cease to exist. The State is continually placing itself in your way, it drivels on, spreads itself out over you, and you are confronted by the State, you are in the midst of it, in its womb, plagued by nausea, yet you mate with it. As saving truth, you are permitted to utter the 200-year-old adages of liberalism. However tactful the State may be, you can decide to take no further notice of it; you go downstairs, take a walk, buy a newspaper, continue your conversation.

5.28.1997

Spandau is aging faster. Whereas in 1982 it sent out invitations to its 750th anniversary five years earlier than its eternal competitor Berlin, today—just 15 years later—it is already celebrating its 800th anniversary as a city. The reason: the first official mention of the site can be dated back to 1197, whereas in 1982 it was the granting of municipal rights in 1232 that was being celebrated. In the course of this year's festivities, Spandau has secured for itself a portion of the Havel river between the Kleine Wall and the Citadel, which from now on will answer to the name "Spandauer See" ("Lake Spandau"). Along the Spandauer See, a new Water City (formerly Wasserstadt Oberhavel) is growing, and of the 12,000 residences planned, over 2,000 are expected to be completed this year.

5.30.1997

Dieter Honisch gives up management of the Neue Nationalgalerie after 22 years. His work is summarized by the exhibit "A Look Backward—Fifty Selected Acquisitions." Through August 17th.

5.31.1997

After more than two years of restoration work, the Grosse Eichengalerie (Large Oak Gallery) at Charlottenburg Castle is reopened for visitors. The costs for the work on the festive hall, built 284 years ago and repeatedly renovated according to the fashion of the times, came to DM 1.5 mill., paid for by the Stiftung Preussische Schlösser und Gärten (Prussian Palace and Garden Foundation).

Beginning of June

The PR Office has moved, at least with some of its staff: This is in order to make room for the Justice Ministry in the building that once housed the GDR PR Office. While waiting for its new building on Dorotheenstrasse, the PR Office will operate out of Neustädtische Kirchstrasse 15.

6.2.1997

Anniversary and convention for historic landmark preservationists in the former Staatsrat (old GDR executive council) building. The themes: Renovating historical buildings for parliamentary and governing functions, the treatment of socialist urban heritage in the Mitte district, as well as the treatment of old and new open spaces and of transportation facilities as part of the unification process. An enumeraton of Berlin's listed buildings and a fresh yearbook give evidence of the Berlin preservationist's successes and failures. On the occasion of the convention, the Staatsrat building opens an exhibit on the history of this house. The material was assembled by the Berlin firm Architektur und Denkmalpflege Kroos & Marx.

6.3.1997

Two days before the 50th anniversary of the Marshall Plan, a cornerstone is laid at Gendarmenmarkt for a new permanent branch of the Kreditanstalt für Wiederaufbau, where a consulting service for Central and Eastern Europe will soon move in. The KfW, founded in 1948 in Frankfurt/Main as a non-dividend-paying public-law bank for Marshall Plan aid, belongs to the federal government and the states. Architects: ABB Architekten, Frankfurt/Main, with Keller, Bachmann and Partner, Switzerland.

6.4.1997

Topping-out ceremony for an 8-story house for GEWOBAG with offices, and shops on the ground floor and first floor as well as 49 condominiums, on the corner of Lietzenburger Strasse and Welserstrasse in Schöneberg. Architects: Hans Schröder, Winfried Ringkamp, Berlin; construction cost: approx. DM 20 mill.

6.5.1997

Fifty years ago today, U.S. Secretary of State George C. Marshall gave the honorary commencement speech at Harvard University, in which he formulated the plan — prepared and worked out by diplomat-scholar George Kennan — for the economic and social reconstruction of Europe. The anniversary is being commemorated with conferences and festive events scheduled throughout the month. This includes the orga-

6.1.1997

The oldest private radio station in Berlin, Radio Hundert,6, celebrates its 10th anniversary. Shortly before this date, the sale of the station to Munich media entrepreneur Thomas Kirch (who also owns Pro 7 and Kabel 1) is announced.

6.2.1997

30 years ago today, the visit of the Shah led to a riot. The student Benno Ohnesorg was shot to death by a policeman. No official commemoration is held.

6.2.1997

The last steel arch for the new building of the Chamber of Industry and Commerce is erected. Architect: Nicolas Grimshaw, London.

6.2.1997

Quadrupeds in a dual deployment system: The police riding squadron will be reduced from 65 to 45 horses, distributed across only two sites and (following a new policing concept) put into use in Berlin's parks as well as (for example) during demonstrations.

6.3.1997

A historical reminder: On June 3rd, 1972, 25 years ago today, the so-called "Four Power Agreement" on Berlin went into effect after being signed by the foreign ministers of the four Allied powers.

6.4.1997

Eight months of renovation work on the 24-story double highrise at Leipziger Strasse 40–41 ends. The Wohnungsbaugesellschaft Mitte invested DM 45 mill. in work on the facade as well as on the total renovation of the heating and sanitary facilities. The two highrises are part of an ensemble of four residential buildings of 22–25 stories each, interspersed with two-story shopping centers and service complexes as well as three transverse structures of 11–14 stories with public facilities in the lower two stories. Planned in the late 1960s, the complex was completed in 1979 as the largest residential development close to the city center. Original architects: Werner Strassenmeyer, Günter Wernitz. Urban planning: Jochen Näther, Peter Schwelzer. Architect: Edwin Busch, Berlin. Execution: R & M Fassadentechnik GmbH, Munich; Gerhard Sillaber.

6.4.1997

Late chance of winning: In its most recent official gazette, the Berlin Senate Office announces that it is looking for a licensee to the rights for the signature and bear-cub logo used by the Berlin Olympic campaign.

6.5.1997

The Coca-Cola Erfrischungsgetränke AG (Coca-Cola Refreshment Corporation, newly merged in January with Cologne's Coca-Cola Rhein Ruhr GmbH) announces its decision to erect its headquarters for Germany in Berlin. The exact site is still not clear. So far there is a distribution base and bottling plant in Hohenschönhausen, which will continue to be used, but which is too small for the headquarters and insufficient as a company showcase.

6.5.1997

Topping-out ceremony for an office and commercial building belonging to Trigon on Schönhauser Allee 188 at the corner of Torstrasse in Prenzlauer Berg. Construction began in August 1996. By year's end the 7-story building, wich will house 2,250 sq. m of office and 300 sq. m of retail space along with six penthouse apartments, will be completed. The building closes the last construction gap on the northern edge of Rosa-Luxemburg-Platz. Architects: Rhode, Kellermann, Wawrowsky, Düsseldorf.

nization of a Marshall Conference by the German Marshall Fund and Citibank on June 27th in the Prussian Parliament building, where the participants include US Vice-President Al Gore, Czech Prime Minister Vaclav Klaus, Polish Foreign Minister Dariusz Rosati, German Foreign Minister Klaus Kinkel, and German Federal President Roman Herzog.

6.6.1997

The American kinetic artist George Rickey turns ninety. Since 1968, Rickey has regularly spent his winters in Berlin, where he engaged professional mechanics to set up his sculptures. One of these, "Four Rectangles in Square," has been staying for 27 years in front of the Neue Nationalgalerie. Five years ago the Berlinische Galerie set up its own "George-Rickey-Room" for him.

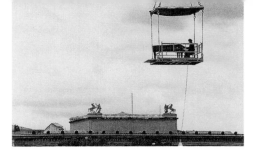

6.6.1997

Today is Environment Day. The cleaning company Kärcher, a Swabian family business, has taken on the assignment of cleaning one monument in each of 15 cities for free on this day. In Berlin, Karl Marx and Friedrich Engels on the Karl-Marx-Forum get the benefit of a high-pressure shower, liberating both from graffiti and red paint.

6.7.1997

An "Open Door Day" is taking place in the Berlin Parliament, where Berliners are invited to pose questions about politics, including media politics, and to eat sausages. The main topic—on the occasion of its 10th anniversary—is the city partnership between Berlin and Paris. An Internet Homepage is switched on with the address www.parlament-Berlin.de.

6.11.1997

The IHK (Chamber of Industry and Commerce) has a new honorary president: Werner Gegenbauer, managing partner of Gegenbauer GmbH & Co. KG, a Berlin business with around 10,000 employees in the building cleaning, management, caretaking and security service, as well as in catering, and running parking lots.

6.11.1997

The BDA (Federation of German Architects) in Berlin has elected Kay Puhan-Schulz to an additional term as chairperson.

6.11.1997

Berlin has a new club: "99 in Berlin." There is nothing really suspicious about this; the organisation is an alliance of 28 Berlin business representatives as well as 15 associations from Bonn. Under the chairmanship of Parliament President Herwig Haase, and with the support of "Partners for Berlin," the club is attempting to help potential new Berliners moving from the Bonn region get a new start via an Info-Hotline, New-home-Parties, and other integration aids. Office: Constanze-Haus, Kurfürstenstrasse.

6.11.1997

The exhibition "Städtebau in Berlin—Ansichten einer Metropole" ("Urban Planning in Berlin—Views of a Metropolis"), organized by the Senate Administration for Urban Development, Environmental Protection, and Technology, opens today in the Arata Isozaki building on Potsdamer Platz. On view through August 30th.

6.12.1997

Berlin and all his friends are still awaiting the groundbreaking of his new building for the Academy of Arts with the controversial glass facade on Pariser Platz. Today is his 75th birthday. Congratulations to Günter Behnisch.

6.12.–14.1997

The German Architectural Convention—held every three years in a different location—is being held in Berlin this year. For three days, around 2,000 architects debate "The Future of Building Culture—Berlin as an Example: The Open City in Transformation." In addition to the open-air opening event

6.9.1997

As of today, the BVG's subway network will be the first worldwide to be equipped completely for mobile telecommunications.

6.9.1997

Bundestag President Rita Süssmuth issues an invitation to view the Reichstag under the new dome being installed.

6.10.1997

In the German Architecture Center DAZ, an exhibit is opened with the title "Beirut—Berlin, a Comparison of Two Cities after the Division" (Stefanie Bürkle: painting/photography; Thomas Sakschewski: texts). The exhibit conjures up the similarities between the two city centers during reconstruction. Through July 26th.

The promise of the future instead of an epilogue: In the S-Bahn a paperback book accidentally slid out of my coat pocket. It bothers me that now I will never be able to read the end of the novel about the Jew who flees to the States. As consolation, I try to imagine who might find unexpected pleasure in the book. A student perhaps, or a retiree, or a foreigner who wants to improve his German, or someone who has never read a novel and now gets excited about it. In accord with the law of series, in which I believe (and with which I am presumably cooperating unconsciously), shortly after losing the paperback, I lost my new gloves as well. I asked for them in vain at the Lost and Found. But I got the book back.
Richard Christ, 1996

6.12.1997

Cornerstone laying for the so-called "Monbijou-Haus" across from the Museumsinsel (Museum Island). The house is the first of three seven and eight story office and commercial buildings that will jointly make up the "Quartier an der Museumsinsel"—a complex with shops, restaurants, cafés, 52 privately financed housing units, 30 studios, a conference center, and an underground garage. Among the future users are the Bundesverband Deutscher Banken (Federal Association of German Banks) and the Bayrische Versorgungskammer. Total investment: 180 mill., space: 26,500 sq. m (on a 6,000 sq. m building lot); developer: HANSEATICA and Deutsche Immobilien Anlagegesellschaft (Frankfurt Berlin); architect: Steffen Lehmann & Partner, Berlin; planned completion: December 1998.

on Schlossplatz, there is an offering of lectures, city tours, construction site visits, a variety of exhibits, and a film series on the theme "Film and Architecture—Reflections on Times, Places, and Actors." The BDLA (Federal Association of Landscape Architects) lets "Temporary Gardens" grow in the Mitte district.

6.12.1997

Under the title "Airports—Vision and Tradition. Impulses for an International Berlin-Brandenburg Airport," the International Design Center IDZ sponsors an exhibit at Tempelhof Airport. Through July 27th.

6.12.1997

Cornerstone laying at Gendarmenmarkt for the Berlin branch of the Wissenschaftszentrum (Scholarship Center). The building, whose DM 50 mill. cost will be assumed by the VW Foundation, will house the Berlin representatives of Germany's most important large scholarly organizations.

6.12.1997

Topping-out ceremony for the Mitte district's new municipal building on Karl-Marx-Allee. The office building will be on the lot of the former Berolina-Hotel, the first modern hotel building after the war, erected 1961–64 according to plans by architects Josef Kaiser, Heinz Aust, Gunter Kunert, and Horst Bauer, and torn down 1996 as unfit for renovation. As the landmark protection authority demands, the new city hall building will be oriented around the shape of the old hotel, in its external dimensions as well as its facade. A political peculiarity: The project will be privately financed, and the state of Berlin will rent the entire complex with its 20,000 sq. m for the district office. Investors: Trigon, Architects: Bassenge, Puhan-Schulz, Heinrich, and Schreiber, Berlin; construction cost: 140 mill.

6.15.1997

Hermann Noack's picture foundry (Varziner Strasse in Friedenau) celebrates its 100th year. They all came here: Ernst Barlach, Wilhelm Lehmbruck, Käthe Kollwitz, Georg Kolbe, and many others. Henry Moore knew no better workshop. An exhibit in the Georg-Kolbe-Museum honors the artistic crafts made here by four generations of a Berlin family. Through August 31st.

6.15.1997

Topping-out ceremony for the first building segment of a new elementary school at Falkenseer Damm in Spandau. Total investment: DM 33 mill.; architect: Spandau District Authority.

6.16.1997

Topping-out ceremony for a low-energy, multi-family house at Flämingstrasse in Marzahn. Low-energy homes are already tested in Spandau and in Tiergarten (erected for IBA, the International Building Exhibition, 1987); two more homes are under construction in Rudow and Pankow. The 7-story house with 56 two and three room apartments costs DM 17 mill. (construction and property). DM 1,3 mill. of subsidies from the state of Berlin go for technology. Developer: WBG (Wohnungbaugesellschaft Marzahn), architects: Assmann, Salomon, Scheidt, Berlin.

6.17.1997

Cornerstone laying for the Berlin branch of the Deutsche Genossenschaftsbank at Pariser Platz 3. Architect: Frank O. Gehry, Santa Monica, California; costs: DM 250 mill.; scheduled completion: end of 1998.

6.18.1997

The results of the limited competition for the completion of the so-called "Oraneum" between Bertolt-Brecht-Platz and Friedrichstrasse are announced. The first prize went to the Hamburg firm of Bothe, Richter and Teherani. The design proposes a nine-story curved corner building and two wings in which an existing building is to be incorporated. The old building will be renovated and its stucco facade restored. Client: Ravenna AG; construction start: 1998; costs: approx. DM 100 mill.

6.18.1997

Today, in its third discussion forum, the series of events entitled "Castle—

6.19.1997

As of today, in an exhibit in the former Staatsrat building, entries of a two-stage urban design competition held EU-wide for the completion of "new residential building for federal government staff at the former Gatow airport" may be viewed. The first prize, which is also meant to serve as a master plan, went to the Berlin planning firm "Linie 5." In addition, the results of the competition for the former Karlshorst barracks grounds in Lichtenberg are in: no first prize, but three second prizes that must still be optimized. Scheduled construction start: 1999. Exhibit through July 4th.

6.25.1997

The Labor Court rejects a petition from the Fachgemeinschaft Bau (representing construction industry employers) for a temporary injunction against measures taken by IG Bau (the construction workers union) in a labor dispute. This means that ongoing warning strikes in the construction industry are legal.

6.25.1997

Topping-out ceremony for the WISTA-Business-Center at the Adlershof Science and Business Site. The facility consists of four five-story blocks in concrete and glass, linked to each other by atriums. There will be a solar energy plant on the

6.13.1997

Topping-out celebrated for 483 residences and, thereby, for the last of a total of four building segments in the new Altglienicke region in Treptow. Client: Stadt und Land Wohnbauten-Gesellschaft; total cost 900 mill. By the end of next year a total of 2,400 residences, 65 individually owned homes, two schools, six daycare centers, a shopping center, a pedestrian bridge, and a public park will be completed.

6.15.1997

First official crossing of the new Südbrücke (south bridge) across the Oberhavel, which connects both parts of the "Wasserstadt am Spandauer See" now under construction. The 264 m long bridge is not for through-traffic and heavy trucks, but primarily for pedestrians and cyclists. Official opening is the end of September. Design: Engineering firm Leonhardt, Andrä, and Partners; cost: approx. DM 44 mill.

6.15.–8.31.1997

As was already the case last year, the most important construction sites in Berlin are turned into exhibition sites for eleven weeks, on the occasion of International Architecture Day, which is taking place in Berlin and Brandenburg two weeks earlier than in the rest of the Federal Republic. The opportunity (initiated by "Partner für Berlin") to get tours of city sites and federal projects, of residential and development zones as well as newly completed buildings— whether by bus, boat, helicopter, or on foot— is being supplemented by special events. These include the long open night at roughly 25 museums, performances of "Don Giovanni" in the E-Werk (staged by Katharina Thalbach), or even a Pitch-In-Construction-Site for kids at Leipziger Platz. Through August 31st.

6.16.1997

With a symbolic pile-driving stroke, construction work begins on the extension of the subway line number 2 from Vinetastrasse to the Pankow rapid transit station. The costs for the 400 m long stretch come to around DM 126 mill.; completion is scheduled for 1999.

Palace—House Fatherland" poses the question of legitimacy for architectural reconstruction. At issue are the different political and practical approaches toward rebuilding after the war in both the GDR and the Federal Republic and different positions on landmark preservation.

6.19.1997

For the grounds of the Lindenstrasse synagogue in Kreuzberg—plundered and then exploited for other purposes by the National Socialists before being bombed out in the war—Israeli artists Zvi Hecker, Micha Ulman, and Eyal Weizman have fashioned a "Memory Site" to be unveiled today: In a publicly accessible courtyard, now belonging to the outdoor facilities of the Barmer Ersatzkasse health insurance fund's Berlin office, benches have been arranged in the order of the rows of pews inside the synagogue after the fire.

6.25.1997

Andreas Nachama, director of the "Topography of Terror Foundation," is voted the new chairperson of the Jewish Community in Berlin by its newly elected (June 18th) board of representatives.

6.25.1997

In a nighttime meeting, the Coalition Committee (representing the governing parties in Berlin) under the direction of Mayor Eberhard Diepgen, passes several resolutions to salvage the budget, including a municipal district reform, which will allow Berlin to reduce its number of districts from 23 to 12.

roof with solar collectors over an area of 2,000 sq.m. In October 1996, construction work began and should be completed by the start of 1998. Developer: WISTA-Management GmbH; architects: Dörr, Ludolf, Wimmer, Berlin; costs: DM 55 mill.; main useable space: 16,070 sq. m, 120 parking spots in the underground garage.

6.26.1997

The southern facade of the landmark-protected Reichstagspräsidenten-Palais (Reichstag Presidential Palace) has gotten cracks from the construction work on the Dorotheenblock. Provisional construction stop within a 20m radius around the palace.

6.26.1997

Environmental Senator Peter Strieder plants the first trees for "Neue Wiesen" ("New Fields"), the newly emerging park on the city's edge, just at the border between Weissensee and Hohenschönhausen. The park, with over 215 acres, is meant to provide recreation for future inhabitants of the newly emerging precinct Neu-Karow. Landscape design: Schirmer and Kernbach, Berlin. Cost: approx. DM 8 mill.

6.27.1997

Topping-out ceremony for the 2nd and 4th construction segments in the Wendenschloss Residential Park in Köpenick. On 13 acres between the Salvador-Allende-Viertel and Altstadt Köpenick, the Köpenicker Baugesellschaft mbH is constructing a total of four building ensembles: "Spree" (127 subsidized residences), "Dahme" (52 residences), "Langer See" (87 residences), and "Müggelsee" (52 residences). Total investment: DM 120 mill.

6.30.1997

Helmut Kohl meets the press to present plans for the CDU's office in Berlin. The new 6-story building will be on the Klingelhöfer Dreieck, at the corner of Klingelhöferstrasse and Lützowufer. It is divided into a pedestal zone, a mid-section, and an attic floor. Formed into a twisted diamond with rounded edges, it is fronted by a glass winter garden.

July

Berlin Interior Senator Schönbohm announces the hit list of the thirty most dangerous places in Berlin. Breitscheidplatz, Alexanderplatz, Kurfürstenstrasse, Ahornstrasse (Steglitz), and Kottbusser Tor are among the flashpoints for "robbery, assault, crimes in homosexual and prostitution milieus, violations of the narcotics laws, car theft, residential and commercial burglaries, illegal cigarette sales, or the 'Hütchenspiel' ('little hat trick') coin game."

Beginning of July

Burda Media Enterprise becomes a shareholder in "Partners for Berlin." Still not a member of this federation: "Time Magazine," "Newsweek," and the Holtzbrinck publishing group.

7.1.1997

Macedonia's ambassador and vice-premier issue an invitation to the opening of their embassy and ambassadorial residence on Koenigsallee in Grunewald. One cannot help thinking that the task of moving an embassy from Bonn to Berlin is more of a burden for some, for whom one might have expected it to be easier, and vice versa.

7.1.1997

Presentation of the results from the international workshop proceedings for the Klingelhöfer Dreieck on the basis of the urban master plan by Machleidt + Stepp, Berlin. On Stülerstrasse, the Rentaco Group, following a Machleidt + Stepp design, is planning a senior citizens residence along the future embankment promenade (closed to auto traffic) called "Corneliusstrasse".

7.2.1997

The meeting of the Curatorium for the Promotion of Capital City Culture decides to commission the architectural firm Hilmer & Sattler with the construction measures needed to improve the entrance situation, climate control, and security technology in the Martin-Gropius-Bau, and to employ DM 20 mill. from federal funds for this purpose. Scheduled construction start: 1998.

Beginning of July

The building formerly housing the U.S. radio station AFN ("American Forces Network") at Saargemünder Strasse 28 in Zehlendorf is being demolished. In its place, the district government envisions a new building with rental apartments for upper-level officials of

6.26.1997

Cornerstone laying for the easternmost of two gatehouses at the corner of Luisenstrasse and Hannoversche Strasse. The gatehouses are part of a larger project, to which the Prisma Commercial House on Invalidenstrasse and three additional residential houses with 34 condominiums also belong. The gatehouses are 16 x 14 m large in plan, 8 m high, und they are thereby (as well as by their brick construction) modeled historically after Schinkel. In the summer of 1998 everything will be finished. Architect: Josef Paul Kleihues; client: Bayrische Hausbau; cost for both gatehouses: DM 3 mill.

6.27.1997

The southern route around the Brandenburg Gate, or, to be more precise, 263 m of Behrenstrasse with four lanes and a segment between Wilhelmstrasse and Glinkastrasse, are open to traffic. Work on the extension began on August 20th of last year.

End of June

Shortly before signing a contract, Tip Restaurations GmbH withdraws from its project to run a restaurant and a canteen in the Ratskeller of the Rotes Rathaus (Berlin's City Hall). This means that the Ratskeller, renovated and modernized at a cost of over DM 10 mill., remains orphaned. The future leaseholder's problem: For several years to come, subway construction work is going to make the area in front of the Rotes Rathaus a site impeding the operation of a business.

The latter feature is being touted as a model of ecology. Architects: Petzinka, Pink, and Partners, Düsseldorf; developer: Groth + Graalfs GmbH; anticipated construction start: April/May 1998; anticipated completion: end of 1999; cost: unknown.

End of June

The Haus Huth has a basement with the wrong height for the surrounding building projects. For this reason, the landmark-protected building on Potsdamer Platz is raised by two centimeters and provisionally placed on a steel construction, so that a new, deeper cellar can be placed underneath. This will be part of a subterranean pedestrian way, the shortest distance between the Potsdamer Platz railway station and the Daimler-Benz area.

Beginning of July

The Administrative Court rejects an urgent petition from the City of Potsdam to stop construction of three multiplex cinemas on the grounds of the former border-crossing station at Dreilinden in Kleinmachnow. This clears the way for the completion of a commercial and amusement park after the model of the Europarcs. The Kleinmachnow variant (bordering on Berlin city district Zehlendorf) is supposed to be on 100 acres and cost the investors (Societé Generale, Thyssen Rheinstahl Technik GmbH, Westdeutsche Landesbank, and Philipp Holzmann AG) around a billion DM. Potsdam fears that its own city center will become deserted.

There will be luxury homes (architects: Hilmer & Sattler, Munich); on Klingelhöferstrasse, embassies or trade associations will be able to rent space in the floors of four houses, and singles will also be able to find lodgings in 35 singles apartments. On the corner of Rauchstrasse will be the Embassy of Mexico, on the southern point the CDU's federal office. A 6,000 sq. m large park is envisioned for the interior of the block. The property, which (together with the Tiergarten quarter) was expanded to become the Diplomatic Quarter in 1937 before being destroyed during the war, has seen plans for it come and go for over 25 years. Everyone surely remembers the vision of a World Trade Center at the beginning of the Nineties, for which the design by Léon/Wohlhage from Berlin won first prize, but whose realization nonetheless foundered because of (among other things) the estimated price of the property.

the revenue service; a building permit has already been granted. The last broadcast of AFN was transmitted on July 15th, 1994, after which its rooms were used for different purposes.

Beginning of July

The city electric company BEWAG and the Landmark Protection Office have reached agreement on a concept for renovating the Shell-Haus on the Landwehrkanal in the Tiergarten district. The house was designed in 1930 by architect Emil Fahrenkamp and is one of the first steel frame houses in Berlin. Since 1989, barriers cordoning off the building have signalled a will to renovate. The barriers still stand, but in the interim they have taken on the idyllic, washed-out air of shutdown train tracks.

7.8.1997

The Senate Building Administration grants a permit for partial demolition of the Kranzler-Eck. For this property, "Difa" is planning, together with architect Helmut Jahn, a 120 m long and 55 m high building, consisting of two houses with 9 and 15 floors respectively, on which 43,000 sq. m of office and commercial space will be distributed. The Victoria-Haus, the Café Kranzler, and the Bilka department store are to remain. For now, the shops in the passage between the Kranzler and the Victoria-Haus are also to remain standing. A permit for a highrise construction as part of the controversial design is still pending, though there are partial permits.

7.8.1997

Presentation at the DAZ on the topic "Berlin Scrapes Heaven—Highrises in the West of the Federal Capital?" Among

7.9.1997

"Initial groundbreaking ceremony" for an office center between Brunsbütteler Damm 75–77 and Altonaer Strasse 70–72 in Spandau. Groundbreaking in quotation marks, since there was already an excavation as far back as 1995 on this site. A standstill ensued for lack of financing. Now the same gentlemen have signed on under new names. The commercial space will amount to 13,740 sq. m, the total volume of investment to DM 96 mill. Planning: Henn Architekten und Ingenieure, Munich.

7.12.1997

9th Love-Parade in Berlin, even bigger than before, with 1,000,000 participants. Connoisseurs of the scene forecast that the Love-Parade will now have reached, or even surpassed, its zenith of success and commercialization. Plans for decentralized events next time are making the rounds. The Hate-Parade, a counter-demonstration in the struggle for increased bpm (beats per minute), is cancelled owing to uncool planning; the fans split and head toward gentle big sister.

7.3.1997

In Hohenschönhausen, on the corner of Konrad-Wolf-Strasse and Weissenseer Weg, the commercial and office house "Hohenschönhauser Tor" opens. The complex consists of two eight-story buildings with facades of polished granite linked by glass bridge passages. Architect: Gustav Schulze, Dortmund; developer: Trigon Unternehmensgruppe; investment total DM 127 mill.; shopping space: 13,500 sq. m.

7.6.1997

The Berliner Ensemble distributes free tickets with a special stipulation: anyone named Brecht, Weigel, Eisler or Weill can visit a performance for the Brecht Summer gratis. Whoever brings along someone holding such a name pays half. If, in addition, the first name is correct—Bertolt, Helene, Hanns and Kurt—, then the invitation is good for all performances.

July

7.4.1997

Topping-out ceremony for the so-called "Rosmarin-Karree" on Friedrichstrasse. The complex for offices, retail trade, and residence is being built on a space of 3,500 sq. m and is divided into two building sections with two interior courtyards. Developer: Hines and Büll, Dr. Liedtke Projektentwicklungs GmbH, Hamburg; architects: Jürgen Böge, Ingeborg Lindner-Böge, Hamburg (office and commercial house), Kahlfeld Architekten, Berlin (residential house). Total investment: DM 300 mill.

7.7.1997

Diagnosis: too maintenance-intensive and technically antiquated. For this reason, the 28 year old, 38 m long antenna tip on the television tower is taken down. The new tip allows the tower to grow another three meters to a height of 368 m. On July 27th the installment of the antenna carrier will be done.

7.7.1997

Westin Hotels & Resorts signs a management contract with the Interhotel Group for the Grand Hotel on Friedrichstrasse, whose future company name will be the "Westin Grand Berlin." Within the year, the hotel is to be renovated. Estimated cost: DM 17 mill. The management contract is valid for 20 years.

the discussants: Senate Building Director Barbara Jakubeit, President of the Federal Building Management Florian Mausbach, and architects Christoph Mäckler and Meinhard von Gerkan.

7.9.1997

From the daily press we derive a list of fine rental objects and their beneficial effect on the Berlin city budget. For example: the Rathaus Schöneberg (district municipal hall, formerly West Berlin's city hall) garnered around DM 350,000 in non-political rental bookings, the Prussian Parliament building DM 200,000. Especially profitable is the assembly room of the Berlin City Parliament. Rarely rented out, and therefore with hardly any impact on the books, is the Rotes Rathaus (Berlin's red-brick City Hall), at DM 10,000 annually. Highly coveted for films are, among other sites, the foyer and outdoor steps at Rathaus Schöneberg and the Moabit Criminal Courthouse.

7.9.1997

The cornerstone for an annex to the future Federal Economics Ministry on Invalidenstrasse in the Mitte district is lain. The new four-story building replaces the mid-section (destroyed during the Second World War) of an ensemble originally made up of three houses erected in 1748 as a facility for the care of the war-disabled. Since the autumn of 1994, work for the Federal Economics Ministry has been going on in the old building (renovated for DM 157 mill.) next door on Invalidenstrasse, formerly the government hospital of the GDR. Altogether, the renovation of these buildings and the construction of the new one will cost around DM 550 mill. Completion of the new building is scheduled for the autumn of 1998, and the ministry's subsequent move there is planned for July 1999. Architects: Baumann and Schnittger, Berlin.

7.11.1997

The glittering white circus world of Cirque du Soleil has again slid in among the construction cranes on Potsdamer Platz. Today the international Canadian troupe commences with its staging of "Alegria," which celebrated its 1994 premiere in Montreal. The guest performance is one of the highlights of Berlin's "SummerTime," a centrally organized and marketed program of cultural events sponsored by the associations "Partner für Berlin" and "Berlin Tourismus Marketing."

Mid-July

The Building Senator offers his department's mobile bar to the highest bidder. Description of the item: 15 x 15 meters, collapsible, suitable for enclosed rooms, and world-traveled. It has already been in the U.S. and Brazil and served for quite some time in the Reichstag.

7.16.1997

The Tiergarten district office has assigned names to the public streets on Potsdamer Platz, which must now receive the blessing of the elected district assembly: Rudolf von Gneist, Marlene Dietrich, Herbert von Karajan, and Tilla Durieux are among the chosen. For the private roads that traverse the debis Quarter, the owner has naming rights. Under consideration: Joseph von Eichendorff, the Grimm brothers, Friedrich Wilhelm Schelling, Theodor Fontane, Ludwig Beck, Varian Fry.

The Chancellor visits the Tiergarten *Diether Huhn*

If, one morning in his office at the beautiful and undemocratic Bellevue palace, the Federal President looks for history and does not find it, I suggest that he throw on a jacket, sneak past his bodyguards, and go to the right. Maybe in the Tiergarten he can be alone for a quarter of an hour or so. Unfortunately, we non-presidents have a harder time finding solitude there; when I visited the Tiergarten, I was watched by nine border guards in combat uniform. I wanted to have a look from outside the fence at what the President now sees on his little stroll.

The President thinks: I've seen this before. A construction pit, a yellow bulldozer, Brandenburg sand. "The Berlin hybrid: great plans, diminutive execution; great demands, tiny achievements; perfect criticism, liberal ideas, courtiers on the streets, the museum and the academy and the sand." When Felix Mendelssohn wrote these words during his time in Berlin, the Tiergarten was simply the natural landscape between the Friedrichstadt and Charlottenburg. What the President sees through the eyes of Mendelssohn is his own headquarters: the Federal President's Office, in death-black granite or marble, will look like the headquarters of a bank where not everyone can get credit.

And it will stand on the exact spot where the Baroness Spitzemberg waited for Bismarck on February 25th, 1872. The Baroness was 29 years old, the Chancellor almost 57. The evening before, during a visit by the Queen of Württemberg, a kind of agreement had been made. The Chancellor had come on horseback, not an easy thing at his age; a bit before—maybe right where the automobile traffic now piles up—he had dismounted and ordered his officers to wait behind. A groom must also have been there, but history tells us nothing of him.

7.16.1997

As of today, the flags belonging to the member states of the European Council are flying again on Ernst-Reuter-Platz in Charlottenburg. Until now, lack of funds had kept the interior department's administration from being able to replace the battered flags. Private sponsoring is envisioned for next year, although the Europa-Center is only offering sponsorship on the condition that it may put up its own flag next to the others. A decision is awaited. For the moment, the square—and especially its fountain—has to be cleaned, disinfected, and refurbished with new plants for the greenery as a consequence of the Love-Parade's ecstasies.

7.16.1997

A study on the situation and outlook for business in the Mitte district's urban renewal zone "Rosenthaler Vorstadt" displays resignation and a downward trend. Unsettled property relations leading to vacancy and short rental contracts, not to mention neverending construction sites, are leading to lost sales and a discordant mood.

7.17.1997

The topping-out ceremony for the future Federal Presidential Office will be celebrated after a construction period of only 16 months (and thereby four weeks earlier than planned) in the presence of Federal President Roman Herzog, his predecessor Richard von Weizsäcker, Berlin's Mayor Eberhard Diepgen, Federal Building Minister Klaus Töpfer, and 500 additional guests. Architects: Helmut Kleine-Kraneburg, Martin Gruber, Frankfurt/Main; developer: Bundesbaudirektion (Federal Building Management); cost: DM 91 mill.; scheduled moving-in date: July 22nd, 1998.

7.16.1997

Last concert in the established Franz-Club on Schönhauser Allee in Prenzlauer Berg. The Treuhand Liegenschafts-Gesellschaft (TLG, real estate company for the trustee agency that privatized former GDR state enterprises) had classified the club as a commercial seller and increased the rent to DM 35 per sq. m. The club will move out over the next few weeks. The "Arena" in Treptow purchases its gigantic sphinx sculpture and safe. At the same time, the TLG approves DM 100 mill. for the renovation of the "Kulturbrauerei" ("Culture Brewery"). On the roughly 25,000 sq. m grounds, a cinema multiplex is planned along with other cultural installations, services, and restaurants. The "Kulturbrauerei" will remain as it is. In November 1995, the TLG took over the grounds. The Franz-Club had been subleasing at the "Kulturbrauerei."

7.17.1997

Topping-out ceremony for the public events building of the Konrad Adenauer Foundation on the corner of Tiergartenstrasse and Klingelhöfer Strasse in the Diplomatic Quarter. The core of the new three-story building is a lecture hall seating 200. On the office floors there will be 25 rooms for 30 staff. The administrative headquarters of the Foundation, which is close to the CDU, remains in Bonn. Architect: Thomas van den Valentyn, Cologne; investment total: DM 30 mill.; completion by mid-1998.

7.18.1997

"Die Franken—Les Franc, Wegbereiter Europas—Précurseurs de L'Europe" ("The Franks—Europe's Trailblazers") is the title of an exhibit on view as of today at the Museum for Prehistory and Ancient History in the Kulturforum on Matthäikirchplatz. Through October 26th.

An entanglement threatened. In principle, the Chancellor had nothing against entanglements; they were his business, he was a master at them. But would the feelings the Baroness was capable of mustering be worth having lifted his thin voice in the parliament to speak about a world that wanted to speak about him? He only went a short way with her, acting as if he had trouble remembering the speech.

Perhaps the President doesn't know this story. Hardly anyone does. So now, when he sees the ostentatious Bismarck monument in the copse, he doesn't know that it stands in a highly ironic location.

But the President most certainly does know that the proud-looking man with a flat head and a funny helmet is Bismarck—unlike the young couple I disturbed here yesterday, who acted as if they had come just to view it.

"Who was Bimak?" asked the small dark-haired girl, for only these five letters remained legible on the monument.

"Dunno," said the guy in the leather jacket, and added "not much in the way of boobs." He was referring to the female figure posing at Bimak's feet, covered with green patina, probably meant to represent the German Nation. Her right breast is exposed, like Delacroix's Liberté, but she seems not to know it; she doesn't even notice the lion puttering about under her slightly lifted skirts. Even Bimak looks the other way.

When the President passes by here, he should be glad that no one will think of setting up a monument for him. (The President's headquarters will not look like him. Or like any of us. It will look like Bimak and the boring right breast of the German Reich.)

7.19.1997

The twenty residents of the "Wagenburg" on the Schillingbrücke in Friedrichshain are forced to move. The district government allots them a substitute property with reactivated tap water on Revaler Strasse, also in Friedrichshain.

7.20.1997

In celebration of the 150th birthday of Max Liebermann (July 20, 1847–February 8, 1935), the Alte Nationalgalerie shows a comprehensive retrospective of his work.

July 1997

A working group of participating building firms organizes a special type of public-private partnership for the extension of the Museum for Transportation and Technology. The group

forestalls a construction stop threatening the building (already standing as a shell) by pre-financing construction work at an interest rate of 1.5 %, which the state of Berlin need not repay until the year 2000.

7.21.1997

The Deutsche Klassenlotterie has—following negative evaluations—decided against supporting the planned Bauakademie dummy, which puts the project in a precarious position. Lottery funds amounting to DM 350,000 had been calculated into the building of the dummy of the Schinkel building near Schlossplatz. The society promoting the project, however, has not given up, and will renew its search for (as of now, yet undiscovered) sponsors next year.

Mid-July

Granules are strewn on the spacious and granite-smooth entrance surface in front of the Neue Nationalgalerie. This puts an end to the traditional use of this site by skaters, following numerous accidents, in which the museum's glass panes were involved. The Tango Community, which roamed there to tunes from a ghetto-blaster on warm summer nights, has also been tripped up.

7.21.1997

Today—several months after the start of construction—Federal Building Minister Töpfer (on behalf of the Bundesbaugesellschaft Berlin, BBB) signs a contract for a project committing the BBB—as manager of federal buildings in the Dorotheen-, Alsen- and Luisenblock—not to exceed DM 1.75 billion in costs and to give preference to medium-sized firms in awarding building contracts.

7.24.1997

Three days of farewell parties in the E-Werk, one of Berlins biggest techno clubs, before it is closed.

7.27.1997

A photo exhibit in the Info-Box displays 100 Wall pictures taken by Frenchman Hendrik G. Pastor as photographer for the US Air Force and later for the British Army between 1974 and 1989. Through August 26th.

7.30.1997

Start of a new leftist weekly paper, "Jungle World". It is being brought out by some of the former editors of what had been the most widely read daily paper in the GDR, "Junge Welt (Young World)."

7.30.1997

The Info-Box on Potsdamer Platz is now also renting itself out as a place to hold weddings. The Registry Office is the agent. Price: DM 199 per hour.

7.31.1997

According to the press, around 100 residences belonging to the Gemeinnützige Heimstätten-Gesellschaft (GEHAG) in Karow are still vacant. For several weeks, the company has been soliciting their tenants for assistance and promising an agent's fee of DM 200 for the conclusion of a rental contract.

7.31.1997

The firms of Hilmer & Sattler (Munich, Berlin) and Thomas van den Valentyn (Cologne) emerge as winners of the second stage in the selection procedure for building Oberbaum-City, formerly the Narva Grounds. They are invited to make their design plans more concrete. Hilmer & Sattler are planning an office block on Warschauer Platz, specifically widened for this purpose. Van den Valentyn is planning a row with 330 housing units in the back portion of the grounds. The plans and models will be exhibited through August 15th in the Friedrichshain District Office.

7.31.1997

After 41 years—some Berliners still recall the opening on April 7th, 1956—the picture galleries in Dahlem close their doors. Rembrandt, van Eyck, and Dürer, and all the other celebreties residing for so long in the outskirts of Berlin are wrapped and packed and stored away. On June 12th, 1998, the new picture gallery opening at Kulturforum will proudly present them.

July 1997

In an open letter to Building Senator Jürgen Klemann (CDU), the Federation of German Architects (BDA) protests the secretiveness surrounding the organization of the 1999 Building Exhibition in the north of Berlin. Commissions for 4,500 individually owned homes were awarded without competition, according to the BDA (cf. May 22nd).

July 1997

A fine of DM 35,000 is imposed on Ernst Freiberger, the owner of the "Spreebogen" at Kirchstrasse/Alt-Moabit, for vacancies without permission in two new residences on Kirchstrasse.

End of July 1997

After three years of work on the project, the landscape architects Wörner/Röthig present their design for the reconstruction and reshaping of Treptower Park. The landmark-protected, 210-acres large park space was designed by Gustav Meyer and completed in 1887. Since 1949, the Soviet Monument has also stood here. There are still no deadlines for implementing the plans; the only things already installed are a goldfish pond and bridges for the Heidekampgraben.

8.4.1997

Within the framework of "Site seeing Berlin," a building property between Leipziger Strasse and Voss-Strasse is transformed into a pitch-in-yourself construction site. Through 8–31, children on the property of Berlin investors Dr. Peter and Isolde Kottmair can emulate the big construction works going on at nearby Potsdamer Platz.

8.5.1997

"... man lives poetically. A house for the word. Space through writing." Under this title, through August 19th, the Deutsche Werkbund Berlin is showing an exhibit in which architects present houses for writers.

8.6.1997

The Berlin State Office of Statistics announces: Of the 20,505 residential units completed in Berlin during 1996, 3,600 fell to the smallest city district, Weissensee. Second place is occupied by Pankow with 2,700 housing units, followed by Köpenick with 1,811 units. In the first half of 1997 only 3,600 residences were built; the most (which is to say 511) in Neukölln.

8.6.1997

Also within the framework of "Site seeing Berlin," the German Society for Solar Energy (Deutsche Gesellschaft für Sonnenenergie – DGS) presents an exhibit in the Willy-Brandt-Haus at Wilhelmstrasse on "Solar Building—Architects for Natural Living Spaces." Partly by using completed projects, the show introduces new materials and modern information technologies by which the demand for energy in buildings can be drastically reduced. Through August 31st.

8.7.1997

Topping-out ceremony for 77 residences in Altglienicke, on Bohnsdorfer Weg 82–86. There, DEGEWO is putting up 3 buildings with 18 residences apiece and five rowhouses with 23 residences. Cost DM 21.5 mill.; completion by March 1998.

8.8.1997

The first East-Side artist to do so, Günther Schäfer again donates a restored version of his painting "Vaterland" to the public. From among what had once been 101 large-sized pictures from the East Side Gallery on the former Wall, only 73 have been preserved.

8.12.1997

The Senate issues stipulations in an artistic competition for a monument to the workers' uprising of June 17th, 1953. In the first phase, 90 artists, mostly from Germany, are to be invited. Possible sites are the former House of Ministries on Leipziger Strasse or Karl-Marx-Allee. The jury's verdict is expected by February 1998, and the Senate is anticipating completion by the year 2000. The cost framework amounts to DM 1 mill., to which the federal government will contribute DM 400,000.

July 1997

Statistics show a tendency toward migration out of Berlin. From January to March, 30,400 people moved out of the city, while around 27,600 settled here. Moves between Brandenburg and Berlin are lopsided. There are more Berliners moving into the surrounding area than Brandenburgers heading toward Berlin.

The number of residences, on the other hand, is going up, in the western districts by 0.7 %, and in the eastern part of the city by 2.3 %, compared to the same time period last year.

And yet another trend: Tenants are staying away from student dormitories. Waiting periods of two years for a desired abode, which was the state of affairs still anticipated in 1994, are a thing of the past; more and more students are moving into rental apartments.

End of July 1997

Hans Kollhoff will build a highrise complex on the corner of Ebertstrasse and Potsdamer Platz for the investment bank of Delbrück & Co Privatbankiers. This decision cuts out the firm of Sievers and Platschek, who had to revise their original design of a mitre-shaped glass tower after it was rejected by the building administration. Kollhoff is planning a 35 m high block building and a 70 m high tower. Floor space: 18,000 sq. m for residences and offices. Construction start: mid-1998. Cost: DM 60–80 mill.

8.5.1997

Decision in the new building competition for the Federal Press Conference. Under the direction of Peter Schweger, Berlin, the jury selects a design by architects Gernot and Johanne Nalbach, Berlin. Beginning in mid-1998, the eight-story building for the Federal Press Conference (overall floor space 16,400 sq. m, construction cost approx. DM 90 mill.), will be erected within sight of the Bundestag, on the corner of Schiffbauerdamm and Reinhardtstrasse, by the Allianz Grundstücks-GmbH. Scheduled completion: early 2000.

8.7.1997

The Allianz Grundstücks-GmbH and the Deutsche Krankenversicherung celebrate a topping-out ceremony on Stresemannstrasse. The seven-story building on the 4,500 sq. m large site near the Martin-Gropius-Bau will be called "Stresemann 111" after its address. Architect: Jan Störmer, Hamburg; investment volume DM 170 mill.

8.7.1997

Brandenburg's Premier Manfred Stolpe and Berlin's Mayor Eberhard Diepgen sign a joint state development program for the two federal states. For the first time, there is an agreement on binding cross-border principles and goals for land use and state planning, rules meant (among other things) to prevent wild settlement growth at Berlin's outskirts.

8.9.1997

2,600 "Inline" skaters arrive for the "1st Berlin Speed-Skate-Night" and the "6th City-Night" on Kurfürstendamm. Participants can also, depending on the distance they have rolled, call themselves "10 Kilometer Fanta Night-Speed-Skater" or "5 Kilometer Fanta Fun-Runner," if they so wish.

8.11.1997

Berlin's Building Senator Klemann presents the first Mietspiegel (Comparison of rent levels) for the city's eastern half. It applies to around 263,000 old and 309,000 newly built residences in multi-family houses. By comparison, living in the east at an average of DM 6.49 per sq. m is cheaper than the western average of DM 7.33. In restored buildings, however, the east can be more expensive by up to 20 %.

8.13.1997

Building Senator Jürgen Klemann starts off the streetcar line City-Ost, connecting Mollstrasse to the Hackesche Höfe via Alexanderplatz. The first segment covers 2.9 km, the construction cost comes to approx. DM 48 mill., and completion is scheduled for the end of 1988. It is estimated that 40,000 will ride the streetcar every day.

8.14.1997

In a kind of caravan for advertising purposes, eleven camels pass through Berlin's east-west traffic bottleneck, the Brandenburg Gate. The first European camel race will take place on Sunday, August 17th, on the galloping racetrack in Hoppegarten.

Diepgen's Camels *Steffi Kammerer*

Once upon a time… two summers ago, a magician came to the city and enchanted the Reichstag, and the Berliners right along with it. Now it is summer again and very hot, and since the inhabitants of the city so enjoy being enchanted, they are dreaming of a fairy tale this year too, an economic fairy tale. One that is quickly told.

August

8.14.1997

Big blowup of the PVC globe for the first Berlin Imax-3D spherical cinema, designed by Renzo Piano of Paris/ Genoa, on the debis grounds at Potsdamer Platz. An air-filled rubber sphere with a diameter of 35 m is sprayed out on the inside with layers of concrete to a thickness of up to 30 cm. The cinema will offer 440 seats, and a 600 sq. m large screen. Completion by the end of 1988.

Once upon a time there was an impoverished German capital, so poor that the mayor possessed not a single racing camel. The aged king Zayed in faraway Abu Dhabi could bear this deplorable situation no longer. So one day, Sheik Zayed Bin Sultan Al Nahyan went to his splendid racing stables, chose the most magnificent of his 1,000 camels, and sent them as a loan to his friend Eberhard in Berlin. The latter, in turn, at once placed himself at the head of a movement to enshrine the desert animals as a symbol of new hope for the Berlin economy. For, they say, where there are camels there are Arabs, and where there are Arabs there is money.

Finally in June, Suleika, Hassan, Anwar, and 22 other drome-daries arrived in Berlin, well-preserved but unfortunately 50 kg too heavy—the result of six months' quarantine in Poland. The Arab trainer prescribed a radical diet, with success: the fat is gone and the animals have once again attained their racing speed of 50 km/h. On Sunday, the gates will rise at the Hoppegarten racetrack for the "Sheik Zayed Cup," the first camel race in Europe.

While the Berlin proletariat indulges in belly dancing, bazaars, and Bedouins between races, the financial vultures in the VIP lounge will be getting down to business. They have high hopes: the race is supposed to be an "economic Open Sesame" for Berlin; "business contacts will be transported between Occident and Orient as if on a flying carpet," says Jörg Schlegel, head of the marketing firm that organized the race. "Here a Fata Morgana will become reality for Berlin." In any case, there will be no lack of financially strong partners in dialogue: dozens of delegates from the Gulf region are expected, including three sons of the sheik. Their camels are already being treated like guests of state: tomorrow, the caravan will pass through the Brandenburger Tor, with the camel driver played by—who else?—Eberhard Diepgen.

147

8.15.1997

Three days of hustle and bustle between KaDeWe and Café Kranzler. This year's name for what is supposed to be the biggest street happening: "Kudamm Festival."

8.15.1997

Delivery of Berlin's largest artificial climbing rock in Hohenschönhausen. The cliff consists of 400 dismantled concrete blocks from the balconies of nearby prefab buildings spray-covered with a layer of concrete. Height 15 m, cost DM 242,000. The developer and promoter, the Deutscher Alpenverein (Charlottenburg Section) wants the cliff to convey "respect for the mountains." Another climbing rock — which, at 25m, should evoke even greater respect — is already being planned.

8.17.1997

40,000 spectators follow the first European Camel Race for the Sheik Zayed Cup. The occasion for the race is the 25th anniversary in office of His Royal Majesty Sheik Zayed Bin Sultan Al Nahyan, President of the United Arab Emirates.

8.18.1997

Through September 5th, the architectural gallery Aedes East in the Hackesche Höfe is showing the exhibit "Jo Coenen & Co '87–'97: Building the Territory." The Dutch architect Jo Coenen, known for his Nederlands Architectuur Instituut building, and heretofore unrepresented in Berlin, will soon be building an office building for the DG-Bank on Gendarmenmarkt next to the Hotel Hilton.

8.19.1997

Topping-out ceremony for the Innovation Center for Environmental Technology (Innovationszentrum für Umwelttechnologie – UTZ) on the Adlershof Science and Business Site "Wista" (Wissenschafts- and Wirtschaftsstandort Adlershof). Architects: Eisele, Fritz and Bott, Darmstadt; scheduled completion: mid-1998.

8.15.1997

Next to and above the German Bundestag's exhibit "Questions for German History" in the Deutscher Dom (German Cathedral) on Gendarmenmarkt, an exhibit opens on the changing history of this building. Until further notice, the exhibit may be viewed in the tower. Tuesday through Sunday.

8.15.1997

Ten months after the cornerstone was laid, the developer CEDC at the former Checkpoint Charlie celebrates a topping-out ceremony for the so-called "White House" within the building ensemble they have been planning around former Checkpoint Charlie. Architects: Lauber and Wöhr, Munich; scheduled completion 1998.

8.18.1997

First wedding on the roof of the Info-Box. With rotating construction cranes as background scenery, Andreas Geldhäuser and Maurenis Eday Pérez Correa exchange vows. The wedding night is sponsored by the "Berliner Tourismus and Marketing GmbH," and the happy couple spends it (far from the downtown construction site clamor) in a Grunewald luxury hotel.

8.18.1997

The UFA-Fabrik in Tempelhof presents the results of a competition "Youth Develops Berlin," sponsored by the marketing company "Partners for Berlin" and the Urban Development Administration. The winner in the field of creative urban development is the design for a "Multifunctional Forum Poliquarium" on Spreebogen by Pascal Rambach, 18 years old. In a cross between politics and an aquarium, visitors there should be able to encounter politicians as if in a zoo.

The peaceful animals that are reputed to go more easily through the needle's eye than a rich man to heaven, now enjoy a respect in Berlin that far transcends the boundaries of the Zoological Garden. The ship of the desert has excellent qualities: it is long-suffering and faithful, faithful even to death, for it providently stores quantities of water in a part of its stomach, which touchingly benefits the miserably languishing Arab when he has pierced the breast of the noble animal with his dagger.

In the majority of cases, however, comparison with a camel signifies a certain doubt as to the intellectual ability of a person. Herein lies the principal significance of the camel for the present day. The exclamation of a German fighter — "Schulze, all you need is horns to be a camel" — shows irrefutably that the concrete image of the camel has been lost to the modern Central European. An ideal camel lives in his soul.

Alfred Kerr, September 8th, 1895

8.20.1997

Spoon-fed investors. Urban Development Senator Strieder presents the "Planning Atlas for Berlin." On 20 DIN-A3 color maps, potential investors are given illustrations of general policy and planning parameters for choosing sites in Berlin. A second brochure shows building gaps in the eastern part of Berlin. Here, 22,500 residences could be built on 950 sites.

8.21.1997

Topping-out ceremony for the second construction segment in Neu-Karow. In the presence of Mayor Eberhard Diepgen, the topping-out crown sways above 2,355 residences and over the Neu-Karow shopping center. Developers: Arge Karow-Nord Groth + Graalfs, GEHAG; urban development conception: Moore, Ruble, Yudell, Santa Monica, California.

8.22.1997

Big "Balloon Glow" on Pariser Platz. Under the sponsorship of the Bundestag and the slogan "Berlin on the rise," 34 teams heat up their balloons in the evening hours. Things get started on the 23rd and 24th of August, on the occasion of the Fourth International Balloon Traveller's Meet by the racetrack in Karlshorst.

8.23.1997

At 11 o'clock, Federal President Roman Herzog opens the new Hotel Adlon at Pariser Platz; the ceremonial address is held by Walter Jens, Honorary President of the Academy of the Arts. Afterwards, a luncheon. In the evening, a gala at the Adlon for 800 invitees, with fireworks following the buffet dessert.

8.23.1997

"Second Long Night" for Berlin's museums. With temperatures at a summer high, 50,000 visitors make their way between 6 p.m. and 2 a.m. to the 27 participating museums of all sizes and kinds.

8.25.1997

After three years of construction, district mayor Franz Schulz hands over Ida-Wolff-Platz (Park) in Kreuzberg to the public. The 1,075 sq. m large city square is located on the corner of Stresemannstrasse and Grossbeerenstrasse. Construction cost DM 2.2 mill.

8.25.1997

Cornerstone laying for the retail and office center "Hallen am Borsigturm." Architects: Claude Vasconi and Dagmar Gross; developer: Herlitz Falkenhöh AG; investment volume: approx. DM 500 mill. Scheduled completion: early 1999.

Some thoughts
about the interdependence of arts and rents *Lorenz Schröter*

No other metropolis in the world has rents as cheap as those of Berlin. Last year, after a three-week search for an apartment, I found my 100 sq. m dwelling through a classified ad: 1,000 marks a month for an abode in a respectable location, with balcony, parquet floor, and central heating. In Moscow, you'd look a long time for something like that. They do still exist, those 164-mark apartments with oven heating and Russian toilets (rush down the stairs).

8.23.1997

Recycling. 60 pairs of onetime brides and grooms, now married couples, celebrate (years after their weddings) the 2nd Bridal Gown Ball in the Opernpalais. The ball's goal is the professionally correct reutilization of an item of clothing whose high investment volume in a period of major savings no longer appears to justify onetime use.

8.23.1997

The first "Hemp Parade" from Ernst-Reuter-Platz to the Brandenburg Gate. Between 7,500 and 35,000 potheads demonstrate for the legalization of hemp as raw material, medicine, and stimulant. The police arrest four demonstrators and confiscate several hemp plants.

But the cheap rents also have ill consequences for the city: the dreadful Berlin artists, who for decades have been welding rusty iron plates together and find it incredibly funny to play guitar badly in bizarre amateur combos, blur one experimental Super-8 film after another, or create recycling-fashion from garbage bags. It's only thanks to cheap housing that these Berlin artists can even keep on. If you hardly have to pay rent, you don't have to compromise: you can stubbornly pursue your dream of spending your life as an artist, untouched by the perpetual lack of success. Yes indeed, cheap rents are dangerous. But it's interesting, too, this parallel world of career refusal. Every once in a while, I drop into one of those nameless cellar clubs, where poets with a beer bottle in one hand recite strange sex-lyrics…

Of course, since Berlin has so dreadfully many of these cellars, galleries, and converted apartments, the consumer is up a creek. Every day there are at least four official poetry readings, as well as countless underground events. As a matter of course, ninety percent of them are trash. And since everything is so diffused, a boring opening won't even do as a social event, where at least you could see and be seen. A gentle, icy wind of market economy would establish a little order here.

But on the other hand, this oversupply is also marvelous. Where else could you find at least two top-floor swimming pools open until midnight, a shop for buffalo skins, and one that sells pumps up to size 45? What other city has clubs where, to the sound of drums and bass, you can watch the river, flowing along in shining silver? And then there are the S-Bahn tracks with their biotopes on either side, where Brandenburg foxes sneak into the city to bite the legs off the flamingos in the zoo. In cities where land is expensive, this wilderness along the tracks would long ago have been built over, and the shop with the buffalo skins would be a video rental. Maybe the cheap rents aren't so bad after all.

8.26.1997

The landmark-protected facade of the Titania Palace (architects Jacobi, Schloenbach, and Schöffler, restoration by Dietrich Dörschner) in Steglitz gets a facelift after 69 years. The 27 rings of the 30 m high light tower are beaming, just as they did at the palace's opening in 1928 and the building's heyday after 1945. As one of the city's few big buildings never destroyed, the Titania Palace witnessed the first postwar concert of the Berlin Philharmonic, it accommodated Marlene Dietrich and Josephine Baker, and it is the place where the Free University was founded in 1948 and the Berlin Film Festival its first showing started out in 1951.

149

8.26.1997

The first 80 of a total of 450 apple trees planned for the plateaus around the Velodrome (architect: Dominique Perrault, Paris) receive godmothers and godfathers. Berlin's School Senator, Ingrid Stahmer, hands over certificates of arboreal sponsorship to school-children from Prenzlauer Berg.

8.28.1997

The "Prince of Wales Urban Design Task Force," called into being by Prince Charles, pitches its tents in Berlin for two weeks on the occasion of its Summer Academy. At the invitation of the Building Administration, 18 young architects and city planners develop ideas for the Schloss-platz in the Mitte district. Presentation of the results on September 13th in the Staatsrat (former GDR executive council) building.

8.29.1997

4th public discussion in the series "Castle—Palace—House Father-land" in the Staatsrat building. The writer Pavel Kohut introduces the evening with his "Memoirs of a Socialist City." The discussants

8.29.1997

Second walking tour of monuments in the series "Babylon Berlin, Archi-tects—Planners—Land-mark Preservation" by the Berlin Chamber of Architects. This time: Karl-Marx-Allee. Proceed-ing from the domicile of the Chamber of Architects in the restored block at Karl-Marx-Allee 78, the group heads toward the highrise on the Weber-wiese (Hermann Hensel-mann), then to the Frank-furter Tor (H. Hensel-mann), and finally to Strausberger Platz. In addition to discussions with landmark and land-scape preservationists, residences are viewed and their inhabitants interviewed.

8.27.1997

Three German business lobbies celebrate at the Mühlendammbrücke in the Mitte district. The Federal Union of German Employers Associations (Bundesvereinigung der Deutschen Arbeitgeber-verbände – BDA), the Federal Association of German Industry (Bun-desverband der deut-schen Industrie – BDI), and the German Chamber of Industry and Com-merce (Deutscher Indus-trie- and Handelstag) invite to the cornerstone laying for their joint Berlin domicile. Federal Chancellor Helmut Kohl and Mayor Eberhard Diepgen have accepted and, together with a priest and a foreman, jointly lay the corner-stone for the seven-story building with a covered interior courtyard. Architects: Schweger and Partners, Hamburg; developers: Groth and Graalfs, Berlin; overall floor space: 27,000 sq. m. Scheduled completion: September 1999.

are art historian Werner Oechslin, architect Gustav Peichl, and archi-tectural historian Simone Hain. Moderator: Karl Schwarz. The topic for discussion is: "Econom-ics and the Public— Urban Spaces in Berlin-Mitte."

8.29.1997

Topping-out ceremony for the "Palais am Pariser Platz" 6a, between Haus Liebermann and the Dresdner Bank building. Architect: Bernhard Winking; developers: Allgemeine Hypotheken Bank, Deutsche Immobi-lien Anlagegesellschaft (DIAG), and HANSEATICA; investment volume: DM 46 mill.; scheduled completion: early 1998.

8.30.1997

1,001 meters of Kudamm runway between Olivaer Platz and Knesebeck-strasse make marathon runners out of 500 models and put Berlin in the Guiness Book of Records. The "Big Q"— the striking name of the event organized by the "Mode Centrum Berlin"— presents collections from 60 international designers.

8.30.1997

25 radio stations and 41 TV stations broadcast live from the 41st Inter-nationale Funkausstel-lung – IFA (International Radio and TV Exhibition) 1997 at the Berlin Radio Tower Exhibition Center. Through September 7th, 812 exhibiters from 33 countries will await 450,000 visitors on 130,000 sq. m of exhibi-tion space.

8.30.1997

Lights on for the Radio and TV Exhibition! A Berlin entrepreneur steps in on behalf of a Senate in pecuniary distress and finances three years of nightly lighting for the Berlin Radio Tower.

8.31.1997

End of "Schaustelle Berlin" (Site Seeing Berlin) with a laser show at the Hackescher Markt. In eleven weeks, 240,000 visitors came to view construction sites and take in cultural programs.

9.1.1997

Each Monday evening at 8, in the Schaubühne Theater at Lehniner Platz, talks are held on "Speaking of the Others." Günter de Bruyn opens this east-west west-east writers' dialogue by speaking on Heinrich Böll.

9.1.1997

The Marzahn Accident Clinic opens after six years of planning and construction. 468 beds are available in eleven wards. With its digital x-ray archive, the building is Germany's first paperless hospital. Architect: Karl Schmucker & Partner, Mannheim.

9.2.1997

On the occasion of the 35th Berlin Discussion on Architecture, Berlin's building administration presents realization studies on uses of Schinkel's Building Academy, which is to be reconstructed. The four proposals envision a European Building Academy, a Berlin Architecture Museum, a German Construction Forum, or a branch of the Bonn Kunsthalle.

9.3.1997

"For a Modern Berlin: Homeland in the Metropolis." The Federation of German Architects (BDA) brings together 12 Berlin institutions from culture, the sciences, and media, all contributing their resources to reflect on this topic. The Academy of Arts starts off with two evenings of readings entitled "City Picture—World Picture. On the Changes of Central Europe in Berlin" on the 3rd and 10th of September 1997.

9.3.1997

The planning stage of Biesdorf-South, the last of the major urban-development planning sites, ends with the demolition of a 66m high chimney. 4,750 apartments, two-thirds of them condos, are to be completed in the next 15 years, costing DM 7 billion.

9.4.1997

Rome in Berlin. The Apostolic Nunciature moves its German headquarters from Bonn to Lilienthalstrasse in Berlin-Neukölln. A Kreuzberg citizens' group collects signatures against the relocation of the papal embassy to the park across from Hasenheide. The last nightingale and a falcon are considered endangered by the planned building. The participants in a limited competition have already been selected, but the results will be released in spring of 1998 at the earliest.

9.6.1997

One year after opening, the Berggruen Collection exhibition welcomes its 200,000th visitor.

9.6.1997

Architects play soccer: In the final of the 5th International Soccer Tournament of Architects, the teams of Grüntuch Ernst/Heide v. Beckrath and Herzog & de Meuron faced each other with one woman required in play for both teams at all times. Herzog & de Meuron secures the title with a score of 1:0. Third place goes to last year's winner, the office Engel and Zillich, fourth to the office of Josef Paul Kleihues.

9.7.1997

In the Berlin-Brandenburg Landmark Festival, some 80 craft businesses show off their wares and their work at Gierkeplatz in Charlottenburg.

9.8.1997

Andrea Breth, artistic director of the famous Schaubühne Theater at Lehniner Platz resigns her post and dissolves the theater's permanent ensemble. With this she terminates its unparalleled programming procedure, in which actors and directors collaborate to sett the program.

September

9.1.1997

Start of the school competition "Are Visions the Truth of Tomorrow? Students Ponder Their Future…" Under the sponsorship of the Multimedia-Living group, students are called on to present and develop their ideas of the multimedia apartment of the future. How will the childrens' room change or how should the apartment be designed when parents work at home and are connected to the office via their PCs?

9.2.1997

The Komische Oper Berlin celebrates its 50th anniversary and honors its chief director Harry Kupfer on the occasion. Besides the book, "Harry Kupfer. Musiktheater," the house will also present an exhibition in the Marstall with the same title. Until September 28th.

9.3.1997

The German Historical Museum (DHM) descends into the lower reaches of bohemia until December 16th with its free exhibition "Bohemia and Dictatorship in the GDR: Groups, Conflicts, and Quarters 1970–1989."

9.3.1997

Topping-out ceremonies for new construction and restoration of Charité Hospital's 172-bed wing for internal medicine. Building costs: DM 171 mill.; planned completion: summer 1999.

9.4.1997

Section four of the Gropius-Passagen on Johannisthaler Chaussee are opened. DM 430 mill. reconstruction costs make this shopping center Berlin's biggest, according to the owners. A multiplex movie theater opens in October with 2,000 seats, the first in Gropiusstadt, a development area from the 1960s. Demolition and reconstruction of the Johannisthaler Chaussee U-Bahn station to follow.

September 1997

After an evaluation process, the architecture office of Foster and Partners is recommended as contractor for the restoration and expansion of the Main Building of the Free University in Berlin-Dahlem.

9.5.1997

One day after the death of architect Aldo Rossi, his facade in Schützenstrasse recalling Palazzo Farnese by Antonio da Sangallo and Michelangelo in Rome is unveiled. The facade is part of Aldo Rossi's "Quartier Schützenstrasse," (cf. pp 32–39). Project clients are Dr. Peter and Isolde Kottmair.

9.7.1997

Inaugural of the 47th Berlin Festwochen with a ceremony (speech by Ralph Giordano) to open the exhibition "Deutschlandbilder. Art From a Divided Country" in Martin-Gropius-Bau. 88 artists show over 450 works from both parts of Germany. Readings, theater and film presentations, concerts and radio reports complement the program. On the upper floor of the Gropius-Bau, the Berlinische Galerie offers its own complementary show on divided Germany with "Positions of Artistic Photography in Germany since 1945," also open until January 8th. The Art Forum of the Grundkreditbank presents "Ostwind," five Eastern German painters from its own collection.

9.8.1997

Four German states, three buildings. Presentation of the winners in the competitions for the state representations of Schleswig-Holstein, Lower Saxony, Rhineland-Palatinate, and Saarland in the former Ministers' Gardens. The first two states will share one building. Two first prizes: Cornelsen + Seelinger, Amsterdam, and Jürgen Böge and Ingeborg Lindner-Böge, Hamburg; estimated construction costs: DM 84 mill. Rhineland-Palatinate: First prize to Heinle, Wischer and Partners, Stuttgart, estimated construction costs: DM 40 mill. State Representation Saarland: The commission goes to Alt & Britz, Saarbrücken, estimated construction costs DM 20 mill.

9.10.1997

The grounds surrounding the printing press and office highrise of the Axel Springer Publishing House on Kochstrasse are to be redesigned. Management, the District Administration, and the Municipal Offices of Urban Development, Construction, and Transit agree on a development plan. The landmark-status printing press from the 1960s is to be demolished and replaced by an office and industrial building. Part of the parking lot in front of the Ullsteinhaus will be closed off by an office and apartment building, with a 5,000 sq. m park to be built behind.

9.11.1997

Berlin landmark preservationists meet in Spandau for a "Landmark Day in the District." The specifics of old town areas are handled in the morning, while in the afternoon current building and landscape preservation in Spandau is addressed.

9.10.1997

The Bavarian hymn, "Gott mit dir, du Land der Bayern," performed by the Bavarian Police Music Corps, lends the proper proto-Bavarian touch to the toppinng-out ceremonies for Bavaria's State Representation. The banking building from 1896 in Behrenstrasse 21/22 will be rebuilt for DM 69 mill. by the autumn of 1998. The saferoom is to be turned into a beer- and wine cellar.

9.12.1997

Flouting all the attendant pseudohistorical kitsch that Berlin feels it needs these days when the city's history is concerned, the private-sector organized "birthday party" for Unter den Linden is opened. Traffic snarls are to be expected between the Brandenburg Gate and Schlossplatz until September 14th.

9.12.1997

Tubrob, the flying robot of the Technical University Berlin; Aquarius, its rocket-like counterpoint; a waterbike, an egg-cooking-and-decapitating machine by two young inventors … all

9.14.1997

The weekend is completely dominated by the Day of Open Landmarks. 150 institutions of all kinds in all districts open their gates to the public.

9.15.1997

Topping-out ceremony for the new capital studios of Germany's ARD network in Wilhelmstrasse 67a, right behind the Reichstag. The curved, glowing red building by architects Ortner and Ortner, Vienna/Berlin, houses television and radio studios, as well as twenty apartments. Developers are the Sender Freies Berlin (SFB) and Westdeutscher Rundfunk (WDR). The property alone costs DM 21.5 mill., costs for construction and technical equipment are expected to reach DM 118 mill. First broadcasting is planned for May 22nd, 1999, the day of the election of Germany's president.

9.18.1997

An 8-peg LEGO block has a side length of 9.6 x 23 x 16 mm; its volume amounts to 4.9152 cc. Identical conditions for all 22 participating architects. The results of their design experiments can be seen in "The Gate of the Present. Architectural Models Made of Lego Blocks," exhibit at the Deutsches Architektur Zentrum (DAZ). Through November 15th.

9.10.1997

Only a few hours after celebrating the topping-out ceremony of the Bavarian State Representation in Berlin, Mayor Eberhard Diepgen can be watched opening the 24th Laubenpieperfest in Bonn. German Chancellor Helmut Kohl stays away, as he does every year, thus missing the Berlin delicacies of fruit flavored blancmange and giant meat balls.

9.11.1997

The cornerstone is laid for the "Forum Landsberger Allee," an office and business center in Prenzlauer Berg. By the end of 1998, a building is to go up at the corner of Storkower Strasse with a net floor area of 36,000 sq. m. Clients are BB Immobilien Service GmbH and Bauwert GmbH. Architects: Rhode, Kellermann, Wawrowsky and Partner, Düsseldorf, investment: DM 250 mill.

9.11.1997

On the grounds of the Exerzierhaus, designed in 1821 by Karl Friedrich Schinkel on Reinhardtstrasse in Mitte, the cornerstone is laid for a building ensemble into which the still-preserved landmark entrance portal is to be integrated. Besides 92 housing and 13 business units, a 930 sq. m rehearsal stage is to be built for the neighboring Deutsches Theater. Client: allbau GmbH, architects: Bellmann, Böhm, Vandreike, Berlin. Total investment: DM 110 mill.

have been invited to the German President's "Festival of Ideas." 5,000 inventors and inventions are on public display for one day in Bellevue Palace.

9.12.1997

Invited by the Marzahn communal housing authority, six photographers, each in his or her own way, approach the giant apartment blocks and inhabitants of Marzahn. "Marzahn— Simply Different. A Changing Berlin District" is presented until November 1st by the Deutsches Architektur Zentrum DAZ.

9.14.1997

After one and a half years of construction, the Hippo House is opened in the Berlin Zoo. Costs: DM 32 mill., architect: Walter Rasché.

9.15.1997

The Brücke-Museum celebrates its 30th anniversary with a major retrospective of its initiator and benefactor, Karl Schmidt-Rottluff. His "Unpainted Pictures," watercolors from the 1940s, are displayed for the first time. Through January 4th, 1998.

9.17.1997

Round five of the round-table discussion, "Castle—Palace—House Fatherland". Today's topic: "Keeping Distant from National Heritage? The Intellectual's Silence and Youth' Disinterest." Participants include Wolfgang Schäuble (Parliamentary Party Leader of the CDU), Klaus Wagenbach (publisher), Wolfgang Pehnt (architectural historian), Michel Friedman (cultural politician), Lothar de Maizière (former Prime Minister of the GDR), and Friedrich Schorlemmer (Theologian). Moderation and summary by Jürgen Engert.

September 1997

The decision is made in Potsdam for the temporary construction of its historic city center. The jury, under the chairmanship of Guido Hager, Zurich, awards first prize (DM 50,000) to the project group freiRaum and Joppien Dietz, Berlin, Frankfurt/Main. In the course of the German Garden Exhibition 2001, the former City Palace, torn down in 1961, will be recreated as a wooden frame with stretched fabric. Multifunctional spaces, which do not interfere with any future construction plans, are thus created for the exhibit.

9.18.1997

36 months after Christo and Jeanne-Claude wrapped the Reichstag, the roof-raising ceremony takes place for the newly-built Reichstag dome. Long before the first parliamentary sheep are counted, an ox moves into the new Reichstag—on a skewer. 500 construction workers and twice as many guests of honor celebrate the completion of building work on the roof platform of the building and under the 12 concrete pillars supporting the dome above the future Plenary Hall. Bundestag President Rita Süssmuth opens the festivities, the architect Sir Norman Foster is present.

9.19.1997

The urban development competition for the barracks grounds in Karlshorst is decided. First prize goes to the Berlin architects Jörg Springer and Jörg Hollricher. For the area between Siewertstrasse, Strasse am Heizwerk, and Zwieseler Strasse 1,175

9.19.1997

146 banks are active in Berlin; two of them are celebrating the roof-raising for their new buildings. At the corner of Augsburger Strasse/Rankestrasse, the Bayrische Handelsbank proceeds toward completion. The bank itself is the developer with an investment of 35 million DM, architect Hasso von Werder. In spring of 1998, the Deutsche Kreditbank will move to Berlin-Mitte, into the listed house of the former Furniture House Trenck in Kronenstrasse 10. A historicized annex, by the architects of the Hotel Adlon, Patzschke, Klotz & Partner, completes the new domicile, 667 employees are to work here. Developer is Bauwert GmbH, Munich. Construction costs: DM 52 mill.

9.22.1997

For the 6th and last time, politicians, architects, and construction industry representatives meet for the discussion series "Castle—Palace—House Fatherland" in the former East German State Council Building. Barbara Jakubeit moderates the topic "Is There an Alternative to the State as Building Client. In Search of the Socially Responsible Developer." With state coffers empty all

9.22.1997

Wielding polished spades, Berlin's political heavyweights join Construction Minister Töpfer and a Thuringian delegation hold the groundbreaking ceremony for Thuringia's State Representation in Berlin. The location on Mohrenstrasse in Mitte has already seen a Thuringia-House which was destroyed in World War II. Until recently, the area served as a parking lot. Developer: Free State of Thuringia; architects: Dr. Worschech + Partner, Erfurt; construction costs: DM 22 mill.; estimated completion spring 1999.

9.23.1997

Slowly, the Europa Sportpark on Landsberger Allee nears completion. Two years after the end of of the European Cycling Championships in the neighboring Velodrome (architect: Dominique Perrault), which was finished in spring, the roof-raising ceremony is celebrated for the swimming and the diving pool, also designed by Perrault and buried 17 meters below ground.

9.26.1997

Time to celebrate, all work stops on the Chancellor's Office construction site. Helmut Kohl and Eberhard Diepgen, Construction Minister Töpfer, Chancellor's Office Minister Bohl, and Undersecretary Pfeiffer lay miniaturized blueprints, coins in circulation, manuscripts of their speeches, and current newspapers into the prepared cornerstone. Lid closed, an ecumenical Our Father, the national anthem, and the work resumes. See also February 4th.

On June 20th, 1884, after the cornerstone of the Reichstag building had been laid, Paul Wallot wrote to his friend Bluntschli: "The period in which this floor plan was created was the most agitated time of my life. I climbed into bed, a few floor plans spread about me; in the night I was jolted out of sleep, a hundredweight of floor plans pressing down on my breast and causing me nightmares. When I arose and looked out into the night, even the old moon seemed to me like a floor plan."

housing units for federal civil servants will be built, beginning in 1999. Completion scheduled for 2000.

9.19.1997

At what cost could you buy a whole housing settlement made of prefabricated slabs? In this case, we are talking about Germany's oldest settlement of this kind. The coveted colony lies in Berlin-Lichtenberg, goes by the name of Splanemann-Siedlung, was built between 1926 and 1930, and awaits a minimum offer of DM 4.6 million. A factory-owning couple from Karlsruhe received the nod for the 27 houses with 118 units with their offer of DM 6.4 mill.

9.20.1997

For the first time in two decades, the Königliche Porzellan Manufaktur Berlin (KPM, Royal Porcelain Manufacture) presents a new coffee and table service. Created by Italian house designer Enzo Mari, the service is given the name Berlin and costs DM 2,595 in the 16-piece version.

9.22.1997

Debis can only move in where debis phosphoresces. One week before the planned move, a construction crane lifts the six-by-six meter company logo onto the roof in what amounts to the last step of construction of the debis-House on Potsdamer Platz. A square of twenty-five green, variously shaped rectangles shines over the city at 100 meters altitude.

over, the discussion panel including German Construction Minister Klaus Töpfer, Berlin Building Senator Jürgen Klemann, the clients Klaus Groth (Industrie- und Wohnungsbau Groth + Graalfs GmbH), Walter Rasch (HANSEATICA), and the architects Wolf R. Eisentraut, and Hans Kollhoff, both Berlin, give their best.

Berlin is still the most political city in Germany. But on public occasions of a political nature, even the Berliners show that quality that Prince Bismarck once called "Wurschtigkeit" (indifference). For the recent celebration of the day of rejoicing, the city was decorated with flags and illumination. But the people who walked about in the glow of the lights were neither politicians nor enthusiasts, nor even opponents. They were — Berliners. They had more criticism for the illumination than for its occasion. They emulated Schopenhauer and withdrew into the territory of the jest, something for which "no paper can be too serious in this thoroughly ambivalent life." They allowed their parodic wit free rein on the statues, the names of shop proprietors, young ladies strolling alone with painted eyebrows, old horses, married couples, and cylinders. But they said nothing about politics.
Alfred Kerr, April 7th, 1895

9.26.1997

Roof-raising ceremony in Mitte. After long haggling with the Landmark preservation office, the complex between Rosenthaler, Gips- and Sophienstrasse approaches completion. The apartment house with 99 units stands as a carcass, and the modernization of the former Wertheim department store at the corner of Sophienstrasse, as office building is about to begin. Planned completion mid-1999, architects: Meyer and Munzinger, Stuttgart, developer: Opus Gesellschaft für Projektentwicklung, total investment DM 240 mill.

9.29.1997

Hannelore Kohl christens the central section of the rail tunnel under the Tiergarten. The four tubes now carry the names Hannelore I–IV. Following an old tradition much cherished in Berlin, she represents Saint Barbara, patron saint of miners and excavators.

9.30.1997

The municipal housing authority DeGeWo celebrates a roof-raising in Gorkistrasse 205–215 in Tegel. The architects Gibbins, Bultmann and Partner are erecting 176 housing units in two-story row houses. Investment DM 49.5 mill., completion mid-1998.

9.30.1997

Pop quiz: If there are 107 shops open for business on Opening Day in the new Gesundbrunnen Center in Wedding, and 150,000 customers come in the first 12 hours, how old are the first two patrons, received at 8 a.m. with bouquets of flowers? 70 and 75 of course, their names are Maria Friede and her husband Alexander.

10.1.1997

Peter Stein, co-founder of the Schaubühne Theater and one of Germany's premier contemporary theater directors, turns 60. His "Faust I and II" production, conceived for the Hanover Expo 2000 (17 hours in 5 evenings), may possibly come to Berlin first.

10.3.1997

Peter Joseph Lenné's Invalidenpark in Mitte, dating from 1843, has been restored and opend to the public. During World War II, the park and its monument, the famous column, were distroyed. The park partially lay in the shadow of the Wall. Architect for the reconstruction: Christophe Girot, France. Cost: approx. DM 11 mill.

10.6.1997

Russian photographer and war reporter Yevgeni Khaldeii dies at the age of 80 in Moscow. Probably his most famous work is his—staged—photograph of Red Army troops raising the Soviet flag on the Reichstag on May 2nd, 1945.

Early October

The German Chancellor's Office and the German Parliament approve plans for renaming the streets in and around the future government quarter on the Spree Bend. Moltkestrasse will become Willy-Brandt-Strasse, Kronprinzenufer will change to Ludwig-Erhardt-Ufer. Also planned are a Konrad-Adenauer-Strasse as well as a Heinrich-von-Gagern-Strasse.

1997	September	October

9.27.1997

The Central European Development Corporation (CEDC), developer of the "Philip Johnson Haus," postpones the projected completion of two office complexes at the former Checkpoint Charlie after the withdrawal of an investment partner. Whether and when both buildings by architects David Childs and Jürgen Engel are realized remains unclear.

9.27.1997

Even weeks afterward, 42 km of blue double stripes will testify to this year's Berlin Marathon, which was held today.

9.29.1997

The conflict escalates between Berlin's culture ministry and Amnon Barzel, Director of the Jewish Museum pending a court ruling. An immediately effective dismissal follows one giving proper advance notice from June 1997.

10.1.1997

Wolfgang Bocksch, Mannheim, takes over the Schiller Theater GmbH, after the retreat of Peter Schwenkow and the German Entertainment AG. The concept of a musical theater remains unchanged. Schwenkow would rather keep an eye on the more promising two large sporting halls, the Velodrom and Max-Schmeling-Halle, in Prenzlauer Berg.

10.1.1997

The equestrian statue of Friedrich II on Unter den Linden is removed for restoration work. The statue was created by Christian Daniel Rauch in 1851. The two year long restauration will cost DM 2 mill. paid for in equal halves by the Deutsche Stiftung Denkmalschutz and the State of Berlin.

10.2.1997

Roof-raising ceremony for the reconstructed museum for post and communication history on Leipziger Strasse/corner Mauerstrasse. Architects: Henze, Vahjen, Braunschweig. The post museum looking back on 125 year's history is the eldest in the world. For the place in front, "The Giants", a group sculptured by Ernst Wenck, has been reconstructed.

10.9.1997

A decision has been announced for the architectural competition of the Mexican embassy. First prize among the exclusively Mexican participants wins the design by Teodoro González de Léon and Francisco Serrano who already built the embassies in Brazil and Guatemala. The new building will be situated on the corner of Klingelhöfer- and Rauchstrasse, the design therefore had to answer to the urban scheme by Machleidt and Stepp. 18-meter-high concrete lamellas along Klingelhöferstrasse make a facade that both suits the closed-block structure and strikes its own chord, with a diagonally-cut portal and a compact, five-story cylindrical building behind. Construction is to begin in spring 1998, completion planned for late 1999. Exhibition in the Galerie Aedes until November 9th.

10.10.1997

Under the title "CULTURE rabble," discussions, theater, film, and photo presentations take place for one week on the topic of homelessness. Organized by UNTER DRUCK kultur von der strasse e.V. and ACUD e.V. Until October 18th.

10.10.1997

Biesdorf Palace in Marzahn is the third venue in the presentation series "Babylon—Berlin. Architects—Planners—Landmark Preservation."

10.10.1997

"EXILE, Flight and Emigration of European Artists 1933–1945" opens at the Neue Nationalgalerie. The exhibition with 130 paintings, sculptures, and drawings by 23 artists who fled to America is complemented by letters, magazine articles, and other contemporary documents. The exhibition was conceived and assembled by the chief curator of the Los Angeles Museum of Art, Stephanie Barron, who five years pre-

10.12.1997

The exhibition "Berlin City Quarters—Inner City Planning" at the Märkisches Museum in Mitte informs of the latest steps in the jigsaw puzzle of Berlin city planning. Results are presented for the quarters Molkenmarkt, Spittelmarkt, Kulturforum, and Breitscheidplatz; their guidelines were proposed by individual workshops. A resolution by the Berlin City Council confirms the guidelines for inner-city development. In early 1998, the city government is due to present a progress report on current planning. Exhibition until January 14th, 1997.

10.13.1997

Opening of an exhibition in the Märkisches Museum: "Berlin. From its Foundation to the Great Elector."

10.13.1997

Construction start for the extension of underground line No. 5 at Pariser Platz and at Reichstag.

10.15.1997

The Houseball, a nine-meter-high sculpture by Claes Oldenburg and Coosje van Bruggen is unveiled on Bethlehemkirchplatz in front of the Philip Johnson Haus.

10.15.1997

The inventory of the Palace of the Republic on Schlossplatz is disassembled and removed. The building is to be emptied by May 1998, when work is supposed to begin on asbestos removal. According to their value and historical importance, the objects are used in various federal-owned buildings, are given to the German Historical Museum, are sold, stored, or discarded. As yet undetermined is the fate of the glass tree by Richard Wilhelm, as its size and weight would make removal difficult. Costs for the clearance

10.20.1997

Dedication of the "Karl-Philipp-Moritz-Haus" on Moritzplatz in Kreuzberg. The ecologically-oriented new building, boasting solar panels on the roof, a car-sharing station, and its own launderette, completes a block destroyed during the war. Architects: tgw, Markus Torge, Sebastian Gaa, Klaus Wercker, Berlin; client: GSW, Berlin, cost: DM 28 mill.

10.21.1997

SFB begins a six-week series named "City, Country, River—Berlin," designed to contribute to the discourse on the city's future face. Half an hour every Tuesday.

10.21.1997

Some 4,000 traffic- and transportation experts from around the world meet for the 4th World Congress for Intelligent Traffic-Control Systems in the International Congress Center (ICC). 170 international associations, firms, and institutions from 17 countries

10.23.1997

The new Forum Köpenick in Bahnhofstrasse opens today, six months after the roof-raising ceremony on April 14th. The building houses 148 shops and snackbars. Architects: gmp, von Gerkan, Marg and Partner, Hamburg. Developer: Fundus Gruppe. Construction costs: DM 350 mill.

10.23.1997

Under the auspices of German Construction Minister Klaus Töpfer the Wasserstadt GmbH opens a congress on "New Addresses Along the Riverside." For three days, participants share their experiences in the planning of cities at the water, examples are Amsterdam, Barcelona, Madrid, Berlin, Budapest, Cardiff, Hamburg, Lisbon, London, Rotterdam, and Vienna.

viously was responsible for the reconstruction of the 1937 "Degenerate Art" exhibition in Nazi Germany. Exhibition design: Frank O. Gehry.

10.12.1997

End of season for velotaxis. The results are positive: DM 150,000 profit, 150 new jobs. For the next season, due to begin at Easter, a new route is being planned starting at Oranienburger Strasse in Mitte.

10.13.1997

Französische Strasse between Mauer- and Glinkastrasse is now open to traffic.

October 1997

Eight 13x3 m pictures by the artists Irene Niepel and Jürgen Villmow, financed by the Köpenick communal housing authority (Köwoge), have been painted on the street facades of the five- to eight-story new buildings in Wuhlheide 86–104 and 96–104 in Berlin-Köpenick.

10.14.1997

The Cologne Fundus-Gruppe, developer of the famous Tacheles site on Oranienburger Strasse opened part of the area to the public. A daily market is to become the core of the site, water mains and electric lines have already been laid, while snackshops and soup kitchens move into refurbished old commuter train cars. A survey had revealed that the profusion of bars left local residents with hardly any places to shop. By the way: Berlin's School of Fine Arts presents today the results of its project INBETWEEN, dealing with concepts and designs for new functions of the Tacheles.

10.16.1997

Exhibition at Kulturbrauerei: "Left Property from the Central Committee and the Ministerial Council," displaying furniture and objects from the two buildings. Until February 12th, 1998.

are put at DM 3.234 mill., the Federal Government having already gained DM 4.2 mill. through inventory sales.
The Federal and Berlin governments have devised the conditions for a future building on the site in a public-private partnership. The paper has been forwarded to more than 30 investment groups worldwide. Their financial propositions are expected by the end of the calendar year. A suitable investor is to be chosen next year, an architectural competition will follow.

inform about their products and services. Through October 24th.

10.21.1997

The embankment Hauptstrasse 7 in the Rummelsburger Bucht Development area has been restored. The Wasserstadt GmbH has freed the riverbank path from concrete and planted a reed strip along the new pathway. Cost: approx. DM 1 mill.

10.23.1997

Werkbund celebrates its 90th anniversary with an exhibition "1907. A Showcase Installation of the Werkbund Archive."

10.24.1997

Queen Silvia of Sweden in person opens the exhibition "Elective Affinities. Scandinavia and Germany 1800–1914" in the German Historical Museum (DHM). The exhibition is organized jointly by the National Museum in Stockholm and the Oslo Norsk Folkemuseum. From Berlin it will move to Stockholm (next year's European City of Culture) and Oslo. Until January 6th, 1998. Incidentally, in a few days, on 10th of October, the DHM celebrates its 10th anniversary. Let's recapulate: 170 full-time and 30 part-time employees, 700,000 collected objects, over 100 exhibitions in various locations, 40 catalogues, 21 magazines, a two-volume publication on the permanent exhibition.

10.24.1997

Grand festivities open the debis-House by Renzo Piano on Potsdamer Platz. Some 1,000 guests are invited and numerous speakers, the Academy of Arts President György Konrád giving the main address. The "Atrium," venue for the celebration, is to become a gallery with changing exhibitions. Debis employees have already moved in the new building. Besides various divisions of debis AG, DASA is also to establish its Berlin offices there.

10.26.1997

The 6th Berlin-Brandenburg Book Weeks start with a reading by Turkish author Yasar Kemal, recipient of the Peace Prize of the German Book Trade on October 20th. In the next four weeks, 109 events under the title "Open World" take place in bookshops, libraries, and cultural institutions, 36 of them in Brandenburg. The laudatory address given by Günter Grass to prizewinner Yasar Kemal caused a scandal due to its biting criticism of the German government's asylum policy.

10.28.1997

The Berlin Government and the Jewish Congregation in Berlin agree on a concept for the continuance of the Jewish Museum. It is to receive the status of a dependent foundation within the Stadtmuseum, but have its own board, budget, and planning authority. The museum's mission remains the integration of Jewish and Berlin history.

10.30.1997

The Ring Center II opens on Frankfurter Allee in Lichtenberg. On a retail space of 20,000 sq. m 45 shops offer their wares. Architects: HPP, Hentrich, Petschnigg and Partner, Düsseldorf, and Manfred Stanek, Jost Hering, ECE, Hamburg. Investor: ECE Projektmanagement. Cost: DM 120 mill.

10.31.1997

A retrospective of the work of Sigmar Polke opens at the Hamburger Bahnhof Museum. Until February 20.

10.30.1997

Architect Daniel Libeskind is awarded an honorary doctorate from the Humboldt University.

10.30.1997

The second "art forum berlin" opens to the public on the Funkturm Exhibition Grounds in Charlottenburg. On a floor space of 7,000 sq. m 135 gallery owners from 23 countries present art works chiefly from the last two decades. The show presented itself last year as an alternative to the Art Cologne. This year's presentation established the show's reputation, according to the press.

10.31.1997

The Press and Visitor Center, first phase of construction for the new Federal Press Office, is finished. The so-called Press Cube is dedicated today. Architects: KSP, Engel—Kramer—Schmiedecke—Zimmermann, Cologne. Cost: DM 38 mill. The Federal Press Office's final move to Berlin is planned for the second half of 1999.

10.31.1997

The "Cultural Department Store" Dussmann, the second major department store for books and media after Hugendubel on Tauentzienstrasse, opens its doors on Friedrichstrasse 90. Four floors of the new building are dedicated exclusively to interactive media, three will house the company's main offices. Architect: Miroslav Volf, Saarbrücken. Client: Dussmann Gruppe. Costs: DM 65 mill.

10.24.1997

Munich business consultant Dr. Seebauer & Partner receives the nod for the development and marketing of the Olympic Grounds. 22 businesses had participated in the Europe-wide competition. A general concept for economic usage and renovation of the Olympic Stadium is to be presented by year's end.

10.27.1997

Roof-raising for the new Japanese-German Center in Saargemünder Strasse 2 in Dahlem. Architects for new construction and rebuilding: RTW Klaus Reichardt and Peter Billerbeck, Berlin. Construction costs: DM 12.5 mill.

10.27.1997

The cornerstone is laid for the new building to accompany the rebuilt Zollernhof, Unter den Linden 36/38, to house the new Berlin studio of the ZDF television network. ZDF and VEBA AG, Düsseldorf—which will establish its Berlin offices there—, are the joint developers. Cost: DM 300 mill. Planned completion: late 1999. The Zollernhof was erected in 1911, its listed facade was designed by Bruno Paul.

10.30.1997

The plans for the Berlin Animal Sanctuary's new building in Falkenberg/Hohenschönhausen are presented to the public. Accomodations for 530 dogs, 700 cats, for birds, hedgehogs, and exotic animals, as well as a lecture hall, veterinary facilities, a children's zoo and show gardens are to be placed on a 39,5 acres site. Architect: Dietrich Bangert, Berlin. Construction is to begin mid-1998. The far too small animal sanctuary in Dessauerstrasse in Lankwitz is to be dissolved.

In Berlin we are standing, perhaps not on "the eve of great events", as the Corsican Buonaparte once put it, but certainly on the eve of great festivities. At times, that may be the opposite of great events ... This folk who lives on the Spree, the Panke, and the Landwehrkanal cannot usually restrain its parodic tendencies; and, much more strongly than would appear from the magazines and newspapers — the official heralds of the popular soul — there lives here a ruthless, genuinely Aristophanean urge, much more radical and disrespectful than for example in France, a country famous for it. The difference is that in France, the relatively moderate mood of sarcasm comes to expression undiminished; in Berlin, on the other hand, the existing parody, three times more audacious, never even remotely sees the light of day in print.
Alfred Kerr, September 1st, 1895

10.31.1997

Roof-raising festivities for the Hellersdorf town hall on Alice-Salomon-Platz. Besides offices and a plenary hall for the district council, the 6-story privately financed building will house the registry office and a citizens' center, a pub and three shops. The district administration is to rent the building from the developer, the MEGA-Entwicklungs- und Gewerbeansiedlungs GmbH. Architects: Brandt & Böttcher, Berlin. Investment: DM 30 mill., planned completion in March 1998.

Late October

The Friedrichshain municipal housing authority WBF is awarded the German Developer's Prize 1997 for its exemplary modernization of the 10-story landmark apartment block on Platz der Vereinten Nationen. The prize is awarded

11.1.1997

Berlin facilitates construction with a revised building code. From now on, building permits are no longer required for the construction of private homes and small building projects up to three full stories.

11.1.1997

Decision is made concerning the last new building in the government district. Gustav Peichl, Vienna, emerges as winner of the two-phase Europe-wide competition for the Bundestag daycare center. The daycare center, to be built 100 m from the Reichstag between the Alsenbrücke and the Kronprinzenbrücke, is to be completed by the time the Bundestag begins work in Berlin in mid-1999. Cost: DM 9.9 mill.

11.6.1997

The global player of art, the Solomon R. Guggenheim Foundation of New York in cooperation with the Deutsche Bank, opens another European branch in addition to Venice and Bilbao: the Deutsche Guggenheim Berlin. In the new Deutsche Bank building Unter den Linden, the two sponsors have installed a showroom of 300 sq. m. The first exhibition, devoted to the work of the Parisian painter Robert Delaunay, is on view until January 4th, 1998.

11.10.1997

Opening of the 11th Jewish Culture Days in the Art Library of the Preussischer Kulturbesitz. "Jewish Culture from New York" will come to Berlin until November 23rd in the form of films, concerts, and an Erwin Blumenfeld exhibition.

11.12.1997

First decision for the Berlin Building Exhibition 1999 "Wohnen im Eigentum—ein Haus im Garten" ("Private Dwelling—a House in a Garden"). Helge Sypereck, Berlin, wins the realization competition for Elisabethaue in Pankow; his urbanistic concept calls for the division of the terrain into 16 building sites interspersed with green areas. All competition projects are on view until November 26th at the Jannowitz-Center on Brückenstrasse.

11.16.1997

Like its predecessor, the second competition for the Berlin Holocaust Memorial produces no unequivocal results (cf. BBA '96, 6.25.1995 and 4.24.1996). Instead, the jury selects four of the eight designs for further discussion until January (Gesine Weinmiller, Berlin; Jochen Gerz, Paris; Daniel Libeskind, Berlin; and Peter Eisenman/Richard Serra, New York). The projects are on view December 10th, 1997 to January 21st 1998 in the Marstall in the Mitte district.

11.18.1997

The Berlin "Milljöh" moves into the Ephraimpalais. For the first time, the foundation Stadtmuseum Berlin shows its combined collections of the works of Heinrich Zille, as well as works on paper from the Wilhelm Busch Museum in Hanover. The 300 drawings, studies, and photographs are on view until January 11th, 1998.

11.21.1997

Roof raising in Nöldnerstrasse 1–7 in Lichtenberg. Housing complex with 74 subsidized housing units, 16 shops and 36 parking spaces. Architect: Werner Wöber, cost: DM 26 mill., completion planned for February 1998.

October   **November**

---

jointly by the Federation of German Architects, the German Council of Cities and the Bundesverband Deutscher Wohnungsunternehmen. Architect: Planungsbüro Klaus Theo Brenner, Berlin.

End October

Winner of the invited competition for the Dependance of the Deutsche Bundesbank on Leibnizstrasse/corner Bismarckstrasse is the architects' office Bangert Scholz, Berlin. 2nd prize: Günter Hermann, Stuttgart; 3rd prize: Benedict Tonon, Berlin.

11.2.1997

"Fine dining in Berlin has the advantage of being tremendously circumscribed." In order to improve on this image, "Partner für Berlin" presents the six "Master Chefs of Berlin 1997" in the Hotel Interconti, one chef per course: Rolf Schmidt (Restaurant First Floor) "Dove galantine with autumn salad and truffle," Herbert Beltle (Altes Zollhaus) "Grilled zander on sweet-and-sour pumpkin," Karl Wannemacher (Alt-Luxemburg), "Thrice Kaiser prawns," Johannes Klings (Grand Slam), "Little soup aria," Manfred Heissig (Borchardt), "Saddle of young venison roasted on cinnamon sticks with leaves of Brussels sprouts and Topinambur noodles," and for dessert, Franz Ranneburger (Bamberger Reiter), "Variation on Valrhona chocolate." Bon appetit.

11.9.1997

Today, after a long period of uncertainty and on the eighth anniversary of the fall of the Berlin Wall, construction officially begins on the Wall Memorial on Bernauer Strasse. The design by the Stuttgart architects Kohlhoff & Kohlhoff will be realized, calling for the preservation of a 210-meter-long section of the Wall, terminated on both ends by two steel plates, 60 and 45 m long and 7 m high. A documentation center will move in the adjacent Protestant Savior church, scheduled to open on November 9th, 1998.

11.13.1997

Behind closed doors and under cover of wintry temperatures, the Berlin chamber of deputies enacts a new ordinance regulating behavior in public parks. Bicycling, ball-playing, sunbathing, and above all grilling will now be allowed only in designated "recreational and special purpose areas"; violators are punishable with up to DM 10,000 in fines. In an interpretation true to the letter of the law, Horst Porath, city building commissioner for Tiergarten, wants to designate the entire Tiergarten park a recreational zone; on pleasant days, as many as 15,000 people grill there, who should not be prevented by law from enjoying themselves.

11.18.1997

The prizes fly thick and fast: in the Berlin Pavilion, Senate building director Barbara Jakubeit presents the winners of the architects' competition "Das städtische Haus" ("The Urban House"). In the context of "Eigentumsstrategie 2000" ("Property Strategy 2000"), houses are to be erected in five Berlin locations providing 100 sq. m of living area for not more than DM 200,000. The winners: F. Arnold and M. Gladisch with 34 rowhouses for Hellersdorf, M. Gussmann and L. Valentin with 57 houses for Hohenschönhausen, B. Seifert and M. Peper with 33 houses for Köpenick, and Eckert, Negwer, Sommer, Suselbeek (ENSS) with 38 houses for Zehlendorf. For Marzahn, Salomon Schindler developed a module house that can be expanded from 114 sq. m to 200 sq. m. All architectural firms are from Berlin.

11.25.1997

Final decision: With the inauguration of the Reichstag in April 1999, the federal parliament will begin its move to Berlin, and after the summer break, from their first session on, the parliamentarians will do their work from here. The majority of the Bundestag, disregarding any political color, voted in favor of the timetable.

11.27.–30.1997

The former Kongresshalle in Tiergarten, today "The House of the World Cultures", sees the "6th European Wohnbund Conference". The issue in question: "Migration. How Cities Change".

12.1.1997

With a symbolic turn of the spade, Federal Moving Commissioner Klaus Töpfer marks the beginning of renovation and remodeling work on the Bendlerblock in Tiergarten, which will house the Berlin office of the Federal Defense Ministry. Built in 1911–14 by the architects Süssenguth and Reinhardt as the Reichsmarineamt (Imperial Naval Office), the Bendlerblock was the seat of the supreme army command during World War II. Today, the German Resistance Memorial on Stauffenbergstrasse serves as a reminder of the failed assassination attempt on Hitler on July 20th, 1944. In 1999, the political leadership of the ministry will be transferred to Berlin with 354 employees; the major part will remain in Bonn. Cost: DM 107.7 mill.

12.2.1997

The Berlin society "Kunst im Bau" ("Art in Prison") organizes theater behind bars. A troupe of professional actors and inmates performs the play "Mausoleum—Agamemnons Grab" ("Mausoleum—Agamemnon's Tomb") in the Moabit penitentiary. For the first time, the three performances are open not only to inmates, but also—under strict guard—to the public.

12.3.1997

Topping-out ceremony for the new outpatient building of the Center for Specialized Medicine at the Bundeswehr hospital in Berlin. 15 years are estimated for the modernization, renovation, and new construction in the 17-acres-area of the former Volkspolizei hospital, which also includes buildings of the Royal Prussian military hospital from the mid-18th century. Total cost: ca. DM 200 mill.

12.3.1997

Topping-out ceremony for a 7-story office and commercial building in Lichtenberg. The new building is part of the redevelopment of the area around the Ostkreuz rail station and functions as an entrance gate to the service center. Architect: Helmut Joos, JSK. Investor: Helmut Joos.

12.4.1997

Premiere of the new play "Café Mitte" by Volker Ludwig—in the young spectators Grips-Theater, where else?

12.1.1997

Inauguration of the "Spandauer See Brücke," the eighth bridge over the Havel and the 1,000th traffic bridge in Berlin. The 264-meter-long bridge connects the development area Wasserstadt Spandau with the Rhenaniastrasse in the center of Haselhorst (see June 15th).

12.1.1997

John R. Krebs, director of the British Council for Environmental Research, gives a lecture at the Technische Universität Berlin on "Wissenschaft und Nachhaltigkeit" (Science and Sustainability). The event reopens the series of annual "Queen's Lectures" by prominent British scholars and scientists, begun in 1965 as an endowment of the Queen of England but discontinued in 1975. In the context of this year's program, the exhibition "Die Technische Universität und Grossbritannien" (The Technical University and Great Britain) opens in the atrium of the main building.

12.2.1997

A final transitional solution for the exhibition "Topographie des Terrors" is found and realized. During construction work, the 435 panels, which up to now were accommodated in a tent at the edge of the construction site, will hang in a covered walkway along the excavations at Niederkirchnerstrasse. Construction on the new building has been underway since July. Scheduled date of completion: 1999. Architect: Peter Zumthor, Switzerland. Building costs have increased from DM 36 mill. to DM 45 mill., with the contribution of the federal government remaining the same; what remains to be seen is how the city of Berlin will finance its increased share.

12.4.1997

The "2. Berliner Gespräche" (2nd Berlin Dialogues) with Josef Paul Kleihues and Winy Maas (MVRDV, Rotterdam) take place at the Deutsche Architekturzentrum (DAZ) on the subject of "Innovation and Repetition. Images between Stagnation and Vision." The event is followed by the opening of an exhibition of competition designs for the French embassy on Pariser Platz, on view until January 31st, 1998.

Café Mitte *Volker Ludwig*
Those who came here long before
plugged their names in Berlin's core
Be they French, or Russian, Polski
say Fontane or Tucholsky
Rocchigiani and Safranski
Mendiburu and Spolianki
Bisky Gysi and Ossietzky
Adlon Mira Chodowiecki
Devrient Lefèvre Bondy
Isang Yung Rogacki Szondi
Karajan Lassalle Kempinski
Ensikat de Bruyn Kuczinsky
Say Geschonnek and Djembritzki
Rutschky Jaeggi or Kudritzki
Radunski Stroux "la Grande Durieux"
Kollo Schily and Lenné
Kowalski Ossowski Jachowiak Ostrowski
Kaleko Scharnowski Pudelko Gotzkowsky
Wapnewski Jankowski Schamoni Kempowski
Bassenge Abramowski Remé and "La Gsovski"
Some of them are no angels at all
Some of them, sure, are rather rascal
As was our Garski, was our Schabowski
as Mister Nawrocki, as Mister Landowsky.
The Mongolian woman and the Zulu man
make Berlin metropolitan
Forget all those terrors legalized
forget all those Bonners subsidized
For without you, dear immigrant
Berlin would still be a heap of sand A heap of sand A heap of sand

12.4.1997

Topping-out ceremony for the new "Charlotten-palais," a historicizing 8-story residential, office, and commercial building on Charlottenstrasse 35/36 in the Mitte district. Client: Bauwert GmbH, Munich. Architects: Patzschke, Klotz and Partner, Berlin. Cost: DM 60 mill. Usable space: 3,700 sq. m. Date of completion: spring 1998.

12.5.1997

After a year of renovation, the Brecht-Weigel-Memorial on Chaussee-strasse in Mitte reopens today.

12.5.1997

Dedication of a new organ with 3,227 pipes in the Nikolaikirche at Nikolaikirchplatz in Mitte.

Early December

The 120 employees of the Berlinische Galerie, along with boxes full of paintings, photos, and architectural models, move into their temporary quarters at the Schultheiss brewery on Methfesselstrasse in Kreuzberg. In the search for a new permanent location for the collection, formerly housed in the Gropius-Bau, the post transport office on Oranienburger Strasse in Mitte is still under consideration.

12.11.1997

After a three-year struggle initiated by a jury decision in favor of Giorgio Grassi, the advisory council of the cultural foundation Preussischer Kulturbesitz decides to commission the British architect David Chipperfield with the reconstruction of the Neues Museum by Friedrich August Stüler on the Museumsinsel, which was heavily damaged in World War II. Construction will begin in the year 2000 at the earliest.

12.13.1997

Starting today, measures are taken to alleviate the high-accident area at Grosser Stern: a traffic light and new lane markings help steer traffic in the right direction.

12.13.1997

Tragedy during sport's event: At the Women's Handball World Championship in Max-Schmeling-Halle, during a game between Denmark and Russia, a Berliner fatally stabs two Danish handball fans.

12.15.1997

Official opening of the branch office of the Dresdner Bank at Pariser Platz 6, with a reception in the covered atrium. Architects: gmp, Hamburg. Cost: ca. DM 165 mill.

12.18.1997

Opening of the sixth and most important S-Bahn (rapid line) section between Treptower Park and Sonnenallee in Neukölln.

12.19.1997

Walter Höllerer, writer, founder of the "Literary Colloquium Berlin", and editor of the magazine "Akzente" and the poetry anthology "Transit" celebrates his 75th birthday.

December 1997

The residential development company Marzahn WBG moves into its new home, a 7-story office and residential building on Mehrower Allee 52 in Marzahn. Architect: Walter von Lom and Partner, Cologne. Client: WBG Marzahn.

12.19.1997

The Berlin Volksbank signs a contract for the purchase of building C2/C3 in the debis complex at Potsdamer Platz (Architects: Arata Isozaki, Steffen Lehmann).

12.20.1997

A 750-meter-long section of streetcar track opens, connecting the S- and U-Bahn station Friedrich-strasse to the streetcar net from the Weidendammer Brücke on. It represents the completion of Linie 50 from Buchholz to Kupfergraben via Schön-hauser Allee, Zions-kirche, and Invaliden-strasse. Cost: DM 7.3 mill.

12.22.1997

The financial ministry of Saxony announced today that the federal state of Saxony has acquired a building from the year 1905 on Brüderstrasse 11/12 for the offices of its state representatives. The building, whose facade is under historic preservation, is to be remodeled by the end of 1999. Cost: DM 25–27 mill.

12.5.1997

In the "Hofgarten" at Gendarmenmarkt in the Mitte district, eight artists have furnished six dwellings. The whole can be seen as an exhibition under the title "muster-wohnen" ("Model Living") until February 1st, 1998.

12.5.1997

Hessen is the first German state to buy land in the Ministergärten ("Ministe-rial Gardens"). On the 3,100 sq. m plot between Ebertstrasse and Voss Strasse in Mitte, the Hessian state represent-atives' office will be built in early 1999. An archi-tectural competition will be announced early next year. In addition to Hessen, the states Bran-denburg, Mecklenburg-Western Pomerania, Rhineland-Palatinate, Saarland, Lower Saxony, and Schleswig-Holstein will also erect their representatives' offices here.

12.8.1997

The 8-story residential building Checkpoint Plaza on the corner of Schützen-strasse and Charlotten-strasse, named after former Checkpoint Charlie, is completed. Architects: Gisela Glass, Günther Bender, Berlin. Client: SBB Stadtprojekt, Cologne.

12.13.1997

In the middle of other-wise fallow land, two completed single-family model homes on a like-wise completed model street in Biesdorf-Süd, Marzahn, open today as a preview of the Building Exhibition 1999. Purchase contracts are available.

Mid-December

At the Oberbaumbrücke in Kreuzberg, a light box by the artist Thorsten Goldberg showing the hand positions of the stone-paper-scissors game marks the former border crossing between Friedrichshain and Kreuz-berg. Next year, artists' installations will be created to preserve the memory of all seven former border crossings in the city.

12.15.1997

Cornerstone-laying for the extension of the future service building of the Federal Transporta-tion Ministry on Invali-denstrasse in Mitte. The remodelling of the old building, erected in 1878 as the Geologische Landesanstalt und Berg-akademie (National Geological Society and Mining Academy), is al-ready underway. Archi-tect of the extension: Max Dudler, Berlin. Total cost of remodeling and new construction: DM 220 mill. Date of comple-tion: September 1998.

12.18.1997

Extremely icy roads paralyze the city from noon on. You can still drive; you just can't brake. Walking involves dance-like motions. Bus service is down, ambu-lances are in top deploy-ment. Still, spirits are high: apparently it takes a state of emergency to thaw Berlin out a little.

12.19.1997

Cornerstone-laying for a new 11-story office building on Budapester Strasse 31, erected by the Deutsches Institut für Normung (German Institute for Standardiza-tion) as an extension of its main building on Burggrafenstrasse. The building is being con-structed on the grounds of the former Hotel Schweizerhof; on another part of the site, the owners of the latter are planning a new hotel. Architect: Johannes Heinrich, Berlin.

12.19.1997

Today a privately fi-nanced eye clinic opens in a building from the year 1893 at Brebacher Weg 15 in Marzahn. The building, now under historic preservation, is located on the grounds of the Wilhelm-Griesinger-Hospital. Client and pri-vate investor: Schindler Immobilien KG, Berlin. Renovation cost: DM 27 mill.

12.23.1997

The Comic Opera on Unter den Linden has been celebrating its 50th birthday all this season with premiäres, exhibi-tions, interviews, and other events. Today is the climax: exactly 50 years ago today, the opera house presented its first performance with Strauss' "Fledermaus", mise-en-scène by Walter Felsenstein.

12.31.1997

With "Menschen—Tiere—Sensationen" ("People—Animals—Sensations"), a sold-out Deutschland-halle celebrates what is really no cause for celebration: the closing of the arena where ca. 3,000 sporting events, concerts, and shows have taken place since its reopening in 1957. Presumably, the Deutsch-landhalle stands as an unwanted rival to the new Max-Schmeling-Halle and the Velodrom. The build-ing's fate remains to be seen. It can't be torn down; there's no money for demolition.

Credits

Literature
56–59 Vicki Baum, Grand Hotel, London, 1930.
118 Heinrich Heine, Gesammelte Werke in sechs
Bänden, Bd. 3, Reisebilder 1822–1830, Berlin 1954
119 Alfred Andersch, Efraim, Zurich 1967
119 Arthur Eloesser, Unter den Linden, in: Der Berliner
zweifelt immer, ed. by Heinz Knobloch, Berlin 1977
119 Christa Wolf, Unter den Linden, Berlin and
Weimar 1974
122 Ben Hecht, A Child of the Century, New York
1982
123 Alfred Kerr, Wo liegt Berlin? Briefe aus der Reichs-
hauptstadt. 1895–1900, Berlin 1997
123 Lothar Heinke, Berge von Blumen auf den Gräbern
in Friedrichsfelde, in: Der Tagesspiegel, 1.15.1997
124 Mathias Remmele, Ein Hauch von Monarchie, in:
Junge Welt Nr. 19, 1997
124 Walter Mehring, Sechstagerennen. Schall und
Rauch 1919–1921, Hamburg 1958
125 Erwin Blumenfeld, Durch Tausendjährige Zeit,
Frauenfeld/Huber, Switzerland 1976
125 Heinz Knobloch, Meine liebste Mathilde, Berlin
1986
126 Cees Nooteboom, Berliner Notizen,
Frankfurt/M. 1991
128 Rahel Varnhagen, Rahel. Ein Buch des Andenkens
für ihre Freunde, Munich 1983
129 Dorothee Wenner, Protest Placement, in: taz, Die
Tageszeitung, 3.10.1997
130 Jurek Becker, Irreführung der Behörden, Rostock
1973
131 Wolfgang Kil, in: Der Architekt No. 7, 1997
132 Volker Braun, Die Irrtümer teilen viele, die Maß-
stäbe setzen wenige, in: Freibeuter 72, Berlin 1997
132 Stephan Hermlin, Die Zeit der Wunder, in: Traum
der Gemeinsamkeit, Berlin 1985
134 Roman Herzog, Berliner Rede 4.26.1997
135 Ernst Heilborn, E.T.A. Hoffmann, Berlin 1926

136 Heinrich Heine, Gesammelte Werke in sechs
Bänden, Bd. 3, Reisebilder 1822–1830, Berlin 1954
138 György Konrád, Der Stadtgründer, Munich 1975
139 Heinrich Mann, cit. in: Dieter Hildebrandt, Berliner
Enzyklopädie, Munich 1991
140 Richard Christ, in: Berlin—ein Ort zum Schreiben.
347 Autoren von A–Z, Berlin 1996
142 Dieter Hildebrandt, Berliner Enzyklopädie,
Munich 1991
144 Diether Huhn, Kanzlerbesuch im Tiergarten,
in: Frankfurter Allgemeine Zeitung, FAZ Magazin,
No. 901, 6.6.1997
147 Steffi Kammerer, Diepgens Kamele, in: Süddeutsche Zeitung, 8.13.1997
148 Alfred Kerr, Wo liegt Berlin? Briefe aus der Reichs-
hauptstadt. 1895–1900, Berlin 1997
149 Lorenz Schröter, in: Süddeutsche Zeitung,
Magazin "jetzt" No. 30, 7.21.1997
153 Paul Wallot an Friedrich Bluntschli,
in: Michael S. Cullen, Der Reichstag. Die Geschichte
eines Monuments, Berlin 1983
153 Alfred Kerr, Wo liegt Berlin? Briefe aus der Reichs-
hauptstadt. 1895–1900, Berlin 1997

Photos
Erik-Jan Ouwerkerk
122, 124 (2x), 126, 127 (top), 129 (top), 133 (2x), 140
(2x), 143 (2x), 145 (3x), 147 (3x), 148, 150(3x), 152,
153 (bottom), 154, 156
123 Ullstein Bilderdienst, p/f/h
127 Sony (bottom)
139 Jens Willebrand
141 CEDC American Business Center GmbH & Co
Checkpoint Charlie KG
153 Rudi Meisel (top)
155 Velotaxi GmbH Berlin
158 David Baltzer

Berlin's New Buildings 1996/97

The difficulty or near impossibility of putting together a comprehensive list of new buildings in
Berlin for one year—or rather, for the current year
and part of the previous one—was described in
detail in the preface to the list for 1996. Here it
would be superfluous to reiterate the ins and outs
of this process; and so we are all the more anxious
to express our thanks to the architects, clients, and
institutions that have supported our efforts. A list of
buildings is toilsome for everyone who comes into
contact with it. The magazine Bauwelt repeatedly
published our urgent appeals to architects and
clients; the BDA Berlin mailed our questionnaires
with the necessary authority, and the city sanitation
department sent us regular faxes letting us know
where to look. ibau was a reliable partner, as always. The Verband Freier Wohnungsunternehmen
(Association of Free Housing Enterprises) Berlin/
Brandenburg undertakes efforts for its yearbook
that are similar to ours, and from which we were
able to profit. Some clients filled out our questionnaires with loving attention to detail, others did not;
the former can easily be distinguished from the latter in the list of buildings. The same holds true for
the architects. All who in their own eyes fulfilled
the simple criteria "new building" and "Berlin" will
find themselves in this list—and those who were
forgotten this year, or forgot themselves, are hereby
offered space in next year's book, the Bauwelt
Berlin Annual 1998. *Michael Goj*

Charlottenburg

Danckelmannstrasse 9
"Engelhardthöfe"
Petra and Paul Kahlfeldt, Berlin
Client: Brau + Brunnen AG,
Engelhardt Brauerei
Construction of an industrial building
and an apartment house to complete
the preserved historic brewery
complex. The new buildings restore the
former block structure,
gross floor area 6,500 sq. m, 16 housing
units, 5 shops, 14 office units,
investment: DM 20 mill.,
built 1995–1996

Dovestrasse 1–5
"Spreeresidenz Charlottenburg"
Apartment and Commercial Building
Steinebach & Weber, Berlin
Client: Optima Aegidius, Munich
3 row buildings, 10 stories, 254 housing
units, gross floor area 17,000 sq. m,
cost DM 85 mill.,
completion 1st building phase
April 1997,
2nd building phase December 1997

Dovestrasse 9
Housing Complex
Hans-Peter Störl, Berlin
Client: Realwert, Berlin
183 housing units, private,
2 retail units,
completion 1997

Fasanenstrasse
"Ludwig-Erhard-Haus"
IHK Central Office Building
**Nicholas Grimshaw & Partners,
London/Berlin**
Client: Berlin Chamber of Commerce
and Industry (IHK)
Block alignment, 15 constructive bows
7 suspended stories, 36,200 sq. m
gross floor area 22,000 sq. m,
cost DM 310 mill.,
built 1994–1997,
completion stock exchange June 1996,
2nd building phase December 1997

Haubachstrasse 41
Apartment Building
with Daycare Center
Rolf D. Weisse, Berlin
Client: Charlottenburger Baugenossen-
schaft eG;
Charlottenburg District Authorities
31 subsidized housing units, standard
sized daycare center (128 places),
completion September 1997
(see BBA 1996)

Heckerdamm 235
Daycare Center
Schmidt-Thomsen and Ziegert, Berlin
Client: Charlottenburg Dictrict
Authorities
Standard sized daycare center
(128 places), 2,527 sq. m usable space,
cost DM 7.7 mill.,
completion December 1997

Kuno-Fischer-Strasse 22–26
Elementary School
Freitag, Hartmann, Sinz, Berlin
Client: Charlottenburg District
Authorities
Elementary School for 800 children
cost approx. DM 23 mill.,
competition May 1992,
built January 1995–December 1997

Kurfürstendamm 63,
Giesebrechtstrasse 9
Apartment and Commercial Building
Pysall and Stahrenberg, Berlin
Client: Albeck & Zehden
Conversion and new construction,
7,467 sq. m new floor area,
completion September 1997

Messedamm
Extension of Berlin Fair Ground
Oswald Mathias Ungers, Cologne
Client: The Senate of Berlin,
represented by Berlin Building,
Housing, and Traffic Department
3rd building phase, 12 halls:
2 halls 100 x 50 m; 4 halls 100 x 63 m;
6 halls 30 x 42 m, office wing with
105 units added to hall 7,
gross floor exhibition area of Berlin fair
ground, July 1997, 135,000 sq. m,
cost DM 1.125 billion,
built July 1994– July 1997

Osnabrücker Strasse 7
Apartment and Commercial Building
Klaus Lattermann, Berlin
Client: Friedrich Weigand, Berlin
7 stories, 39 housing units,
2 retail spaces,
gross floor area 1,848 sq. m,
cost approx. DM 3 mill.,
built April 1996–April 1997

Teichgräberzeile 13–17,
Reichweindamm 3–3b
Apartment Buildings
**Hans-Joachim Garsztecki,
Michael Hartmann, Berlin**
Client: GEWOBAG
Two free standing buildings. 3 stories,
usable space 2,315 sq. m,
36 apartments, pivately financed,
cost approx. DM 6.1 mill.,
built December 1996–October 1997

Friedrichshain

Andreasstrasse 7–8 /Langestrasse
City-Carré II
Fischer and Fischer, Köln
Client: DGI Deutsche Gesellschaft
für Immobilien,
28,500 sq. m gross office area,
built 1995–1997

Boxhagener Strasse 102/103,
Kreutziger Strasse 17/17a
Apartment and Commercial Building
Stadler and Besch, Berlin
Client: COMMERCIAL
Wohnungsbaugesellschaft mbH
Block alignment, 7 stories,
56 housing units,
commercial space 1,549 sq. m,
investment DM 24.2 mill.,
built 1997

Frankfurter Allee 111
Shopping Center "Ring-Center Berlin II"
**HPP and Manfred Stanek, Jost Hering,
Hamburg**
Client: ECE Projektmanagement GmbH
Retail space approx. 20,000 sq. m,
Investment approx. DM 180 mill.,
built June 1996–December 1997

Friedenstrasse 9
Apartment Building
Gerhard Pfannenschmidt, Berlin
Client: Wohnungsbaugesellschaft
Friedrichshain
Apartment house, 11 stories,
20 housing units, penthouse,
cost DM 7.9 mill.,
built 1995–1996

Gubener Strasse 21, Torellstrasse 7
Apartment and Commercial Building
Carlos Zwick, Berlin
Client: Grundstücksgesellschaft
Gubener Strasse 21/Torellstrasse 7
corner building, 7 stories,
9 housing units, 1,734 sq. m,
completion 1996

Karl-Marx-Allee 131 A
Cinema "Kosmos UFA-Palast"
**Architekten RKW Rhode, Kellermann,
Wawrowsky + Partner, Berlin**
Client: UFA-Theater AG, Düsseldorf
Conversion of the preserved Kosmos
cinema to a Multiplex, 10 cinemas with
3,395 seats, 14,000 sq. m,
cost approx. DM 39 mill.,
built March 1996–February 1997

Krautstrasse 52, Blumenstrasse 44
Apartment Building
**BSP Klaus Baesler, Bernhard Schmidt,
Martin Schwacke, Berlin**
Client: HKW
Block alignment, angled building,
8 stories, 150 housing units,
16,000 sq. m gross floor area,
construction cost approx. DM 30 mill.,
investment DM 85.2 mill.,
built 1995–96

Landsberger Allee,
Petersburger Strasse
Housing Complex
**Hans-Peter Harm, Hamburg, and
Thomas Michael Krüger, Berlin**
Client: Wohnungsbaugesellschaft
Friedrichshain and
Wohnungsbaugenossenschaft
Friedrichshain eG, Berlin
Row buildings as block alignment,
222 housing units,
gross floor area 44,671 sq. m,
20 retail and office spaces,
built March 1996–October 1997

Landsberger Allee 48
Cemetery Administration Building
**Andreas Brückner
in Brückner + Rummel, Berlin**
Client: Verwaltungskommission
der Ev. Friedhöfe Friedrichshain
Brick courthouse, 1 story, green roof,
gross floor area 925 sq. m,
cost DM 4.2 mill.,
built June 1994–May 1997

Pettenkofer Strasse 15–17
Apartment and Commercial Building
von Haehling, Berlin
Client: G + J Bau
6 stories and 1 staggered floor,
approx. 13,000 sq. m gross floor area,
cost approx. DM 35 mill.,
completion 1997

Richard-Sorge-Strasse 37
Housing Complex
**BSP Klaus Baesler, Bernhard Schmidt,
Martin Schwacke, Berlin**
Client: Rocloplan
Urban infill, 12 housing units,
2 retail units,
1,600 sq. m gross floor area,
cost approx. DM 3 mill.,
built 1995–1996

Wilhelm-Stolze-Strasse 24
Apartment Building
Gerhard Pfannenschmidt, Berlin
Client: Wohnungsbaugesellschaft
Friedrichshain
Urban infill, apartment building,
7 stories,
20 privately owned apartments
cost DM 6.3 mill.,
built 1995–January 1997

Waterfront district
"Rummelsburger Bucht"

Quarter Stralau-Stadt

Quarter area; 77.35 acres
Housing units planned: 1,951
Office space planned: 77,985 sq. m
Retail space planned: 4,200 sq. m
Social infrastructure:
3 daycare centers, 1 youth center

Urban Design
Herman Hertzberger, Amsterdam
Landscape Design
Atelier Loidl, Berlin

Bahrfeldtstrasse,
Friedrich-Junge-Strasse
Client: VEBA Immobilien AG,
DePfa Immobilien Management AG
Architects:
**Arnold & Bezzenberger,
Bad Homburg;
Architektengemeinschaft
Bartels + Wittwer, Berlin;
Braun & Voigt and Partner,
Frankfurt/Main;
Bremmer-Lorenz-Frielinghaus,
Friedberg;
Herman Hertzberger, Amsterdam
O&S Architekten AG with Schenker &
Stuber Architekten AG, Bern**
Investment approx. DM 200 mill.,
Housing units planned 450
completion 1997/98

Alt-Stralau 13–18
Housing complex "Spreeferresidenz"
**WLP– Werner Lehmann & Partner,
Bonn/Potsdam**
Client: Concordia Bau + Boden AG,
Berlin
Three 5-storied apartment buildings,
129 housing units,
investment DM 36 mill.,
built 1995–1997

Alt-Stralau 17, 19, 22
Client: Zschokke GmbH, Berlin
42 housing units planned
investment DM 12 mill.,
completion 1998
Inken Baller, Berlin
(Alt-Stralau 17, 19)
**A. de Reus/G. Fell,
Gravenskin/Denmark**
(Alt-Stralau 22)

Daycare Center, 140 places
Client: Friedrichshain District
Authorities
Vollmer & Larisch, Berlin
construction cost DM 8 mill.,
built 1996–1997

Section Stralau-Dorf

Quarter area: 45.22 acres
Housing units planned: 546
Office space planned: 2,705 sq. m
Social infrastructure:
elementary school, daycare center

Urban Design
Klaus Theo Brenner, Berlin
Landscape Design
Thomanek & Duquesnoy, Berlin

Tunnelstrasse 30–35
Client: HANSEATICA
Wohnungsbaugesellschaft mbH, Berlin
Faskel & Partner, Berlin;
Müller & Keller, Berlin
Investment DM 38.2 mill.,
95 housing units planned,
completion 1997/98

Alt-Stralau 30–31
Client: INCO Baupartner GmbH, Berlin
Klaus Theo Brenner, Berlin
Investment DM 13 mill.,
45 housing units planned,
completion 1997/98

Section Rummelsburg I

Social infrastructure:
2 daycare centers
Green public space: 53 acres

Urban Design
Klaus Theo Brenner, Berlin
Landscape Design
Thomanek & Duquesnoy, Berlin

Hauptstrasse 4–6, Hofgärten
Housing Complex
Pudritz + Paul, Berlin
Landscaping:
Büro für Stadt/Landschaft,
Hermann Barges, Berlin
438 housing units,
built 1996/97

Hauptstrasse 4, Stadtpalais
Housing Complex
Pudritz + Paul, Berlin
106 housing units,
2.200 sq. m retail space,
completion 1998

Hellersdorf

Hellersdorf District Center
"Helle Mitte"

Alice-Salomon-Platz
Hellersdorf Town-Hall
Brandt & Böttcher, Berlin
Client: MEGA AG, Berlin
Town hall, part of Hellersdorf district
center, 10,000 sq. m office space,
1,000 sq. m retail space,
cost DM 22 mill.,
1996–1997, completion March 1998

Alice-Salomon-Platz
Apartment and Commercial Building
(Block 30)
Walter Rolfes and Partner, Berlin
Client: MEGA AG, Berlin
gross floor area 10,000 sq. m,
built 1995–1997

Hellersdorfer Strasse
"Mark(t) Brandenburg" (Block 11)
Walter A. Noebel, Berlin
Client: MEGA AG;
Otremba Baubetreuungsgesellschaft
Shopping Center, Offices, Apartments,
gross floor area: approx. 18,000 sq. m,
built 1995–1997

Henny-Porten-Strasse 10/12,
Janusc-Korczak-Strasse 23/25,
Stendaler Strasse
Apartment and Office Building
Schattauer and Tibes, Berlin
(Block 3.1)
Liepe and Steigelmann, Berlin
(Block 3.2)
Client: MEGA-Entwicklungs- und
Gewerbeansiedlungs AG
Block, 5 stories, 5th floor staggered,
each half of the building designed by
one of the offices,
retail space on ground floor,
96 housing units,
6,577 sq. m usable space,
built 1995–1997

Janucs-Korczak-Strasse 31,
Quedlinburger Strasse 6
Apartment and Commercial Building
(Block 4.2)
Horst Hielscher,
Bernward Derksen, Berlin
Client: MEGA Entwicklungs- und
Gewerbeansiedlungs AG, represented
by ITAG: Immobilien-Treuhand- und
Vermögensanlage, Berlin
Brick building, 5 stories,
retail space on ground floor 587 sq. m,
4 office units, 484 sq. m,
24 housing units,
cost approx. DM 7.5 mill.,
built October 1995–May 1997

Quedlinburger Strasse
Apartment and Commercial Building
(Block 5)
Christine Jachmann, Berlin
Client: MEGA-Entwicklungs- und
Gewerbeansiedlungs-AG
5 housing wings above a continuous
ground floor retail area,
60 housing units,
gross floor area: 5,292 sq. m,
cost DM 15 mill.,
built 1995–1997

Stendaler Strasse,
Quedlingburger Strasse
Apartment and Commercial Building
(Block 4.1)
HPP Hentrich – Petschnigg & Partner,
Berlin
Client: MEGA Entwicklungs- und
Gewerbeansiedlungs AG
Apartments and retail spaces,
gross floor area approx. 7,000 sq. m,
built 1995–1997

Stendaler Strasse
Multiplex Cinema "CineStar" (Block 12)
Jürgen Sawade, Berlin
Client: MEGA AG, Berlin
12 cinemas, 2,700 seats total
cost DM 35 mill.,
opening September 11th, 1997

"Helle Mitte" District Center (Block 18)
Apartment and Commercial Building
Monika Krebs, Berlin
Client: MEGA AG, Berlin
63 housing units,
office space 1,110 sq. m,
retail space 5,075 sq. m,
built September 1995–September 1997

"Helle Mitte" District Center (Block 24)
Private Medical Center
Monika Krebs, Berlin
Client: MEGA AG, Berlin
Medical practices, 6,037 sq. m usable
space, office space 7,41 sq. m,
4,665 sq. m retail space
built September 1995–September 1997

(end of "Helle Mitte")

Chemnitzer Strasse 148–152
Apartment and Commercial Building
Michael König ,
Michael von Möllendorf, Berlin
Client: BOTAG Bodentreuhand- und
Verwaltungs-AG
Free standing building, 4 stories,
24 housing units,
2,800 sq. m gross floor area,
100 sq. m retail space,
cost approx. DM 13 mill.,
completion 1996

Eilenburger Strasse 1
Gym Hall
GKK + Partner Architekten
Peter Kuhlen, Berlin
Client: Hellersdorf District Authorities
Three-sectional gym hall
(27 x 45 m ground)
cost DM 15.3 mill.,
completion 1997

Landsberger Strasse 230
Office Building, Commercial Halls,
Garage, Section "R"
Fischer + Fischer, Köln
Client: GIP, Gewerbe im Park GmbH
Comb-shaped office building
completing the commercial park,
gross floor area 5,900 sq. m (offices),
5,100 sq. m (commercial space),
built 1996–1997

Landsberger Strasse 230
Office Building, Commercial Halls
Section "S"
Fischer + Fischer, Köln
Client: GIP, Gewerbe im Park GmbH
Comb-shaped office building
gross floor area 3,900 sq. m (offices)
3,700 sq. m (commercial space),
built 1996–1997

Louis-Lewin-Strasse 63–73
Housing Complex at "Branitzer Platz"
CASA NOVA Architekten, Berlin
Ruth Golan and Kay Zareh, Berlin
Kny + Weber, Berlin
Client: WOGEHE,
Wohnungsbaugesellschaft Hellersdorf
330 housing units in all,
built 1995–1997

Schönewalder Strasse 9
Elementary and
"1st Cooperative School"
Berlin-Hellersdorf
Rolf D. Weisse, Berlin
Client: Hellersdorf District Authorities
3 stories, 2 layered three-sectional
sports halls, (27 x 45 m grounds),
gross floor area 17,315 sq. m,
cost DM 60.5 mill.,
built 1995–1997

Strasse an der Schule 13–17
Elementary School
Michael Bürger in der GbR
Bumiller/Bürger Architekten, Berlin
Client: Hellersdorf District Authorities
Elementary school and sports hall,
gross floor area 3,895 sq. m,
cost DM 16.3 mill.,
completion 1997

Hohenschönhausen

Ahrensfelder Chaussee 41
Barnim High School
Stefan Scholz
in Bangert/Scholz, Berlin
Client: Hohenschönhausen District
Authorities
High school (5 flights, 2 gym halls),
two building volumes on a round
platform, high school in the southern
part, sports fields in the west,
gross floor area 14,670 sq. m,
cost DM 63 mill.,
built May 1995–December 1997

Darsser Strasse 97
Comprehensive School
BSP Baesler, Schmidt and Partner,
Klaus Baesler, Bernhard Schmidt,
Martin Schwacke, Berlin
Client: Hohenschönhausen District
Authorities
Comprehensive school (8 flights) with
3 building volumes—bar, bow and
gymnasium—in an urban set,
cost DM 80.5 mill.,
built 1994–1997

Ferdinand-Schultze-Strasse 55
Car Licence Office (East)
Urs Müller, Thomas Rhode,
Jörg Wandert, Berlin
Client: Immobilienvermietungs-
gesellschaft Knappertsbusch
Office building, 4 stories, plus
workshop for safety tests,
6,900 sq. m gross floor area,
cost DM 16.5 mill.,
built 1995–1996

Gärtnerstrasse 54–56
Apartment Buildings
Pudritz + Paul, Berlin
Client: Immobilienfonds Ziel 9 GbR
Row buildings, 6 stories, as block
alignment, 58 housing units,
investment DM 58.8 mill.,
built 1995–1996

Goeckestrasse 30/31
Housing Complex
Martin + Pächter, Berlin
Client: HOWOGE, Wohnungsbaugesellschaft Hohenschönhausen
127 housing units
and 750 sq. m retail space
built 1994–1996

Grosse-Leege-Strasse 49–52,
Simon-Bolivar-Strasse 44–45
Housing Complex
Kerstin and Erhard Rönspieß, Berlin
Client: GEWOBAG Fonds 3 GbR
Corner buildings, 5–6 stories,
plus roof story., 120 housing units,
gross floor area 10,893 sq. m,
8,797 sq. m usable space
cost DM 43 mill.,
built October 1995–July 1997

Hauptstrasse 9–10
Shopping Center "Storchenhof"
Hilde Léon and Konrad Wohlhage,
Berlin
Client: Mübau,
Münchner Baugesellschaft, Munich
3-story building,
16,000 sq. m gross floor area,
investment approx. DM 120 mill.,
1st building phase
completion October 1997,
2nd building phase starting 1998

Küstriner Strasse,
Reichenberger Strasse
Housing Complex
CONNOVA, Berlin
Client: Classico Projekt + Bau GmbH,
Berlin;
40 housing units
cost DM 15 mill.,
completion November 1997

Landsberger Allee 201–205
Service Center
"BCA-Hotel Wilhelmsberg"
Bartels and Wittwer,
with K. Rissé, Berlin
Client: ARWOBAU Apartment- und
Wohnungsbaugesellschaft mbH, Berlin
800-bed-hotel, congress center,
shopping mall, private medical center,
office area,
cost approx. DM 70 mill.,
built 1993–1996

Manetstrasse 85
Apartment Building
Kny & Weber, Berlin with
H. Richter, K. Bock, Berlin
Client: GbR Manetstrasse, Berlin
Extension of an existing building
through a 3 story apartment building,
plus staggered story,
6 housing units,
3 commercial units on ground
and 1st floor
cost DM 2.7 mill.,
built May 1996–May 1997

Plauener Strasse
Printing Plant "Print Media Center"
Heiken & Partner, Frankfurt/Main
Client: Rolf Henke,
"Henke Pressedruck"
Office building and printing plant,
4 stories, ecological pilot project
cost approx. DM 8 mill.,
completion June 1997

Plauener Strasse 163–165
Industrial Court
Architekturbüro Reinhard Müller
GmbH, Berlin
Client: GSG Gewerbesiedlungs-
gesellschaft GmbH, Berlin
Axial arrangement of 13 single
buildings, 4 stories high,
110,300 sq. m gross floor area,
299 commercial units,
cost DM 200 mill.,
built 1994–1997

Prendener Strasse,
Falkenberger Chaussee
Elementary School
Max Dudler, Berlin
Client: Hohenschönhausen District
Authorities
Three-sided elementary school
for 600 children,
gross floor area 5,375 sq. m,
cost DM 23 mill.,
built 1995–1997

Prendener Strasse,
Falkenberger Chaussee
Comprehensive School
Max Dudler, Berlin
Client: Hohenschönhausen District
Authorities
Six-sided comprehensive school,
double sports hall, sports fields,
17,267 sq. m gross floor area,
cost DM 70.45 mill.,
built 1995–1997

Weissenseer Weg 35–38a,
Konrad-Wolf-Strasse 56–60
Office and Commercial Building
"Hohenschönhauser Tor"
Gustav Schulze and Partner,
Dortmund
Client: Trigon Unternehmensgruppe
Two 8-storied office buildings,
bridged on all upper floors,
usable space 20,362 sq. m,
13,500 sq. m retail space,
investment approx. DM 127 mill.,
opening July 3rd, 1997

Zechliner Strasse
Housing Complex
Architekturbüro Werkfabrik, Berlin
Client: HOWOGE Wohnungsbaugesellschaft Hellersdorf
37 housing units,
155 sq. m commercial space
completion 1997

Köpenick

Bahnhofstrasse 33
Shopping Center "Forum Köpenick"
gmp von Gerkan, Marg and Partner,
Hamburg
Client: GP Fundus Gewerbebau und
Projektierung GmbH
Shopping center on
103,423 sq. m gross floor area,
cost DM 350 mill.,
built 1996–1997
opening October 23rd, 1997

Bölschestrasse 137,
Müggelseedamm 163
Apartment Building
Bernhard Winking, Berlin
Client: HANSEATICA, Berlin
5 stories, 25 housing units ,
780 sq. m retail space on ground floor,
built 1995–1997

Freiheit 2–4
Apartment and Commercial Building
Rolf D. Weisse, Berlin
Client: Köpenicker
Liegenschaftsgesellschaft, Berlin
Block alignment,
48 housing units, 3 retail units,
gross floor area 4,664 sq. m,
cost approx. DM 13 mill.,
built 1996–1997

Glienicker Strasse 4–6
Apartment and Commercial Building
Peter Brinkert, Berlin
Client: Limberger und Partner
GmbH & Co.
Housing and retail space,
2,250 sq. m gross floor area,
built 1996–1997

Grünauer Strasse 117–125
Housing Complex
Feige + Partner, Berlin
Client: W. Graf und Maresch GmbH,
Augsburg
Second building phase,
8 out of 11 buildings,
160 housing units,
completion 1997

Mentzelstrasse 25/26/28
Apartment Building
Marianne Wagner, Berlin
Client: Köpenicker Wohnungsbaugesellschaft mbH, Berlin
25 housing units,
built April 1996–April 1997

Ottomar-Geschke-Strasse 83–87
Apartment Building
Peter Möhle
Client: Köpenicker Wohnungsbaugesellschaft mbH, Berlin
33 housing units,
cost DM 11 mill.,
completion May 1997

Salvador-Allende-Strasse 76
Housing Complex "Bullenacker"
Assmann, Salomon, Scheidt, Berlin
Client: Klammt AG, Berlin
Two urban villas,
3 stories, plus staggered story,
8 housing units each,
gross floor area 1,866 sq. m in all,
cost DM 2.8 mill.,
built October 1995–December 1996

Segewaldweg 59
Housing Complex
"Wohnpark Dahmeufer"
Klussmann, Bielefeld,
with Kammann and Hummel, Berlin
Client: R & S Specker-Gruppe, Berlin
Seven apartment buildings,
3 stories,
5,600 sq. m gross floor area in all,
cost DM 13 mill.,
completion 1997

Stillerzeile 30–36
Apartment Building
Meyer, Bach, Hebestreit, Sommerer,
Berlin
Client: Köpenicker Wohnungsbau-
gesellschaft, Berlin
Apartment building,
46 subsidized housing units,
built June 1996–August 1997

Weiskopfstrasse 18,
Ecke Wasserstrasse
Apartment Buildings
Michael König ,
Michael von Möllendorf, Berlin
Client: BOTAG
Two apartment buildings,
48 housing units;
3 stories, plus staggered story,
cost DM 7 mill.,
completion December 1997

Wendenschloss-Strasse 103–123
Housing Complex
Schmidt-Thomsen & Ziegert, Berlin
Client: Köpenicker Wohnungsbaugesellschaft Berlin
Urban grid of apartment buildings
generating streets and courtyards,
subsidized housing,
cost DM 45.5 mill.,
built 1995–2997

Wendenschloss-Strasse 462
Urban Villa
Markus Heller in Bothe, Richter,
Teherani, Hamburg/Berlin
Client: City 7b
Urban villa, 12 housing units,
1,350 sq. m gross floor area;
cost DM 3.0 mill.,
built 1995–1997

Kreuzberg

Askanischer Platz 4,
Schöneberger Strasse 1
Apartment and Commercial Building
Rüdiger Baumann in HPP, Berlin
Client: HABERENT Grundstücks-,
Dienstleistungs ohG
Corner building completing city block,
7 stories high,
gross floor area approx. 5,000 sq. m,
competition 1993,
completion December 1997

Kommandantenstrasse 15,
Oranienstrasse
Federal Printing Plant
BHHS & Partner (Wolfgang Schuster),
Berlin
Client: Bundesdruckerei GmbH, Berlin
Production plant of the Federal Printing
Works, office and production building
behind glass curtain towards street,
treasury as separate building in
courtyard,
gross floor area 21,500 sq. m,
cost DM 115 mill.,
built 1993–1997

Oranienstrasse 50–57
Apartment and Commercial Building
"Karl-Philipp-Moritz-Haus"
tgw Markus Torge, Sebastian Gaa,
Klaus Wercker, Berlin
Client: GSW Berlin mbH
"Social and Ecological Service Center"
gross floor area 8,850 sq. m,
housing space 3,440 sq. m,
usable space 2,760 sq. m,
46 subsidized housing units,
20 commercial units (3,000 sq. m),
plus cafeteria
construction cost DM 28 mill.,
built 1995–September 1997

Stresemannstrasse 126
Transformation Station and
Cooling Plant
Hilmer and Sattler, Munich
Client: Bewag, Berlin
Double edifice supplying the buildings
at Potsdamer Platz with energy
gross floor area 7, 900 sq. m,
built 1995–1997

Lichtenberg

Alt-Friedrichsfelde, Gensinger Strasse
Housing Complex
"Friedrichsfelder Viertel"
Axel Gutzeit, Berlin
Clients: Unternehmensgruppe Gutzeit,
Berlin;
Bavaria Baubetreuung GmbH, Berlin;
565 housing units in 3 semi-circular-
buildings, 5–6-stories high,
one 13-story high-rise
(with privately financed apartments),
8,500 sq. m commercial space
cost DM 205 mill. in all,
built 1995–1997

Hauptstrasse 4–6
Housing Complex
"3 Hofgärten"
in the "Rummelsburger Bucht"
development area
Pudritz + Paul, Berlin
Client: INTECH-Verwaltungs-
gesellschaft, repres. Ziel
Baubetreuungsgesellschaft, Berlin
gross floor area 45,164 sq. m,
438 housing units in all,
270 housing units subsidized,
168 housing units privately financed,
1,483 sq. m retail and office spaces;
cost DM 110 mill.,
completion 1997

Ontarioseestrasse 16/18
Residential Complex
K.-H. Schlusche, Berlin
Client: Trigon, Berlin
U-shaped housing complex,
4–5 stories, 97 housing units;
67 units subsidized,
30 units privately financed,
cost approx. DM 15. mill.,
built February 97–December 1997

Otto-Schmirgal-Strasse 8
Shopping Center "Bärenschaufenster"
**MRL Architekten Markovic, Ronai,
Lütjen, Voss, Hamburg/Berlin**
Client: Mediconsult AG. Düsseldorf;
MC City-Center
18 stories, 50 shops,
15,000 sq. m retail space,
investment approx. DM 103 mill.,
opening November 27th, 1997

Treskowallee, Dönhoffstrasse
Ute Frank, Georg Augustin, Berlin
Office and Commercial Building
Client: GRUNDAG AG
Mini tower, 5 stories, on the grounds of
the former "Kaufhaus Karlshorst";
retail space on ground floor, branch-
bank on 2nd floor, 3rd to 6th floor
offices and medical practices,
completion 1997;
opening of the shops Dec. 15th, 1997

Marzahn

Brebacher Weg 15
Emergency Hospital
Karl Schmucker & Partner, Mannheim
Client: Trägerverein
Unfallkrankenhaus Berlin mit
berufsgenossenschaftlicher
Unfallklinik e.V.
General Hospital with emergency
center for industrial injuries,
3 stories, 468 beds,
cost approx. DM 500 mill.,
built 1991–1997;
opening September 3rd, 1997

Flämingstrasse, Wittenberger Strasse
Apartment Building
**Assmann, Salomon and Scheidt,
Berlin**
Client: Wohnungsbaugesellschaft
Marzahn
Low energy building, curved slab,
7 stories, 56 subsidized housing units,
gross floor area 5,593 sq. m,
cost DM 11.4 mill.,
built May 1996–November 1997

Grumsiner Strasse 27a
Apartment Building
Hierholzer & von Rudzinski, Berlin
Client: WBG Marzahn
Apartment building with 14 owner-
occupied apartments,
completion April 1997

Havemannstrasse 21a
Apartment Building
**Borchert + Hendel,
Planungsgruppe H 3, Berlin**
Client: WGB Marzahn
High-rise, 12 stories,
41 subsidized housing units,
completion August 1997

Mehrower Allee 52
Apartment and Office Building
Walter von Lom and Partner, Köln
Client: WBG Marzahn
Office building ,
1st building of a set,
a low building links four 6-story
apartment buildings,
77 housing units,
completion 1998/99
7-story office high-rise,
completion December 1997

Sella-Hasse-Strasse 2a
Apartment House
Volker Theissen & Partner, Berlin
Client: WBG Marzahn
Corner building , 6 stories,
row building, 4 stories,
56 subsidized housing units,
completion August 1997

Wuhlestrasse 7a/b, 9a, 15a, 19a–d
Apartment Building
Jens Freiberg, Berlin
Client: WBG Marzahn
3-story building
linking 3 existing high-rises,
45 housing units and
7 commercial units
built August 1995–April 1997

Mitte

Ackerstrasse 3, 3a–3e
Apartment and Commercial Building
Hans-Rudolf Kurth, Göttingen
Client: Hans-Rudolf Kurth, Göttingen
Urban infill, 6 stories,
with courtyard building,
49 housing units, 14 commercial units,
cost DM 18.5 mill.,
built 1994–1996

Adalbertstrasse 42
Apartment and Commercial Building
Voidl Tatic, Berlin
Client: TURM Bau- und
Projektentwicklungs GmbH
Gross floor area 1,875 sq. m,
built 1996–1997

Alte Jakobstrasse 76–84
Apartment and Office Building
"Alte Jakobstrasse"
**Planungs AG für Bauwesen
(Neufert, Mittmann, Graf), Cologne**
Client: Concordia Bau- und Boden AG,
Cologne
7–10 stories, 240 housing units;
cost DM 169 mill.,
completion October 1997

Alte Jakobstrasse 81/82
Office Building
Walter Krüger, Berlin
Client: Techniker Krankenkasse
Office building for technicians'
insurance company,
6 stories plus staggered roof story,
gateway to the courtyard house
(22 housing units; 6 stories),
gross floor area 7,498 sq. m in all,
cost DM 15 mill.,
built 1995–1997

Dircksenstrasse 42–44
Apartment and Office Building
**Urs Müller, Thomas Rhode,
Jörg Wandert, Berlin**
Client: Deutsche Immobilien Anla-
gengesellschaft
The office building (gross floor area:
10,700 sq. m) as urban infill, apartment
house in the courtyard (gross floor
area: 1,990 sq. m)
cost DM 24.6 mill.,
built 1996–1997

Dorotheenstrasse 39–43
Boarding House
**Mario Campi and Franco Pessina with
Christian Volkmann, Lugano**
Client: Peter Dussmann, Munich
One new construction and two existing
buildings, 2,900 sq. m gross floor area,
competition 1993,
built 1994–1997

Dorotheenstrasse 74
Press and Visitors Center of the
Federal Press Bureau
**KSP Engel Kramer Schmiedecke,
Cologne**
Client: Bundespresseamt
Glazed cube as the 1st building phase
of the Federal Press Bureau,
cost DM 38 mill.,
completion 1997,
opening October 30th, 1997

*Französische Strasse 8,
Glinkastrasse 34–36*
Apartment and Office Building
Schweger and Partner, Hamburg
Client: Behne-Immobilien GmbH,
Hamburg; BHF-Bank
Corner building closing the block
along Französische Strasse
and Glinkastrasse,
shops on 1st floor, 3 office floors,
6 housing units in 6th and roof floor,
cost DM 21 mill.,
built October 1995–January 1997

*Friedrichstrasse, Dorotheenstrasse,
Mittelstrasse*
Media Department Store
"Haus Dussmann" (Block 210)
Office, Commercial and Apartment
Building
Miroslav Volf, Saarbrücken
Client: Peter Dussmann, Munich
Media Department Store closing the
city block,
gross floor area 17,500 sq. m,
36 housing units,
cost DM 65 mill.,
built 1995–1997,
opening of the department store
October 30th, 1997

*Friedrichstrasse 45–46 ,
Zimmerstrasse 20–25,
Charlottenstrasse 31*
Office and Commercial Building
"Checkpoint Arkaden"
Josef Paul Kleihues, Berlin
Client: GSW, KapHag, Berlin,
Württemberger Hypo
U-shaped block alignment with corner
emphazising ship-shape-elements
along Zimmerstrasse, arcades with
retail space, offices on 2nd to 6th floor,
apartments on 7th floor,
gross floor area 20,700 sq. m,
built 1994–1996

*Friedrichstrasse 61,
Leipziger Strasse,
Kronenstrasse*
Office and Commercial Building
"Atrium", Quartier 203
Volkwin Marg, gmp, Hamburg
Client: ECE Projektmanagement,
Hamburg
Halfblock-sized building with huge
entrance atrium,
5 stories plus 2 staggered stories,
office space approx. 15,000 sq. m,
11 apartments approx. 800 sq. m,
2,500 sq. m commercial space,
cost DM 250 mill.,
built December 1994–April 1997,
opening April 4th, 1997

*Friedrichstrasse 108–109,
Johannisstrasse*
Office and Commercial Building
**gmp, von Gerkan, Marg and Partner,
Hamburg**
Client: Tekton-Baubetreuungs- und
Immobiliengesellschaft mbH
Gross floor area 3,224 sq. m,
built 1995–1997

Friedrichstrasse 185–190,
Mohrenstrasse 13–16,
Kronenstrasse 60–65
Office and Commercial Building
"Kontorhaus Mitte"
Josef Paul Kleihues, Berlin
(House A, C, D, Atrium)
Klaus Theo Brenner, Berlin (House B)
Vittorio Magnago Lampugnagni
Marlene Dörrie, Frankfurt am Main
(House E)
Walter Stepp, Berlin (House F)
Client: Argenta Internationale Anlagen
GmbH Munich, HANSEATICA Consulting
GmbH Berlin
Block designed by four architects,
restoration and hightening of the listed
"Quantmeyerhaus",
gross floor area 34,790 sq. m,
84 housing units, 8 commercial units,
investment DM 360 mill.,
built 1994–1996

Friedrichstrasse 200
Network Office Block
Checkpoint Charlie (Block 106)
Philip Johnson, Ritchie & Fiore
Architects, New York
and PSP Pysall, Stahrenberg &
Partner, Berlin
Client: Checkpoint Charlie KG, Berlin,
Network Office Grundstücks GmbH
"Philip Johnson House",
gross floor area 37,780 sq. m,
18,060 sq. m (offices);
2,990 sq. m retail space,
cost approx. DM 95 mill.,
built 1995–1997

Friedrichstrasse 204
Office and Apartment Building
"Triangel"
Josef Paul Kleihues, Berlin
Client: TCHA-Grundstücke Berlin GbR,
Berlin; Fütterer – Stamp ILK GbR
Free-standing city building, 7 stories,
retail space on ground floor,
offices on 2nd to 6th floor,
apartments on the last two floors,
gross floor area 4,138 sq. m,
built 1994–1996

Hannoversche Strasse 20a–22,
Hessische Strasse
Apartment Building
"Wohnen am Luisen-Carree"
Stefan Ludes, Berlin
Client: VEBA Immobilien AG
Corner building, 7 stories,
65 housing units,
cost DM 32 mill.,
completion December 1997

Heinrich-Heine-Platz 8–12
Housing and Commercial Complex
"Heinrich-Heine-Forum"
K. H. Cammann, Berlin
Client: HANSEATICA
Wohnungsbaugesellschaft, Berlin
U-shaped complex around a listed
cavalry school, 6–8 stories,
164 subsidized housing units,
38 apartments in a private
boarding house,
commercial space approx. 7,000 sq. m,
built 1995–1997

Köpenicker Strasse
Thermal Power-Station Mitte
Jochem Jourdan, Frankfurt/Main
Client: Bewag, Berlin
Modernization and extension,
cost DM 600 mill.,
completion 1997
(see BBA 1996)

Krausnickstrasse 23
Apartment and Office Building
Hinrich Baller, Doris Piroth, Berlin
Client: Hinrich Baller and
Doris Piroth, Berlin
2,400 sq. m gross floor area,
built 1996–1997

Kronenstrasse 8–10
Office and Commercial Building
"Kronen Palais"
Patzschke, Klotz & Partner, Berlin
Client: Bauwert GmbH, Munich
Construction of an office and
commercial building next to a restored
listed building (1902 by Hart & Lesser),
3,429 sq. m office space in all,
730 sq. m retail space,
housing in the roof floors (590 sq. m),
investment DM 52 mill.,
built October 1996–December 1997

Kronprinzenufer, Schiffbauerdamm
Kronprinzenbrücke
Santiago Calatrava, Zürich
Clients: EC and the Federal State of
Berlin,
Bridge crossing the Spree river from
Kronzprinzenufer to Schiffbauerdamm,
73 m span,
built 1992–1997

Leipziger Strasse 15,
Voss-Strasse 22
Office and Commercial Building
"Mosse-Palais"
Hans D. Strauch & Gallagher, Boston
Client: Hans Röder
Verwaltungsgesellschaft mbH & Co.
Mosse-Palais KG,
1st building on Leipziger Platz,
built 1995–1997

Märkisches Ufer 10–12,
Wallstrasse 70–73
Hotel "Art'otel"
Nalbach + Nalbach Architects, Berlin
Client: Sylvia Gädeke, Berlin
Extension of the listed Ermeler House
and reversion in a hotel building,
gross floor area 5,300 sq. m,
built 1994–1997

Mulackstrasse 3–6, Rückerstrasse 1,
Alte Schönhauser Strasse 9–10
Apartment and Commercial Building
Kny & Weber; Anne Kirsch,
Joachim Schroth, Berlin
Client: Hochtief AG
Section A: 4 stories
Section B/C: 4 stories , 1 staggered floor,
Section D: 6 stories,
54 housing units in all, 7 commercial
units, gross floor area: 8,910 sq. m,
cost DM 16.8 mill.,
built January 1995–May 1996

Oranienburger Strasse 31
Gym Hall
Ruth Golan, Kay Zareh, Berlin
Two gym halls piled one upon the other,
both with grounds of 15 x 27 m size,
built June 1996–June 1997

Pariser Platz 5a/6
Dresdner Bank
Berlin Headquarters
gmp, v. Gerkan, Marg and Partner,
Hamburg
Client: Dresdner Bank, Frankfurt/Main
Office building as block alignment,
rooms for representation and guest
apartments, glass roofed inner court,
gross floor area 11,600 sq. m,
built 1996–1997

Pariser Platz 6a /Ebertstrasse 24
Apartment and Commercial Building
Bernhard Winking with Martin Froh,
Berlin
Client: TASCON, Zwölfte Beteiligungs-
gesellschaft mbH, Hamburg
gross floor area 10,504 sq. m,
built 1996–1997

Platz vor dem Neuen Tor 1a+b,2–3,
Hannoversche Strasse 9
"Platz vor dem Neuen Tor"
Josef Paul Kleihues, Berlin
Client: KG Bayrische Hausbau
GmbH & Co, Munich/Berlin
Reconstruction of the corresponding
urban places "Platz vor dem Neuen Tor"
and "Robert-Koch-Platz".
Modern interpretation of the two
Schinkel gate-houses.
Commercial building (Platz vor dem
Neuen Tor 2–3): 7 commercial units,
gross floor area 8,900 sq. m;
apartment buildings (Platz vor dem
Neuen Tor 1a, 1b): 30 housing units,
6 commercial units, gross floor area:
4,300 sq. m; studio house
(Hannoversche Strasse 9): 4 housing
units, 6 commercial units,
gross floor area: 1,480 sq. m,
gate houses (Robert-Koch-Platz 11 +
12): 2 commercial units,
gross floor area: 1,210 sq. m,
built 1994, 1996–1997
(gate houses 1998)

Reinhardtstrasse 31
Apartment and Office Building
Götz Bellmann & Walter Böhm, Berlin
Client: Erich Bonert
8 stories, retail space on ground floor,
offices on 2nd to 7th floor, 6 housing
units on staggered roof floors,
gross floor area 3,123 sq. m,
cost DM 5.8 mill.,
built 1996/97

Schützenstrasse, Charlottenstrasse,
Krausenstrasse
Apartment Block (Quartier 201 B)
"Checkpoint Plaza"
Gisela Glass and Günther Bender,
Berlin
Client: Checkpoint Charlie KG, Berlin,
Network Office Grundstücks GmbH
Above retail space on ground floor
8 stories for housing (134 units),
opening December 5th, 1997

Schützenstrasse 7, 8, 9, 10, 11, 12,
Markgrafenstrasse 56, 57,
Charlottenstrasse 16, 17,
Zimmerstrasse 58, 68, 69
Quartier Schützenstrasse
Masterplan
Aldo Rossi, Milano
in cooperation with
Götz Bellmann, Walter Böhm, Berlin
Design of the neighboring houses
in the block
Aldo Rossi, Milano,
except Zimmerstrasse 69,
Charlottenstrasse 17
(Luca Meda, Milano)
Client: Dr. Peter und Isolde Kottmair,
Munich/Berlin
City block of 12 houses around two
inner courtyards,
10 houses of 5 stories plus 2 staggered
roof stories,
integration of one listed apartment
house on Schützenstrasse and of two
floors preserved in the neigboring
building,
completion 1997

Seydelstrasse 5,6
Office and Apartment Buildings
"Stadtresidenz Spittelmarkt"
Hans-D. Strauch, HDS + Gallagher,
Inc, Boston;
Dieter W. Schneider u. Partner, Berlin
Client: DBM Druckhaus Berlin Mitte &
debis Immobilienmanagement (dIM)
Grundstücksbeteiligungs GmbH & Co.,
Projekt Spittelmarkt KG, Berlin
90 privately owned apartments in two
buildings,
housing space 5,632 sq. m,
completion December 1997

Sophienstrasse 1a
Apartment House
Petra and Paul Kahlfeldt, Berlin
Client: HTV-Immobilien GmbH
The building of 10 housing units
completes the Sophienstrasse
ensemble, preserving the existing
typology,
cost DM 2.2 mill.,
built 1996/1997

Sophienstrasse 21, Gipsstrasse 12
Apartment House "Gipshöfe"
Becker, Gewers, Kühn + Kühn, Berlin
Client: Sophie Gips GbR
Block alignment along Gipsstrasse,
modernization of a former factory
building and addition of a roof story for
a private art collector,
gross floor area 7,850 sq. m,
14 housing units, 11 commercial units,
cost DM 12 mill. in all,
built January 1996–June 1997

Taubenstrasse 45
Office building
Christoph Mäckler, Frankfurt/Main
Client: KPMG Deutsche Treuhand-
Gesellschaft AG,
Urban infill,
7,000 sq. m gross floor area,
built 1996–1997

Unter den Linden 13–15
Deutsche Bank Berlin Headquarters
Benedict Tonon, Berlin
Client: DEBEKO Immobilien GmbH & Co.
Grundbesitz oHG, Eschborn
Modernization, finishing
and upper extension of the existing
building with a new architectural
interpretation of the corner
Unter den Linden/Charlottenstrasse;
gross floor area 23,430 sq. m,
built 1994–1997

Unter den Linden 19,
Friedrichstrasse 84,
Rosmarienstrasse
Apartment and Commercial Building
"Lindencorso"
Christoph Mäckler,
Frankfurt/Main/Berlin
Client: Lindencorso
Grundstücksgesellschaft mbH, Berlin
(Societé Général d'Entreprises,
B. Katz, K. Marks)
"German-French Center for Culture and
Commerce", 23 apartments,
1,800 sq. m housing area,
gross floor area 43,471 sq. m,
cost DM 180 mill.,
built 1993–1996

Unter den Linden 77
Hotel Adlon Berlin
**Rüdiger Patzschke,
Rainer-Michael Klotz and Partner,
Berlin,**
Client: Fundus Fonds-Verwaltungen
GmbH, Cologne;
Bredero Projekt Berlin GmbH
Construction of the new Hotel Adlon on
the historical site at Pariser Platz,
6 stories, plus roof story, 3 basement
stories,346 bed-rooms; 18 shops, 16
offices, gross floor area 49,980 sq. m,
construction cost DM 435 mill.,
built 1994–1997
opening August 23rd, 1997
(see chap.7, pp. 54)

Zimmerstrasse 69
Commercial Building,
Quartier Schützenstrasse
Götz Bellmann & Walter Böhm, Berlin
Client: Dr. Peter and Isolde Kottmair,
Munich/Berlin
Part of Aldo Rossi's Schützenstrasse
block, street and courtyard house,
5,077 sq. m gross floor area,
cost approx. DM 16.8 mill.,
built 1995–1997
(see chap. 4, pp 32)

Neukölln

Böhmische Strasse 38/39
Apartment Building with
Daycare Center
**Linie 5 – Margot Gerke.
Wolf von Horlacher, Gabriele Ruoff,
Berlin**
Client: Stadt und Land
Wohnbauten-Gesellschaft mbH
and Neukölln District Authorities
Block alignment, 4 stories,
9 housing units, daycare center
(112 children) in courtyard,
housing on 769 sq. m,
daycare center 652 sq. m,
cost DM 6.3 mill. + DM 3.0 mill.,
built October 1995–January 1997

Gerlinger Strasse
Daycare Center
**Peter Bendoraitis, BGM Architekten,
Berlin**
Client: Neukölln District Authorities
Child care center
built 1994–1996

Karl-Marx-Strasse 175
Apartment Building
Günther Bender, Gisela Glass, Berlin
Client: N. Kotek, J. Semel, Berlin
Apartment house, 5 stories,
integrated in the open courtyard
of Neukölln shopping center,
gross floor area: 1,200 sq. m,
cost approx. DM 4 mill.
built February 1996–April 1997

Knollstrasse
Residential Park "Katzenpfuhl"
Wolfgang Schwarzer, Bavaria, Berlin
Client: Bavaria Objekt-
und Baubetreuung GmbH, Berlin
Ensemble of 11 free standing houses
with 113 apartments in all,
completion autumn 1997

Lipschitzallee 29
Youth Center
Dörr, Ludolf, Wimmer, Berlin
Client:Neukölln District Authorities
Round building, 2 stories, central hall
with radial wings for youth groups,
approx. 600 sq. m usable space,
cost DM 3.75 mill.,
built 1992–1996

Richardstrasse 15
Apartment Building
Inken Baller, Berlin
Client: Stadt und Land
Wohnbauten-Gesellschaft mbH
Urban infill,
10 subsidized housing units,
cost approx. DM 4,4 mill.,
completion spring 1997

Rudower Chaussee 5
Office and Commercial Building
"WISTA-Business Center"
Dörr, Ludolf, Wimmer, Berlin
Client: Objektgesellschaft WISTA
Business Center mbH + Co. KG
Comb-shaped building, 5 stories,
with 4 arms and 3 glass halls
in between, all connected by
a double-storied retail zone,
gross floor area 24,000 sq. m,
cost DM 38 mill.,
built 1996–1997

Rudower Strasse 48
Neukölln General Hospital
D. Kloster, Berlin
Client: Krankenhaus Neukölln,
Conversion of a listed building
within the ensemble of
the old Neukölln hospital.
New function: central medical
laser services for Berlin
and Brandenburg
cost DM 10.1 mill.,
built 1994–96

Sonnenallee 76
Apartment Building
Hasso von Werder & Partner, Berlin
Client: Sonnenallee 76
Grundstücksgesellschaft b.R. c/o
INVESTCONSULT Baubetreuung und
Projektverwaltung GmbH
Corner Building, 42 housing units,
291 sq. m commercial space,
investment DM 21,6 mill.,
completion 1997

*Tauernallee 31–37, Watzmannweg 27,
Dachsteinweg 20*
Housing Complex
Wolf & Kreis, Berlin
Client: BKatz Baubetreuungsgesellschaft mbh, Berlin
Block alignment, 5 stories,
130 housing units,
9,981 sq. m housing space,
investment DM 75.9 mill.,
completion spring 1996

Thomas-Morus-Strasse 32–40
"Regenbogen" Elementary School
D. Kloster, Berlin
Client: Neukölln District Authorities
Class rooms, auditorium, offices
and gym hall as building addition,
4 stories high,
cost DM 10.7 mill.,
built 1996–1997

Warthestrasse 61/62
Apartment Building
and Daycare Center
Stankovic + Bonnen, Berlin
Client: WIR Wohnungsbaugesellschaft
in Berlin mbH and
Schöneberg District Authorities
Block alignment, 7 stories,
21 housing units,
cost approx. DM 6 mill.,
(daycare center),
DM 4 mill. (housing section),
built 1996–1997

Garden City Rudow

Approx. 1,800 housing units,
Commercial space approx. 5,000 sq. m,
Area: 111 acres,
Public green space: 33 acres,
3 daycare centers,
1 elementary school,
1 high school

Clients:
GEHAG, Stadt und Land
Wohnbauten-Gesellschaft mbH;
R+S Bau, Berlin,
Bavaria Objekt- und Baubetreuung
GmbH, Berlin

January 1992
Development Plan and Urban Design
Martin + Pächter, Berlin
Construction start: spring 1995
Completion of the 1st building phase
December 1996,
of the 2nd building phase,
December 1997,
approx. 1,200 housing units,
3 child care centers
(architects:
Hartmann, Freitag, Sinz, Berlin
landscape design:
Ariane Röntz, Berlin)

Architects (1st building phase):
**Arno Bonanni, Berlin
Maximiliano Burgmayer, Berlin
Martin + Pächter, Berlin
Mussotter + Poeverlein, Berlin
Plessow, Ehlers, Krop, Berlin
Schattauer + Tibes, Berlin
Peter Träger, Berlin
Werkplan, Berlin**

Landscape design
(1st building phase):
**Holm Becher, Berlin
GLF Jurk, Berlin
Stephan Haan, Berlin
Thomanek & Duquesnoy, Berlin
WES, Hamburg**

Architects (2nd building phase):
**Blase + Kapici, Berlin
Borck, Boye, Schaefer, Berlin
GEHAG, Dept. Technik, Stefan
Reinsbach, Berlin
Liepe and Steigelmann, Berlin
Martin + Pächter, Berlin
Mussotter + Poeverlein, Berlin
Nalbach Architekten, Berlin
Plessow, Ehlers, Krop, Berlin
SRRS, Wolfgang Schlicht, Berlin
Volkmar Schnöke, Berlin
Peter Träger, Berlin**

Landscape design
(2nd building phase):
**Holm Becher, Berlin
Becker, Gisecke, Mohren, Richard,
Berlin
Thomanek & Duquesnoy, Berlin**

3rd building phase,
completion planned for December 1998
Clients:
Stadt und Land Wohnbauten-
Gesellschaft mbH; Berlin,
Bavaria Objekt- und
Baubetreuung mbH, Berlin;
Classico, BBT Treuhand
Architects:
**Rainer Oefelein, Berlin;
Schattauer + Tibes, Berlin,
Schmitz, Aachen**

Elementary School
construction start: 1997
Architect:
Anne Rabenschlag, Berlin
Landscape architect:
Regina Poly, Berlin

High School 1997
Competition winner:
Dirk Alten,
Landscape architect:
Harms Wulf, Berlin

Buildings listed by addresses:

Dorothea-Stutkowski-Weg 3, 5
Apartment Building
**Mussotter Poeverlein Architekten,
Berlin**
Client: Stadt und Land Wohnbauten-
Gesellschaft, Berlin
Two urban villas on square floor plan,
4 stories high, 8 housing units and
996 sq. m gross floor area each,
built 1995–winter 1996

Dorothea-Stutowski-Weg 4, 6
Apartment Building
**Mussotter Poeverlein Architekten,
Berlin**
Client: GEHAG, Gemeinnützige
Heimstätten AG
Two urban villas on square floor plan,
4 stories high, 8 housing units
and 943 sq. m gross floor area each,
cost DM 1.27 mill.,
built 1995–winter 1996

Elfriede-Kuhr-Strasse 32, 34, 36, 38
Apartment Buildings
Volkmar Schnöke, Berlin
Client: SF-Projektentwicklungs-
gesellschaft mbH, Berlin
4 apartment buildings,
36 privately owned apartments ,
2,340 sq. m housing space in all,
cost approx. DM 6 mill.,
built 1997

Elly-Heuss-Knapp-Strasse 11, 13, 15, 17
Apartment Building
**Mussotter Poeverlein Architekten,
Berlin**
Client: GEHAG, Gemeinnützige
Heimstätten AG
L-shaped building, 4 stories,
2 apartments on each floor,
48 housing units in all,
gross floor area 5,825 sq. m,
3,200 sq. m housing space,
cost DM 7.3 mill.,
built summer 1995–winter 1996

Elly-Heuss-Knapp-Strasse 14
Apartment Building
Werkplan GmbH, Berlin
Client: GEHAG, Berlin
4 stories, 19 housing units,
housing space: 1,172 sq. m,
completion December 1997

Elly-Heuss-Knapp-Strasse
20, 22, 24, 26
Apartment Building
Karl Pächter and Partner, Berlin
Client: GEHAG, Berlin
4 stories, 36 housing units,
completion winter 1997

Elly-Heuss-Knapp-Strasse
37, 39, 41, 43, 45
Apartment Building
Schulze-Rohr, Schlicht, Berlin
Client: Gagfah, Berlin
row building, 4 stories, 31 apartments,
owner-occupied, project based on
an investors' competition (1993/1994),
cost approx. DM 6 mill.,
built 1995–1997

Friederike-Nadig-Strasse 27, 29, 31, 33
and Käthe-Frankenthal-Weg 6, 8
Apartment Buildings
Mirjam Blase and Osman Kapici,
Berlin
Client: GEHAG, Gemeinnützige
Heimstätten AG, Berlin
L-shaped building complex consisting
of six low energy houses, 4 stories,
42 housing units,
approx. 3,400 sq. m housing space,
built 1996/97

Helene-Weber-Strasse 11–17
Apartment Buildings
Stefan Reinsbach, GEHAG
Dept. Technik, Berlin
Client: GEHAG, Gemeinnützige
Heimstätten AG, Berlin (LBB-Fonds 7)
4 stories, 44 subsidized housing units,
housing space 2,340 sq. m,
built 1995–December 1997

Helene-Weber-Strasse 21, 23, 25, 27
Apartment Buildings
Karl Pächter and Partner, Berlin
Client: GEHAG, Gemeinnützige
Heimstätten AG, Berlin
Row houses, 4 stories,
36 housing units
completion winter 1997

Helene-Weber-Str, 33–39
Apartment Building
Günter Plessow, Reinhold Ehlers,
Peter Krop, Berlin
Client: Stadt und Land Wohnbauten -
Gesellschaft mbH and Bavaria Objekt-
und Baubetreuung GmbH, Berlin
Apartment building, 4 stories,
32 housing units
cost approx. DM 5.93 mill.,
built November 1996–November 1997

Jeanette-Wolff-Strasse 11
Power Plant Rudower Felder
Freitag, Hartmann, Sinz, Berlin
Client: BTB – Blockheizkraftwerks-
Träger- und Betreibergesellschaft mbH
Berlin
Decentralized power plant,
gross floor area approx. 1,280 sq. m,
cost approx. DM 4 mill.
built February 1996–February 1997

Jeanette-Wolff-Strasse 13, 17,
Ursulinenstrasse 27,
Three Daycare Centers
Freitag, Hartmann, Sinz, Berlin
Client: Neukölln District Authorities
3 Daycare Centers
(100 children and approx. 1,050 sq. m
gross floor area each),
competition 1992,
cost approx. DM 4.8 mill. each,
built October 1995–April 1997

Lieselotte-Berger-Strasse 5
Elisabeth-Seibert-Strasse 34, 36
Apartment Building
Axel Liepe, Hartmut Steigelmann,
Berlin
Client: GEHAG, Gemeinnützige
Heimstätten-AG, Berlin
5 row houses and cubic buildings
(low energy), 4 stories,
26 subsidized housing units,
built 1995–1997

Lieselotte-Berger-Strasse 7–17
Apartment Building
Stefan Reinsbach, GEHAG,
Dept. Technik, Berlin
Client: GEHAG, Gemeinnützige
Heimstätten-AG, Berlin
Row building, 5 stories,
59 subsidized housing units,
housing area 3,920 sq. m,
completion December 1997

Lieselotte-Berger-Strasse 15
Apartment Building
Karl Pächter and Partner, Berlin
Client: Stadt und Land Wohnbauten
5 stories, 11 housing units
and 1 commercial unit,
completion 1996

Lieselotte-Berger-Strasse 21
Apartment and Commercial Building
Mussotter Poeverlein Architekten,
Berlin
Client: GEHAG, Gemeinnützige
Heimstätten AG, Berlin and
Bavaria Objekt- und Baubetreuung
GmbH, Berlin
5-storied building as part of a block
side, 12 housing units,
retail space on ground floor,
gross floor area 1,314 sq. m,
cost DM 1.88 mill.,
built summer 1995–winter 1996

Lieselotte-Berger-Strasse 32
Apartment Building
Karl Pächter and Partner, Berlin
Client: GEHAG, Gemeinnützige
Heimstätten AG, Berlin
Corner building, 5 stories,
12 housing units and 2 shops,
completion winter 1997

Lieselotte-Berger-Strasse 33
Apartment and Commercial Building
Günter Plessow, Reinhold Ehlers,
Peter Krop, Berlin
Client: Stadt und Land Wohnbauten
GmbH and Bavaria Objekt- und
Baubetreuung GmbH, Berlin
5 stories, 12 housing units, 1 shop,
cost approx. DM 1.69 mill.,
built November 96–November 97

Lieselotte-Berger-Strasse 35, 41, 53
Elisabeth-Seibert-Strasse 35, 37
Apartment Buildings
Borck, Boye, Schaefer, Berlin
Client: Stadt und Land Wohnbauten-
Gesellschaft mbH, Berlin, and
Bavaria Objekt- und Baubetreuung
GmbH, Berlin,
5-storied buildings along Lieselotte-
Berger-Strasse, 8 housing units and
2 shops on ground floor (No. 35),
8 housing units; 1 shop (No. 41);
10 housing units (No. 53) and
2 apartment buildings with
8 housing units each along
Elisabeth-Seibert-Strasse,
cost approx. DM 7.5 mill.,
built November 1996–December 1997

Lieselotte-Berger-Strasse 37, 43, 49,
Elly-Heuss-Knapp-Strasse 30, 32, 34
Apartment Buildings
Axel Liepe, Hartmut Steigelmann,
Berlin
Client: Stadt und Land
Wohnungsbaugesellschaft, Berlin
Row houses, 5 stories,
55 subsidized housing units;
retail space on ground floor,
built 1995–1997

Lieselotte-Berger-Strasse 42
Apartment Building
Stefan Reinsbach, GEHAG,
Dept. Technik, Berlin
Client: GEHAG, Gemeinnützige
Heimstätten-Aktiengesellschaft Berlin
(LBB-Fonds 7)
5 stories, 8 housing units and 2 shops,
housing space 500 sq. m,
completion 1997

Lieselotte-Berger-Strasse 44
Apartment and Commercial Building
Günter Plessow, Reinhold Ehlers,
Peter Krop, Berlin
Client: GEHAG/Bavaria, Berlin
5 stories, 12 housing units, 2 shops.
cost approx. DM 1.57 mill.,
built July 1996–November 1997

Lieselotte-Berger-Strasse 51
Apartment Building
Günter Plessow, Reinhold Ehlers,
Peter Krop, Berlin
Client: Stadt und Land Wohnbauten
GmbH, Berlin, and Bavaria Objekt- und
Baubetreuung GmbH
5 stories, 10 housing units,
cost approx. DM 1.75 mill.,
built November 1996–November 1997

Lieselotte-Berger-Strasse 59
Apartment Building
Karl Pächter and Partner, Berlin
Client: GEHAG, Gemeinnützige
Heimstätten AG, Berlin
Apartment building, 5 stories,
13 housing units,
completion winter 1997

Lieselotte-Berger-Strasse 61
Apartment Building
Mirjam Blase and Osman Kapici,
Berlin
Client: GEHAG, Gemeinnützige
Heimstätten AG, Berlin
Corner building, 5 stories,
10 housing units
built 1996–1997

Ursulinenstrasse 15–17,
Elfriede-Kuhr-Strasse 10–16
Apartment Building
Günter Plessow, Reinhold Ehlers,
Peter Krop, Berlin
Client: Stadt und Land
Wohnbauten GmbH, Berlin
4-storied building, 46 housing units,
housing space 3,157 sq. m,
cost approx. DM 7.58 mill.,
built July 1995–December 1996

Waltersdorfer Chaussee 170–176
Apartment and Commercial Building
Arno Bonanni, Berlin
Client: Bavaria Objekt- und Baubetreuung and R & S Specker, Berlin
Block alignment, 5 stories, 52 housing
units, housing area 3,700 sq. m,
1,750 sq. m retail space
9,370 sq. m gross floor area,
cost approx. DM 13 mill.,
built June 1995–February 1997

Waltersdorfer Chaussee 180,
Hiltrud-Dudek-Weg 6–12
Apartment Building
René Berndt, Maximiliano Burgmayer,
Berlin
Client: Bavaria Objekt- und
Baubetreuung and
R & S Specker, Berlin
U-shaped building, 59 housing units,
gross floor area 5,168 sq. m,
cost DM 10.2 mill.,
completion 1997

Pankow

Binzstrasse 5a/5b
Apartment Building
Schwarz & Assoziierte, Berlin
Client: Bonczyk Baubetreuungs GmbH
5 stories plus staggered roof story,
24 housing units,
gross floor area: 2,760 sq. m,
cost DM 4,2 mill.
built November 1996–December 1997

Eschengraben 3-9
Two Apartment Buildings
Baesler, Schmidt and Partner, Berlin
Client: Bau-Herr Verwaltungs
GmbH & Co, Berlin
Block alignment above gas station in
city quarter dating from 1920/30,
2 houses in the courtyard,
137 housing units
housing space 8,800 sq. m,
office space 1,600 sq. m,
cost DM 27.8 mill.,
built autumn 1993–summer 1997

Friedrich-Engels-Strasse 39–43
Housing Complex
Götz Bellmann & Walter Böhm, Berlin
Client: Heinz Wilhelm Schoof
and SESTE GmbH
8 stories, 51 housing units;
gross floor area 6,858 sq. m.,
cost DM 21.9 mill.,
built 1996/97

Garibaldistrasse 4
Apartment and Commercial Building
Peter Ottmann, Berlin
Client: Linde and Paul Ottmann
4-storied building, 8 housing units,
2 commercial units on 790 sq. m
gross floor area;
cost DM 1.77 mill.,
built June 1996–July 1997

Schillerstrasse 2–6a,
Waldowstrasse 22–23a
Residential Area "Heinrich-Böll"
W. Brenne; Eble + Kalepky, Berlin
Client: GSW – Gemeinnützige
Siedlungs- und Wohnungsbaugesellschaft Berlin mbH
114 housing units and
5 commercial units as 1st building
phase of a new settlement,
conceived as an ecological pilot project.
The settlement will consist
of 650 housing units in all,
realized in 5 building phases,
cost DM 25.9 mill.,
1st building phase 1994–1997

Schillerstrasse 9/10, 21/22
Apartment and Commercial Building
Wolf-Rüdiger Borchardt, Berlin
Client: JHD Beteiligungsgruppe GmbH &
Co., Objekt Pankow,
Schillerstrasse KG, c/o DIG
Dom und Partner Immobilien-
Management GmbH
11,000 sq. m gross floor area,
built 1995–96

Waldstrasse 64
Apartment Building
**Schwarz & Schwarz,
Stuttgart/Dresden**
Client: VS Projektregie GmbH, Berlin
Urban infill, 4 stories,
16 privately financed housing units,
investment: DM 5 mill.,
completion 1996

*Wolfshagener Strasse,
Pankgrafenstrasse*
Housing Complex
Schiedhelm + Partner, Berlin
Client: DEGEWO, Berlin (section west)
DEMOS, Berlin/Munich (section east)
69 housing units (in section west) and
102 housing units (in section east), all
of them subsidized, competition 1992,
built 1994–1997

Development Area Buchholz

Clients: ARGE Süd;
diverse Real Estate Funds, represented
by BEB Berliner Eigenheim-Bau

Urban Design
Engel and Zillich, Berlin
Winner of the limited competion 1992
Landscape Design: **Bos, B + J Buse,
Kossel, Breuckmann, Kienle**

Area: 127 acres (incl. Rosenthaler Weg),
cost approx. DM 1 billion,
construction start: September 1995,
completion planned for winter 1998,
investment amount December 1997,
approx. DM 850 mill.,
2,888 housing units planned,
2,500 housing units completed
December 1997.
Public green space 2,47 acres
Approx. 12,000 sq. m
commercial space planned,
approx. 10.000 sq. m,
completed in 1997.
Social infrastructure:
5 daycare centers for 540 children,
youth center, 3-sided elementary
school with special branch for
handicapped children,
daycare centers for 340 children have
been completed by December 1997.

Architects:
Engel and Zillich, Berlin
Erling, Ewald, Graf, Neumann, Berlin
Fabrik 40, Berlin
Faskel and Becker, Berlin
Feddersen, v. Herder and Partners
Frank Friedrich, Berlin
Klaus Kammann, Berlin
Krüger, Schuberth, Vandreike, Berlin
Maschlanka Architekten
Meyer, Ernst & Partner, Berlin
Hans-Jürgen Mücke, Berlin
Richter Architekten, Berlin
Helge Syperek, Berlin
Schröder, Berlin
Schattauer + Tibes, Berlin
Schaper and Noack,
Hannes Sauer, Berlin
C.-A. v. Halle, Berlin

Prenzlauer Berg

Diedenhofer Strasse 2
Apartment Building
MEP Meyer, Ernst and Partner, Berlin
Client: WIP Wohnungsbaugesellschaft
Prenzlauer Berg, Berlin
Corner building as urban infill,
12 subsidized housing units,
cost approx. DM 3 mill.,
built 1995–1997

Driesener Strasse 26
Apartment Building
Dietrich von Beulwitz, Berlin
Client: WIP Wohnungsbaugesellschaft
Prenzlauer Berg, Berlin
Urban infill, 14 housing units,
gross floor area 949 sq. m,
cost approx. DM 2,8 mill.,
completion 1997

Jablonskistrasse 15
Apartment Building
Karsten and Veit, Berlin
Client: CASA-TEC, Berlin
Urban infill, 8 privately financed
housing units, 7 subsidized housing
units, 2 commercial units,
gross floor area 1,700 sq. m,
cost approx. DM 3.5 mill.,
completion February 1997

Kollwitzstrasse 56a
Apartment Building
Stankovic and Bonnen, Berlin
Client: WIP Wohnungsbaugesellschaft
Prenzlauer Berg, Berlin
Urban infill, corner building,
5 housing units in all, 1 supervised
dwelling community,
gross floor area: 875 sq. m;
cost DM 1.2 mill.,
completion 1997

*Ostseestrasse 26a, Sültstrasse 63, 65,
67, Georg-Blank-Strasse 61*
Apartment Building
Grundei and Partner, Berlin
Client: WIP Wohnungsbaugesellschaft
Prenzlauer Berg, Berlin
3-wing-ensemble with
66 subsidized housing units,
cost approx. DM 15.6 mill.,
built 1995–1997

Pappelallee 37–39
Apartment Building
Stankovic + Bonnen, Berlin
Client: WIR Wohnungsbaugesellschaft
in Berlin mbH
Block alignment, 31 housing units in all,
14 seniors' apartments,
gross floor area 3.801 sq. m;
cost DM 6.35 mill.,
built 1996–1997

*Prenzlauer Allee 207,
Sredzkistrasse 66*
Apartement and Commercial Building
**Günter Plessow, Reinhold Ehlers,
Peter Krop, Berlin**
Client: Th. Kohl GbR, Regensburg
7 stories, 28 housing units,
housing space 1,599 sq. m,
3 shops, 3 medical practices,
cost approx. DM 6 mill.,
built February 1995–October 1997

Schönfliesser Strasse 9
Apartment Building
Gerd Neumann, Berlin
Client: WIP Wohnungsbaugesellschaft
Prenzlauer Berg, Berlin
Urban infill, 18 subsidized housing
units, cost approx. DM 4.5 mill.,
built 1995–97

Schönhauser Allee
Office and Commercial Building
"Königstadt-Terrassen"
Müller, Reimann, Scholz, Berlin
4–6 stories above commercial area
on ground and first floor,
gross floor area 22.300 sq. m,
completion 1997

Schönhauser Allee 188, Torstrasse
Apartment and Commercial Building
**Dieter Schmoll, RKW + Partner,
Düsseldorf, Berlin, Frankfurt/Main**
Client: Trigon Consult GmbH + Co,
Schönhauser Allee 188 KG
Corner building, offices on 5 stories,
office space 1,747 sq. m,
3 shops on ground floor,
5 housing units on 7th floor,
built November 1996–December 1997

Reinickendorf

Alt-Hermsdorf 9, 10a
Village "Tegeler Fliess"
Landsberg + Stephan Pinkau, Berlin
Client: GEWINO, Gemeinnützige
Wittenauer Wohnungsbau-
genossenschaft, Berlin
Pairs of 14 square-houses with
2 housing units each, arranged in
a geometrical structure,
cost DM 12.5 mill.,
built August 1995–November 1997

Am Borsigturm 40–50
"Phönix-Innovation Center"
Walter Rolfes and Partner, Berlin
Client: Herlitz-Gewerbepark am
Borsigturm
Gross floor area 10,000 sq. m,
approx. 40 commercial units,
built October 1995–May 1997

Brieseallee 21
5 Urban Villas
Becher and Rottkamp, Berlin
Client: GeHaGe, Berlin
Gross floor area 3,208 sq. m
built 1995–1996

Brusebergstrasse 7, 7e
Three Apartment Buildings
Ewald, Graf, Neumann, Berlin
Client: Köpenicker Immobilienfonds 1 GbR
59 housing units in all, 3 stories each,
usable space 4,294 sq. m,
cost DM 29.9 mill.,
completion 1996

Holländerstrasse 31–34
Office and Service Center
"ANTHROPOLIS"
**HPP Hentrich, Petschnigg & Partner
GmbH, Düsseldorf**
Client: Anthropolis Projektentwicklung
GbR, Frankfurt/Main, Berlin
Eight single building volumes
linked with each other and
with the existing industrial buildings,
40,000 sq. m office space in all,
cost approx. DM 350 mill.,
built 1993–1997

Holzhauser Strasse 175/Triftstrasse
Office Building, Berlin/Brandenburg
Headquarters of Bilfinger + Berger
J.S.K., Berlin
Client: Bilfinger + Berger Bau AG
Gross floor area 9,100 sq. m,
built 1996–1997

Lindauer Allee 39–45
Apartment Buildings
Hentschel + Oestreich, Berlin
Client: GSW, Berlin
5–6 stories high, extending the existing
housing area "Lindauer Allee",
33 housing units,
gross floor area 4,550 sq. m,
construction cost: DM 6 mill.,
built 1997

Neheimer Strasse 8a
Tower C, Apartment Building
Moritz Müller and Götz Keller, Berlin
Client: GEWOBAG, Berlin
One of three towers planned to
continue the row of existing high-rises,
32 housing units,
housing space 1,863 sq. m,
gross floor area 3,336 sq. m,
construction cost approx. DM 7 mill.,
built February 1996–June 1997

*Sommerstrasse 12–15,
Klemkestrasse 102–104*
"House of the Generations"
**Günther Grossmann and
Zsuzsana Damosy, Berlin**
Client: Reinickendorf
District Authorities and DEGEWO, Berlin
Daycare center and
seniors' residence under one roof,
gross floor area 20,310 sq. m,
built 1994–1997

Zabel-Krüger-Damm 22, 24
"Rollberge II", Apartment Building
**Günter Plessow, Reinhold Ehlers,
Peter Krop, Berlin**
Client: GSW, Berlin
Supplementary building
to the existing settlement, 8 stories,
40 housing units, 1 shop,
housing space 2,878 sq. m,
cost approx. DM 7.5 mill.,
built August 1995–September 1997

*Zabel-Krüger-Damm 54–62,
Waldshuter Zeile 10, 12*
Rollberge I, Apartment Buildings
**Günter Plessow, Reinhold Ehlers,
Peter Krop, Berlin**
Client: GSW, Berlin
Seven apartment buildings,
2–6 stories, 63 housing units,
housing space 4,722 sq. m,
cost approx. DM 11.14 mill.,
built June 1995–August 1997

Schöneberg

Dennewitzstrasse, Nelly-Sachs-Park
Housing Complex
Rainer Oefelein, Berlin
Client. WIR Wohnungsbau-
gesellschaft mbH, Berlin (WIR Fonds 9)
Two urban villas, 5 stories,
green roof terraces,
plus long row houses, 6 stories high,
141 housing units,
gross floor area 18,814 sq. m,
daycare center,
built 1995–1997

Kolonnenstrasse 8/Feurigstrasse
Apartment and Commercial Building
**ELW, Georg Eyl & Partner
with Laura Wendt-Mieser, Berlin**
Client: Stadt und Land Wohnbauten-
Gesellschaft mbH, Berlin
Corner building as infill
7 stories, 10 housing units,
3 commercial units,
gross floor area 1,870 sq. m,
cost approx. DM 4.4 mill.
built March 1996–May 1997

Kurfürstenstrasse 129
"Haus der Deutschen Bauindustrie"
Schweger + Partner, Hamburg/Berlin
Client: Hauptverband der Deutschen
Bauindustrie
House of the German Building Industry,
urban infill, office building, 7 stories,
gross floor area approx. 3,675 sq. m,
competition 1994,
built 1996–1997

*Lietzenburger Strasse 9a /
Welserstrasse 30*
Apartment Building
"Lietzenburger Spitze"
**Hans Schröder & Winfried Ringkamp,
Berlin**
Client: GEWOBAG, Berlin
Wedge-shaped building, 8 stories,
subterranean car park,
48 housing units, privately owned,
housing space 2,721 sq. m,
commercial space 252 sq. m,
gross floor area 4,247 sq. m,
construction cost approx. DM 21 mill.,
built August 1996–Dezember 1997

Rubensstrasse 125
Department of Internal Medicine
Project Partnership
Baumann and Niedballa, Berlin
Client: Department für Public Health
and Social Affairs, represented by
Schöneberg Hospital Administration
Modernization of the existing building
and new wing with a 300-bed capacity,
gross floor area 12,500 sq. m,
net floor area approx. 24,000 sq. m
cost approx. DM 80 mill.,
built 1994–1997

Welserstrasse 16–22
"Finow" Elementary School
**Bayerer, Hanson, Heidenreich,
Schuster (BHHS), Berlin**
Client: Schöneberg District Authorities
Conversion and extension of "Finow"
elementary school,
gross floor area 7,502 sq. m
built 1992–1997

Spandau

*Residential Park
"Aalemannufer"*

Ensemble of 29 buildings,
536 apartments in all,
480 subsidized housing units,
approx. 750 sq. m commercial space,
quarter area approx. 15.6 acres;
approx. 2.97 acres public green space,
2 daycare centers

Client: Bauwert AG, Munich,
Bauwert Immobilienverwertung GmbH
& Co. Aalemannufer KG

Landscaping:
EXTERN, Stephan Haan, both Berlin

Investment DM 350 mill.
architects' workshop August 1993
real estate acquisition 1993/94
built December 1994– autumn 1996
(1st building phase),
spring 1997 (2nd building phase)

Aalemannufer 5
Gregotti Associati Int., Milano
Am Teufelsbruch 1 and 3
Gregotti Associati Int., Milano
Am Teufelsbruch 2 and 4
Kramm and Strigl, Darmstadt
Am Teufelsbruch 9–21
**Martin + Pächter with Büttner,
Neumann, Braun, Berlin**

Am Teufelsbruch 6–12
David Chipperfield Architects, London
Am Teufelsbruch 14–18
Kramm and Strigl, Darmstadt
Am Teufelsbruch 20–26
Kramm and Strigl, Darmstadt
Zum Erlengrund 1 and 3
David Chipperfield Architects, London
Zum Erlengrund 2 and 4
Feige and Partner, Berlin
Zum Erlengrund 5 and 9
Kramm and Strigl, Darmstadt
Zum Erlengrund 15–17
David Chipperfield Architects, London
Zum Erlengrund 6 and 8
**Martin + Pächter with Büttner,
Neumann, Braun, Berlin**
Zum Erlengrund 10 and 20
Feige and Partner, Berlin
Zu den Fichtewiesen 1 and 3
**Martin + Pächter, with Büttner,
Neumann, Braun, Berlin**
Zu den Fichtewiesen 2–12
Gregotti Associati Int., Milano
Zu den Fichtewiesen 5 and 7
Feige and Partner, Berlin
Zu den Fichtewiesen 9–13
**Martin + Pächter with Büttner,
Neumann, Braun, Berlin**
Zu den Fichtewiesen 16–36
**ASP Planungs- and Bauleitungs-
gesellschaft mbH, Nolte, Reese +
Partner, Kassel**

"Water City on the Spandauer See"

"Quartier Havelspitze"

Client: Grundstücksgesellschaft
Wasserstadt Oberhavel Quartier
Havelspitze GbR;
Bavaria Objekt- und Baubetreuungs
GmbH (LBB) in cooperation with
Siemens (SBB), Berlin

Urban design:
Kees Christiaanse, Rotterdam
Landscape design:
**Gustav Lange, Hamburg,
WES & Partner, Hamburg
Ariane Röntz, Berlin**

Total investment DM 1 billion,
1,600 housing units planned,
813 subsidized units, 219 privately
financed units finished,
commercial area (retail and service
space) 45,000 sq. m planned,
1 daycare center finished.

"Spandauer See Bridge" (South Bridge)
crossing the havel river from
Havelspitze to Haveleck
completed December 1st, 1997,
architect: **Walter A. Noebel, Berlin**
engineers: **Andrä, Leonhardt &
Partners**

North Bridge planned

Building phase WA 1
*Sigmund-Bergmann-Strasse,
Hugo-Cassirer-Strasse,
David-Frank-Strasse*
**Kees Christiaanse ASTOC, Rotterdam
A & P Suter & Suter GmbH**
Completion July 1997

Building phase WA 2
*Hugo-Cassirer-Strasse,
David-Frank-Strasse,
Franz-Meyer-Strasse*
J.S.K. Perkins & Will, Berlin
Completion July 1997

Building phase WA 3
*Hugo-Cassirer-Strasse,
Franz-Meyer-Strasse*
Josef Paul Kleihues, Berlin
Completion July 1997

Building phase WA 4
Sigmund-Bergmann-Strasse
Otto Steidle, Munich
Completion September 1997

Building phase WA 5
Josef Paul Kleihues, Berlin
Completion July 1998

Building phase WA 6 and WA 7
AG SIAT with Albrecht
Completion August 1998

Quartier Pulvermühle

Client: GSW Gemeinnützige
Siedlungs- und Wohnungsbaugesellschaft Berlin mbH

Urban design:
Nalbach + Nalbach, Berlin
Landscaping:
**Häfner & Jeminez;
Alkewitz & Armbruster, Berlin**

1,038 subsidized housing units,
88 owner occupied apartments,
3,500 sq. m commercial space
2 daycare centers,
elementary school, gym hall,
public green space 95 acres,
construction start November 1994,
completion planned 2000

Architects:
**Bernd Albers, Berlin
Theodora Betow, Berlin
Hentschel & Oestreich, Berlin
ENSS, Berlin
Faskel & Becker, Berlin
Geske & Wenzel, Berlin
Jahn & Suhr, Berlin
Mayer, Ruhe, Voigt, Wehrhahn, Berlin
Nalbach Architekten, Berlin
Klaus-Rüdiger Pankrath, Berlin
Plessow, Ehlers, Krop, Berlin
Carola Schäfers, Berlin
Benedict Tonon, Berlin**

Quartier Maselake Nord

Client: Kommanditgesellschaft für
Warenhandel, Goetsche & Granobs mbH

Urban Design:
David Chipperfield, London
Architects:
Grobe & Grobe, Berlin

Housing units planned: 271 in all,
53 owner occupied apartments,
completion planned summer 1998

*Quartier Parkstrasse on the site of
the former Schultheiss-Brewery
Neuendorfer Strasse 19–20*

Client: Bayer. Beamtenversicherung
Grundstücksentwicklungs AG (BBV),
Munich

Architects:
**Reichen & Robert, Paris,
Benedict Tonon, Berlin**
(Daycare center)
KSV, Berlin
Landscape Design:
Gustav Lange, Hamburg
Landscaping:
**WES & Partner; W. Betz, H. Wehberg,
P. Schmidtke, P. Schatz, G. Eppinger**

Housing units planned: 700 in all,
1 high-rise building of 16 stories,
retail space on ground floors, hotel,
old people's home, daycare center.
construction start spring 1997,
completion planned for 1999

*Projects finished in 1997,
listed by addresses:*

Romy-Schneider-Strasse 9–11
Apartment Building
Bernd Albers, Berlin
Client: GSW Gemeinnützige Siedlungs-
und Wohnungsbaugesellschaft Berlin
mbH
5 stories, 48 housing units, shops
gross floor area 7,960 sq. m,
cost DM 14 mill.,
built April 1996–October 1997

Olga-Tschechowa-Strasse 2–14
Apartment Buildings
**ENSS Eckert, Negwer, Sommer,
Suselbeek; Berlin;
Nalbach + Nalbach, Berlin**
Client: GSW – Gemeinnützige
Siedlungs- und Wohnungsbau-
gesellschaft Berlin mbH
10 buildings, 137 housing units
cost DM 25.9 mill.
built April 1996–August 1997

*Romy-Schneider-Strasse 2–6,
Grützmacherweg 16–18*
Apartment Building
Bernd Albers, Berlin
Client: GSW – Gemeinnützige
Siedlungs- und Wohnungsbaugesellschaft Berlin mbH
6 stories, 40 housing units, 11 office
units, 6 commercial units
cost DM 15.0 mill.,
built April1996–October 1997

Quartier Siemens, WA 2
Apartment and Commercial Building
J.S.K Dipl. Ing. Architekten, Berlin
Client: Siemens Beteiligungsgesellschaft GmbH and Bavaria Objekt-
und Beteiligungsgesellschaft, Berlin
Apartment Building with shops on
ground floor, daycare center,
gross floor area 24,800 sq. m,
175 subsidizend housing units,
72 privately financed apartments,
built 1996–1997

Residential Area "Wohnpark Staaken"

Contractors: bewoge, Berlin, and
Bauwert, Munich/Berlin

Section Bauwert GmbH, Munich

Bergstrasse, Hauptstrasse
17 buildings, 158 housing units in all,
145 subsidized housing units,
13 privately financed apartments
in 3 urban villas,
real estate area 44.5 acres,
housing space 14,700 sq. m,
commercial space approx. 200 sq. m,
public green space 3,000 sq. m,
investment DM 105 mill.,
planning since 1993,
built December 1994– December 1996

Architects:
**Feige and Döring, Berlin
ASP (Nolte, Plaßmann, Reese), Berlin,
Kassel, Leipzig**
Landscape Design:
Stephan Haan, Berlin

Daycare center (130 children):
Client: bewoge, Berlin
Architects:
Augustin and Frank, Berlin
completion spring 1998

Section Bavaria, Berlin

*Wiesenweg, Erna-Sack-Strasse,
Nennhauser Damm*
147 housing units in all, 131 subsidized,
16 privately financed, 4 housing units
for handicapped people, 10 senior units

Architects:
Burckhard, Emch and Berger, Berlin

Section Trigon, Berlin

1st building phase:
580 housing units, daycare center
cost DM 290 mill.,
completion 1996

Client: Grundstücksgesellschaft
Cosmarweg 91–121 mbH & Co.
Beteiligungs KG

Architects:
**Bendoraitis, Gurt, Meissner, Berlin
Hansen & Kellig, Berlin
Reinhard Müller, Berlin
Barna von Sartory, Martin Focks,
Berlin
Schiedhelm + Partner, Berlin
Bernhard Winking, Berlin**

2nd building phase:
184 housing units,
commercial area on ground floor,
daycare center

Client: Grundstücksgesellschaft
Cosmarweg 91–121 mbH & Co.
Beteiligungs KG
completion winter 1997

Architects:
**Georg Heinrichs, Berlin
Reinhard Müller, Berlin
Barna von Sartory, Martin Focks,
Berlin
Schiedhelm + Partner, Berlin**

3rd building phase
47 owner occupied apartments

Client: Trigon Consult GmbH & Co
Staakener Felder KG

Architects:
**Barna von Sartory, Martin Focks,
Berlin**
completion winter 1997

*Projects finished in 1997
listed by addresses:*

Cosmarweg 29–41
Apartment Buildings
Bernhard Winking Architekten, Berlin
Client: Grundstücksgesellschaft
Staaken 2.8. b.R.
Building volume split up in seven parts,
5 stories, 76 housing units,
gross floor area 8,947 sq. m,
built January 1996–May 1997

Cosmarweg/Pfarrer-Theile-Strasse
Apartment Building
Schiedhelm + Partner, Berlin
Client: Trigon, Berlin
Block structure, 4 stories,
79 housing units,
5,159 sq. m housing space,
built 1995 – 1997

Richard-Münch-Strasse (11–23)
Apartment Buildings
Schiedhelm + Partner, Berlin
Client: Trigon, Berlin
Building row, 3–6 stories high,
26 housing units,
housing space 1,973 sq. m,
built 1995–1997

Wohnpark Staaken 1.3
**Barna von Sartory , Martin Focks,
Berlin**
Client: Trigon Consult GmbH & Co.
47 housing units,
completion 1997

Wiesenweg
Daycare Center
Ute Frank, Georg Augustin, Berlin
Client: Arge Kita Spandau
(bewoge, Bauwert, Berlin)
Daycare center for 130 children,
gross floor area 1,711 sq. m,
cost DM 7.2 mill.,
built April 1997–December 1997

*(End of Residential Area
"Wohnpark Staaken")*

Falkenseer Chaussee 242–256
Apartment Building
ELW and Feddersen/von Herder, Berlin
Client: WIR Fonds 7;
WIR Wohnungsbaugesellschaft
in Berlin mbH
128 housing units; 1 commercial unit
built 1995–1997

Goldbeckweg 8–14
Center for Electric and Energy
Engineering Training
Klaus-Rüdiger Pankrath, Berlin
Client: Spandau District Authorities
Gross floor area: 2,705 sq. m,
built 1995–1996

Nonnendammallee/Paulsternstrasse
Power Station
Kny + Weber, Berlin
Client: Siemensstadt Grundstücksverwaltung GmbH + Co. oHG
Transformation Plant 110/10 KV,
gross floor area 1,623 sq. m,
construction cost DM 5.3 mill. in all,
built March 1996–November 1996

Paulsternstrasse 34
Fire-station
**Kny + Weber with Holger Drechsler,
Berlin**
Client: Siemensstadt-Grundstücks-
verwaltung GmbH & Co. KG, Berlin
Prototype for a new generation of
decentralized fire-stations,
801 sq. m gross floor area,
cost DM 5.9 mill. in all,
built October 1995–June 1996

Weinmeisterhornweg 147
Housing Complex
**H. Schreck, G. Hillmann, J. Nagel,
I. Lütkemeyer; IBUS, Berlin**
Client: GSW – Gemeinnützige
Siedlungs- und Wohnungsbau-
gesellschaft Berlin mbH
One "Zero-Energy-House"
and 12 housing units
cost DM 5.6 mill.,
built August 1996–August 1997

Steglitz

Amalienstrasse 9, 9 a
Two Urban Villas
Siegfried Tschirley, Berlin
(Realization)
Client: BOTAG Bodentreuhand- und
Verwaltungs-AG
Two urban villas, 2–3 stories high
plus roof story, 17 housing units,
investment DM 8.2 mill.,
completion winter 1996

*Hanielweg 13–19,
Malteserstrasse 150–158*
Apartment Building
**BSP Klaus Baesler, Bernhard Schmidt,
Martin Schwacke, Berlin**
Client: Bau-Herr Zweite Verwaltungs
GmbH & Co. Hanielweg oHG
Combination of row houses and square
houses, 4 stories high (5 stories high
on Malteserstrasse),
187 housing units and
1 commercial unit
14.002 sq. m usable space,
cost DM 103.8 mill.,
built November 1995–June 1997

Hindenburgdamm 4–4c
Apartment Building
Thomas Langenfeld, Berlin
Client:Haschtmann
Baubetreuungsgesellschaft, Berlin
Housing complex, 2 stories high,
38 housing units,
investment DM 19.4 mill.,
completion 1996

Hindenburgdamm 31
"Tibor-Diamantstein-Haus"
Halbach Architects, Berlin
Client: Berlin Building, Housing,
and Traffic Dept.;
Benjamin Franklin University Clinic
laboratories,
3-storied "Research Container",
cost approx. DM 6 mill.,
completion February 1997

Schünemannweg 25
Housing Complex
**Planungsbüro P & R,
Michael C. Reinelt, Brigitte Kreutel,
Berlin**
Client: Trigon, Berlin
24 housing units,
completion 1997

Tempelhof

Alarichstrasse 12–17
Office Center Tempelhof,
Gothaer Versicherung
Kahlen + Partner, Berlin
Client: Kahlen + Partner
Bau- und Umwelttechnologie
GmbH & Co. KG, Berlin
Office and commercial space for
the Gothaer Insurance Company,
gross floor area 18,200 sq. m,
built 1995–1996

Kaiserin-Augusta-Strasse 83
Apartment Building
M. Paal, Berlin
Client: Eigentümergemeinschaft
Dürckheim
Urban infill, 4 stories, 1 roof story,
23 privately owned housing units,
housing space 1,490 sq. m,
built March 1997–November 1997

Kirchhainer Damm 66
Home for Young Prisoners Upon Trial
**Urs Müller, Thomas Rhode,
Jörg Wandert, Berlin**
Client: Berlin Dept. for Justice
The softly curved building is organized
as a small town offering many
functions, housing, workshops,
instruction and service rooms,
gross floor area 6,663 sq. m,
cost DM 20.5 mill.,
built 1995–1997

Mariendorfer Damm 19–21
Office, Commercial and Apartment
Buildings "Mariendorfer Hof"
Arno Bonanni, Berlin
Client: GbR Wohn- und Geschäftspark
am Mariendorfer Damm
Office and commercial building,
8 stories high, aligning the street,
apartment houses, 4 stories high,
130 housing units,
gross floor area approx. 21,293 sq. m,
commercial space 2,833 sq. m,
construction cost approx. DM 35 mill.,
built November 1994–January 1997

Schichauweg
Research Institute for Water, Soil and
Air Pollution
Jan, Roosje, and Rolf Rave, Berlin
Client: Umweltbundesamt Berlin
Institutional building and shed hall on a
12 x 12 m steelcolumn grid covering an
artificial channel.
Cost approx. DM 32 mill.,
built 1995–1997

*Wenckebachstrasse 23,
Albrechtstrasse, Colditzstrasse*
"Wenckebach Hospital"
Borck, Boye, Schäfer, Berlin
Client: Wenckebach Hospital, Berlin
gross floor area 13,000 sq. m,
construction cost approx. DM 200 mill.,
built 1993 (1990)–1997

Tiergarten

Bissingzeile 17–19
Daycare Center
Schmidt-Thomsen & Ziegert, Berlin
Client: Tiergarten District Authorities
Daycare center for 125 children,
brick block, 3 stories high
gross floor area 1,650 sq. m,
cost DM 6.8 mill.,
built 1993–1996

Bredowstrasse 27/28
Apartment Building and
Daycare Center
**tgw Markus Torge, Sebastian Gaa,
Klaus Wercker, Berlin**
Client: GSW – Gemeinnützige
Siedlungs- und Wohnungsbaugesellschaft Berlin mbH
Block alignment along Bredowstrasse
with a 2-story-doorway leading to a
public green space,
gross floor area 5,630 sq. m,
housing space 3,440 sq. m,
32 subsidized housing units,
daycare center for 130 children,
construction cost DM 14.4 mill.,
built September 1996–April 1997

Friedrich-Krause-Ufer 24
Corner Office Building
Walter Arno Noebel, Berlin
Client: State of Berlin
New construction and addition
to an existing office block, 4 to 7 stories
high, gross floor area 11,000 sq. m,
built 1994–1996

Huttenstrasse 8/9
Apartment and Commercial Building
Bertelsmann and Partner, Berlin
Client: HUGA Grundstücksverwaltung
New construction, 6 stories high,
24 housing units, 3 commercial units,
cost DM 6.6 mill.,
completion 1997

Kaiserin-Augusta-Allee 104–106
Office Building
**SJ Planungsgesellschaft Schuler
Jatzlau Partner mbH**
Client: Vereinigte
Haftpflichtversicherung
Usable space approx. 16,000 sq. m,
construction cost approx. DM 60 mill.,
built 1994–1997

*Levetzowstrasse 10/10a,
Agricolastrasse 24/24a*
Apartment, Office and Commercial
Building
**Hahnenfeld, Bäppler, Günther,
Frankfurt/Main**
Client: GbR Götz and Konstanze Diehl;
Frankfurt/Main
Modernized building raised by 1 to 2
stories, 24 housing units
cost DM 15.2 mill. in all,
built 1995–1996

*Lützowufer 26,
Landgrafenstrasse 14–15,
Wichmannstrasse 5*
Office Building "Lützow-Center"
**Günter Plessow, Reinhold Ehlers,
Peter Krop, Berlin**
Client: Lützow Center GmbH & Co KG,
Berlin
Block completion through new building
sections and addition in height,
modernization of the existing
substance, 26 office units,
usable space approx. 12,5000 sq. m,
cost approx. DM 45 mill.,
built March 1995–October 1997

Paulstrasse 4, 11
Apartment Buildings
Peter Träger, Berlin
Client: Kausch & Partner, Berlin
Urban infill through two buildings
covering the gable-ends,
44 housing units,
completion 1996

*"Potsdamer Platz"
Reichpietschufer,
Corner Linkstrasse/Eichhornstrasse*
Office and Commercial Building
"C2" and "C3"
**Arata Isozaki & Ass., Tokyo,
Steffen Lehmann & Partner, Berlin**
Client: debis Gesellschaft
Potsdamer Platz, Projekt- und
Immobilienmanagement mbH, Berlin
Two 10-story building arms parallel to
each other connected by bridges
on 8th floor,
gross floor area 38,000 sq. m,
One of the winning competition
entries of May 1992,
built May 1994–July 1997

*"Potsdamer Platz"
Reichpietschufer*
Office and Commercial Building
"debis-Headquarters"
Renzo Piano, Genova
Client: debis Gesellschaft
Potsdamer Platz, Projekt- und
Immobilienmanagement mbH, Berlin
Gross floor area 46.000 sq. m,
built 1995–1997

*"Potsdamer Platz"
Linkstrasse/Eichhornstrasse*
Apartment Building and
Daycare Center
Lauber & Wöhr, Munich
Client: debis Gesellschaft
Potsdamer Platz Projekt- und
Immobilienmanagement mbH, Berlin
Gross floor area approx. 11,000 sq. m,
built 1995–1997

Schöneberger Ufer 81–91
Office Building
Fischer + Fischer, Cologne
Client: DEVK Deutsche Eisenbahner
Versorgungskasse
New office building around
existing substance,
3-story subterranean car park,
gross floor area 23,600 sq. m,
built 1993–1997

*Schöneberger Ufer,
Gluckstrasse*
Apartment Building
Fischer + Fischer, Cologne
Client: DEVK Deutsche Eisenbahner
Versorgungskasse
Apartment House as urban infill
bordering the office building of the
DEVK, 15 housing units,
built 1994–1996

*Schöneberger Ufer,
Genthiner Strasse*
Apartment Building
Fischer + Fischer, Cologne
Client: DEVK Deutsche Eisenbahner
Versorgungskasse
Urban infill, next to the DEVK building,
10 housing units,
built 1995–1997

Treptow

Housing Area Altglienicke

Altglienicke 1.1–1.4

2,433 housing units in all,
1,582 subsidized units,
786 privately financed housing units,
65 owner occupied apartments,
3,000 sq. m commercial space,
public green space 247 acres

Client: Stadt und Land Wohnbauten-
Gesellschaft mbH;

Urban Design
**PLANWERK, Heinz Tibbe,
Carlo Becker, Berlin**

Housing Area 1.1
587 subsidized housing units,
41,470 sq. m housing space,
cost approx. DM 218 mill. in all,
construction start March 1993,
completion December 1995

Architects:
**Frank Dörken, Volker Heise, Berlin
Dieter Rühle, Berlin
Borck, Boye, Schaefer, Berlin
Joachim Ramin, Berlin**

Housing Area 1.2
971 subsidized housing units,
housing space 69.980 sq. m,
cost DM 375 mill.,
construction start December 1996,
completion July 1997

Architects:
**Braun & Voigt and Partner, Berlin
Dörken and Heise, Berlin
Findeisen and Partner, Berlin
Heide and v. Beckerath, Berlin
Hillig and Witte, Berlin
HOPRO Bauplanung, Brandenburg
Kennerknecht,
Kneffel,
Liepe and Steigelmann, Berlin
Meik, Berlin
Mussotter + Poeverlein, Berlin
Pieper + Partner, Berlin
Plessow, Ehlers, Krop, Berlin
Georg Procakis, Berlin
Rühle and Partner
Yamaguchi and Essig, Berlin**

Housing Area 1.3
482 subsidized housing units,
housing space 36.890 sq. m,
65 privately owned detached houses,
3 commercial units,
cost approx. DM 323 mill.

Architects:
**Assmann, Salomon, Scheidt +
Schmidt, Berlin
Dähne + Dahl, Berlin
Grünberg and Partner
Jeromin, Berlin
Kny and Weber, Berlin
Madebach, Redeleit + Partner, Berlin
Pininski, Berlin
Eckhard Schmidt, Berlin**

Housing Area 1.4
328 subsidized housing units,
housing space 23,252 sq. m,
cost approx. DM 125 mill.,
construction start March 1995,
completion June 1997

Architects:
**Dörken and Heise, Berlin
M.E. Gehrmann and Partner, Berlin
MKH Mahraun, Kowal, Heieis, Berlin
K. Manfred Pflitsch, Berlin**

EURO Residential Park

Client: Bayerische Städte- und
Wohnungsbau GmbH, Munich
Site Area 331 acres,
construction start March 1994,
completion planned for 2000,
cost DM 190 mill. in all,
housing units planned approx. 1,000,
daycare center,
public green space approx. 104 acres

Architects:
Lehmann + Lachawitz, Munich
Bunge + Resch, Munich
Bayerische Städte- und
Wohnungsbau, Munich

Landscaping:
Cooperative Prof. Schmidt, Munich

Buildings listed by addresses

Altglienicke III.1
north of Wegedornstrasse,
18 Apartment Houses and
2 Apartment and Office Buildings
ARGE urbanistica Berlin
and Kny & Weber, Berlin
Row and free standing houses ,
3–4 stories high, 260 housing units,
8 shops, 1 restaurant,
gross floor area 29,814 sq. m,
cost DM 58.5 mill.,
built 1995–1997

Chorweilerstrasse 1–9,
Kalker Strasse 2–12.
Ehrenfelder Strasse 2–12
Apartment Buildings
Günter Plessow, Reinhold Ehlers,
Peter Krop, Berlin
Client: Stadt und Land Wohnbauten
GmbH; Berlin
Eight apartment houses, 4 stories,
174 housing units in all,
housing space 10,951 sq. m,
cost approx. DM 26.3 mill.,
built February 1996–November 1997

Mohnweg 20
Elementary School and Gym Hall
Urs Müller, Thomas Rohde,
Jörg Wandert, Berlin
Client: Treptow District Authorities
4-sided elementary school following
the acute-angled site with a long
curved wing for the class rooms,
gross floor area 8,260 sq. m,
cost DM 21.6 mill.,
built 1994–August 1997

Nippeser Strasse 20
Daycare Center "Am Wäldchen"
Frank Dörken, Volker Heise, Berlin
Client: Treptow District Authorities
Daycare center for 120 children,
gross floor area 1,753 sq. m,
construction cost DM 6.6 mill.,
built May 1995–October 1996

Porzer Strasse 33–37/67–79
Apartment Building
Axel Liepe, Hartmut Steigelmann,
Berlin
Client: Stadt + Land Wohnungsbau-
gesellschaft mbH, Berlin
L-shaped buildings, 4 stories high,
supplemented by cube houses
forming a block like structure toward
the street, 69 housing units (Porzer
Strasse 67–79), 29 housing units
(Porzer Strasse 33–37),
built January 1996–January 1997

Porzer Strasse 123
Daycare Center "Am Wegabogen"
HOPRO Bauplanung, Rühle, Berlin
Client: Treptow District Authorities
Daycare center for 120 children,
gross floor area 1,672 sq. m,
net floor area 1,367 sq. m,
cost DM 7.0 mill.,
built September 1994–January 1996

Schneller Strasse 99–101,
Rudower Strasse 1
Apartment and Commercial Building
Günter Plessow, Reinhold Ehlers,
Peter Krop, Berlin
Client: Stadt und Land Wohnbauten
GmbH,
4 to 6 stories, 47 housing units, 1 shop,
housing space, 2,967 sq. m
cost approx. DM 15.2 mill. in all,
built September 1995–spring 1997

Siriusstrasse 17–21
Apartment Building
Arge Altmann + Pflitsch, Berlin
Client: Stadt und Land Wohnbauten-
Gesellschaft mbH, Berlin
Corner building, 5–8 stories,
102 subsidized housing units,
cost approx. DM 36 mill.,
built autumn 1995–spring 1997

(End of Housing Area Altglienicke)

Baumschulenstrasse 28
Youth Center "Rumbar"
AIG mbH, Berlin
Client: Treptow District Authorities
Youth center, 3 stories high, steel
construction, gross floor area 611 sq. m,
cost approx. DM 2.3 mill.,
built October 1995–December 1997

Büchnerweg/Zinsgutstrasse
Apartment Building
Axel Liepe, Hartmut Steigelmann,
Berlin
Client: Trigon Consult,
Wohnpark Adlershof KG
U-shaped building group,
5 stories high, part of
a meandering urban structure,
gross floor area 8,700 sq. m,
92 housing units,
built 1996–1997

Büchnerweg
Apartment Building
Martin and Pächter + Partner, Berlin
Client: Trigon Consult GmbH + Co,
Adlershof KG
144 housing units,
completion winter 1997

Dörpfeldstrasse 54–56
Remodelling of a listed school building
Treptow Building Authorities,
Stubendorf Architects
Client: Treptow District Authorities
Renovation and reorganization of
an existing school building
to house a cultural center,
addition of a new one-story library,
cost DM 4.3 mill. in all,
built October 1995–December 1997

Eichenstrasse/Fanny-Zobel-Strasse
Office Center "Twin Towers"
Kieferle & Partner, Stuttgart
Investor: Walter Immobilien EAW,
Augsburg
Developer: Roland Ernst
Städtebau, Berlin
Two 16-story towers connected
by a 3-story basement,
plus two carrées of 6 stories,
two staggered stories,
gross floor area 11,203 sq. m (towers);
20,289 sq. m (carrées)
completion autumn 1997

Elsenstrasse/Ecke Hoffmannstrasse
Office Center "Treptowers"
Schweger + Partner, Hamburg/Berlin,
Reichel + Stauth, Braunschweig;
Gerd Spangenberg, Berlin
Client: Allianz Versicherungs-AG,
Munich, represented by AGRAG
Allianz-Grundstücks GmbH, Stuttgart
31-story tower, 125 m high,
on square floor plan (32 x 32 m),
1,000 sq. m office space per floor,
plus rows of 6 to 10 stories around
11 inner courtyards
gross floor area 165,000 sq. m in all,
investment DM 1 billion in all,
completion winter 1997

Lohnauer Steig 1–17
Sports Center
HL-Investition GmbH, Hennigsdorf
Client: Treptow District Authorities
Multi-functional hall built
of prefabricayted slabs,
gross floor area 635 sq. m,
cost DM 1.6 mill.,
built July 1996–June 1997

Ostwaldstrasse 7–51
"IBZ Adlershof"
Fin Bartels, Christoph Schmitt-Ott,
Berlin with Gernot Wagner, Berlin
Client: The State of Berlin, represented
by the Alexander-von-Humboldt-
Foundation, Bonn
Apartments for the scientists of
WISTA Adlershof;
gross floor area 3,343 sq. m,
built 1996–1997

Peter-Kast-Strasse, Büchnerhof
Apartment Building
Karl Pächter and Partner, Berlin
Client: Trigon Consult, Wohnpark
Adlershof KG, Berlin

Wedding

Badstrasse 4, Behmstrasse,
Bellermannstrasse
"Gesundbrunnen-Center"
Jost Hering, Manfred Stanek,
Hamburg
Client: ECE Projektmanagement GmbH,
Hamburg; Wollank'sche
Familienstiftung Berlin
Investor: Immobilien-Kommandit-
gesellschaft Dr. Mühlhäuser & Co.
Gesundbrunnen-Center Berlin,
Hamburg;
100 shops, 25,000 sq. m retail space,
office space 2,600 sq. m,
investment approx. DM 300 mill.,
built September 1995–September 1997,
opening September 30th, 1997

Brunnenstrasse
Apartment and Office Building
"Brunnenstrasse"
Josef Paul Kleihues, Berlin
Client: Bavaria Objekt- und
Baubetreuung GmbH
Block alignment for housing, 7 stories,
free standing ship-shaped office
building, 13 stories, retail space,
270 housing units,
gross floor area 52,000 sq. m,
built 1995–1997

Kapweg 3–8
Office and Commercial Building
"Kap Carré"
Wolf-Rüdiger Borchardt, Berlin
Client: Internationales
Immobilieninstitut GmbH
Offices, shops,
gross floor area 30,998 sq. m,
built 1995–1997

Luxemburger Strasse 21a
Students Housing
Linie 5 Architekten,
Gabriele Ruoff, Berlin
Client: Studentenwerk Berlin
Housing units for students, shops,
gross floor area 8,090 sq. m,
built 1995–1997

Luxemburger Strasse 26/28
Apartment and Commercial Building
Klaus Effenberger, Berlin
Client: GSW – Gemeinnützige
Siedlungs- und Wohnungsbaugesellschaft Berlin mbH
Corner building, 8 stories high,
49 subsidized housing units,
housing space 3,527 sq. m,
commercial unit 217 sq. m,
cost DM 12.4 mill.,
built June 1995–November 1997

Osloer Strasse 103–107,
Travemünder Strasse
Apartment and Commercial Building
Baesler, Schmidt + Partner, Berlin
Client: DEGEWO
Block alignment, 8 stories high,
104 housing units, 6 shops, 1 cafe,
housing space 7,900 sq. m,
cost DM 24 mill.,
competition 1990,
built winter 1995–1997

Osloer Strasse 103–107
Daycare Center
Baesler, Schmidt + Partner, Berlin
Client: Wedding District Authorities
Daycare center, 3 stories high,
gross floor area 1,500 sq. m,
cost DM 6 mill.,
built summer 1995–spring 1997

Prinzenallee 89/90, Badstrasse 27
Office Building
Steinebach & Weber, Berlin
Client: BfG Immoinvest
7-story building on a Z-shaped floor
plan, commercial units, shopping area,
gross floor area 9,441 sq. m,
cost approx. DM 72 mill.,
built 1995–autumn 1997

Seestrasse 3/Sylter Strasse 1
Wedding Waste Water Facilities
(Berlin IX)
Stefan Schroth, Berlin with
Astrid Kantzenbach,
Daniela McCarthy
Client: Berlin Water Works
Wast Water Pumping Plant,
Caisson-construction,
cost approx. DM 25 mill.,
built 1995–97

Voltastrasse 6
"Media Port"
Josef Paul Kleihues, Berlin
Client: Media Port GmbH, Berlin
Office building for the broadcasting
station "Deutsche Welle",
high-rise of 12 stories
with ad joining 7-story wings ,
gross floor area 14,000 sq. m,
built 1994–1997

Weissensee

*Housing Area Neu-Karow
(former Karow-Nord)*

Clients:
Arge Karow-Nord:
Groth + Graalfs, Berlin;
Gehag, Berlin,
Süba; Berlin

Urban Design
**Moore, Ruble, Yudell,
Santa Monica/Cal.**
Landscape Design
Müller, Knippschild, Wehberg, Berlin

Housing units planned 5,100,
commercial space planned
approx. 13,000 sq. m

Social infrastructure:
10 daycare centers,
2 elementary schools,
1 comprehensive school
2 youth centers

Public green space approx. 62 acres
Investment approx. DM 2.5 billion

Completion until December 1997
approx. 4,500 housing units
approx. 13,000 sq. m commercial space,
4 daycare centers,
1 elementary school,
investment until December 1997
approx. DM 2.1 billion

*Buildings, architects, and clients
listed by streets
(West to east, north to south)*

Pfannschmidtstrasse (odd numbers)
1   **Eckert, Negwer, Sommer,
        Suselbeek (ENSS), Berlin**
        WBG Weissensee/Gesobau
3   **Dörr, Ludolf, Wimmer, Berlin**
        WBG Weissensee/Gesobau
5–7   **ENSS, Berlin**
        WBG Weissensee/Gesobau
9   **Krüger, Schubert, Vandreike
        (KSV), Berlin**
        WBG Weissensee/Gesobau
11   **ENSS Berlin**
        WBG Weissensee/Gesobau
13–17   **KSV, Berlin**
        WBG Weissensee/Gesobau
17–19   **ENSS, Berlin**
        WBG Weissensee/Gesobau
21–23   **Dörr, Ludolf, Wimmer, Berlin**
        WBG Weissensee/Gesobau
25–31   **Casa Nova, Berlin**
        Gehag-Fonds 16 GbR
33–43   **ENSS, Berlin**
        Gehag-Fonds 16 GbR
45–51   **Casa Nova, Berlin**
        Gehag-Fonds
53–55   **Dörr, Ludolf, Wimmer, Berlin**
        Gehag-Fonds 16 GbR
57–59   **ENSS, Berlin**
        Gehag-Fonds 16 GbR
61   **Dietrich Bangert, Berlin**
        Gehag-Fonds
63–65   **ENSS, Berlin**
        Gehag-Fonds 16 GbR
67   **Dietrich Bangert, Berlin**
        Gehag-Fonds 16 GbR

69–71   **ENSS, Berlin**
        Gehag-Fonds 16 GbR
73–79   **Dörr, Ludolf, Wimmer, Berlin**

Pfannschmidtstrasse (even numbers)
2   **Carola Schäfers, Berlin**
        (Daycare center), Weissensee
        District Authorities
4–10   **Maximiliano Burgmayer,
        Berlin**
        WBG Weissensee/Gesobau
12–18   **KSV, Berlin and Dámosy,
        Wiechers + Beck, Berlin**
        WBG Weissensee/Gesobau
        KapHag Fonds 40
        "Wohnen in Berlin Karow" KG
24–30;
44–50   **Jan Rave, Roosje, and Rolf
        Rave, Berlin**
        Bavaria Immobilien Beteili-
        gungs GmbH & Co – LBB Fonds 5
52–58   **Hilmer + Sattler,
        Munich/Berlin**
        Bavaria Immobilien
70   (daycare center), Weissensee
        District Authorities

Karestrasse
2–4   **Schmidt-Thomsen + Ziegert,
        Berlin**
        WBG Weissensee/Gesobau
6–8   **ENSS, Berlin**
        WBG Weissensee/Gesobau

Achillesstrasse (even numbers)
30   **Feddersen, von Herder +
        Partner, Berlin**
        Groth + Graalfs, Berlin
32   **Ferdinand + Gerth, Berlin**
        Groth + Graalfs, Berlin
34–36   **Höhne + Rapp, Berlin**
        Groth + Graalfs, Berlin
38   **Schulze-Rohr, Ruprecht,
        Schlicht, Berlin**
        Groth + Graalfs, Berlin
40   **Ferdinand + Gerth, Berlin**
        Groth + Graalfs, Berlin
42   **Feddersen, von Herder +
        Partner, Berlin**
        Groth + Graalfs, Berlin
44   **Kammann + Hummel, Berlin**
        Groth + Graalfs, Berlin

Commercial complex as building joint
between the two housing areas

Block 13 **Moore, Ruble, Yudell,
         St. Monica**
         Groth + Graalfs, Berlin
Block 15 **Moore, Ruble, Yudell,
         St. Monica**
         Groth + Graalfs, Berlin
Block 19 **Moore, Ruble, Yudell,
         St. Monica**
         Groth + Graalfs, Berlin
Block 20 **Ferdinand + Gerth, Berlin**
         Groth + Graalfs, Berlin
Block 22 **Faskel + Becker**
         Groth + Graalfs, Berlin

Röländerstrasse (odd numbers)
39   **Wiechers + Beck, Berlin**
        WBG Weissensee/Gesobau
41–45   **Zsuzsanna Dámoszy, Berlin**
        WBG Weissensee/Gesobau
47   **Dörr, Ludolf, Wimmer, Berlin**
        WBG Weissensee/Gesobau

Röländerstrasse (even numbers)
12–26   **Brandt + Böttcher, Berlin**
        WBG Weissensee/Gesobau
28–30   **Joachim Ramin, Berlin**
        WBG Weissensee/Gesobau
32–36   **Brandt + Böttcher, Berlin**
        WBGG Weissensee/Gesobau
38–40   **Fissler + Ernst, Berlin**
        Bavaria Immobilien
42   (Daycare center, planned),
        Weissensee District Authorities
44   **Casa Nova, Berlin**
        WBG Weissensee/Gesobau
46   **Horst Hielscher, Berlin**
        Weissensee District
        Authorities (daycare center)

Busonistrasse (odd numbers)
81–85   **Alexander Williams, Berlin**
        Bavaria Immobilien, Berlin
113–117 **Carola Schäfers, Berlin**
        Bavaria Immobilien, Berlin
119–125 **Fissler + Ernst, Berlin**
        Bavaria Immobilien, Berlin
127–131 **Johannes Wiesermann, Berlin**
        Bavaria Immobilien, Berlin
133   Daycare center; Weissensee
        District Authorities
135   **Fissler + Ernst, Berlin**
        Bavaria Immobilien, Berlin
141   Daycare center; Weissensee
        District Authorities

Busonistrasse (even numbers)
90–94   **Feddersen, von Herder, Berlin**
        Groth + Graalfs, Berlin
96–104 Daycare Center; Weissensee
        District Authorities
106–110 **Höhne + Rapp, Berlin**
        Groth + Graalfs, Berlin
118–134 **Kamann + Hummel, Berlin**
        Groth + Graalfs, Berlin
136   (commercial center)
        Kammann + Hummel, Berlin
        Groth + Graalfs, Berlin
138   **Wiechers + Beck, Berlin**
        Bavaria Immobilien, Berlin
140–144 **Hilmer + Sattler,
        Munich/Berlin**
        Bavaria Immobilien, Berlin

Beerbaumstrasse
1–3   **Wiechers + Beck, Berlin**
        Bavaria Immobilien, Berlin
5–15   **Stefan Scholz, Berlin**
        Bavaria Immobilien, Berlin
17–29   **Gehag, Dept. Technik**
        Bavaria Immobilien, Berlin

Achtrutenberg (odd numbers)
16   **Brandt + Böttcher, Berlin**
        Groth + Graalfs, Berlin
18   **Moore, Ruble, Yudell,
        St. Monica**
        Groth + Graalfs, Berlin
20–28   **Joachim Ramin, Berlin**
        Groth + Graalfs, Berlin
30–36   **Moore, Ruble, Yudell,
        St. Monica, Cal.**
        Groth + Graalfs, Berlin
38–48   **Faskel + Becker, Berlin**
        Groth + Graalfs, Berlin
50–54   **Brandt + Böttcher, Berlin**
        Groth + Graalfs, Berlin

Achtrutenberg (odd numbers)
31–33   **Joachim Ramin, Berlin**
        Groth + Graalfs, Berlin
47–51   **Moore, Ruble, Yudell,
        St. Monica, Cal.**
        Groth + Graalfs, Berlin
53–55   **Faskel + Becker, Berlin**
        Groth + Graalfs, Berlin
57   **Joachim Ramin, Berlin**
        Groth + Graalfs, Berlin

Gewanneweg
1   **Brandt + Böttcher, Berlin**
        Groth + Graalfs, Berlin
3   **Faskel + Becker, Berlin**
        Groth + Graalfs, Berlin
5   **Joachim Ramin, Berlin**
        Groth + Graalfs, Berlin
7   **Moore, Ruble, Yudell,
        St. Monica**
        Groth + Graalfs, Berlin

Ballonplatz 1–4, 5–8
Jan, Roosje and Rolf Rave, Berlin
Bavaria Immobilien

Am Elsebrocken
1–3   **Höhne + Rapp, Berlin**
        Groth + Graalfs, Berlin
5–9;
11–17   **Schulze-Rohr, Berlin**
        Groth + Graalfs, Berlin
19   **Höhne + Rapp, Berlin**
        Groth + Graalfs, Berlin

Matestrasse
23–27   **Feddersen, von Herder, Berlin**
        Groth + Graalfs, Berlin

Teichbergstrasse
1   **Feddersen, von Herder, Berlin**
        Groth + Graalfs, Berlin
3   **Höhne + Rapp, Berlin**
        Groth + Graalfs, Berlin
5–9,
11–15   **Ferdinand + Gerth, Berlin**
        Groth + Graalfs, Berlin
17   **Höhne + Rapp, Berlin**
        Groth + Graalfs, Berlin
19   **Feddersen, von Herder, Berlin**
        Groth + Graalfs, Berlin

*Achillesstrasse (even numbers)
continued (east of Lossebergplatz)*

70   Youth center; Weissensee
        District Authorities
72   **Eyl, Weitz, Würmle + Partner,
        Berlin**
        Groth + Graalfs, Berlin
74   **Nielebock, Berlin**
        Groth + Graalfs, Berlin
76–80   **Seidel**
        Groth + Graalfs, Berlin
82–86;
90–94   **Heueis + Fritzsche, Berlin**
        Groth + Graalfs, Berlin
96–102;
104–106 **Krüger, Schubert, Vandreike,
        Berlin**
        Groth + Graalfs, Berlin
108–110 **Hierholzer, von Rudzinski**
        Groth + Graalfs, Berlin
112–120 **Pysall + Stahrenberg, Berlin**
        Groth + Graalfs, Berlin

*Achillesstrasse (odd numbers)
continued (east of Lossebergplatz)*

55–63   **Moore, Ruble, Yudell,
St. Monica, Cal.**
Groth + Graalfs, Berlin
65–67   **Faskel + Becker, Berlin**
Groth + Graalfs, Berlin
69–75   **Ferdinand + Rapp, Berlin**
Groth + Graalfs, Berlin
77   Library
79–107   Comprehensive school

Lossebergplatz
1   **Nielebock, Berlin**
Groth + Graalfs, Berlin

Münchehagenstrasse (even numbers)
2–6   **Neumeyer + Schönfeld,
Berlin**
Groth + Graalfs, Berlin
8–12;
14–22   **Heueis + Fritzsche, Berlin**
Groth + Graalfs, Berlin
24–26;
28–32   **Hermann + Valentiny**
Groth + Graalfs, Berlin
34–38   **Thomas Sieverts, Bonn**
Groth + Graalfs, Berlin
40–44;
46–50   **Kammann + Hummel, Berlin**
Groth + Graalfs, Berlin
52–56   **Thomas Sieverts, Bonn**
Groth + Graalfs, Berlin
58–62   **Moore, Ruble, Yudell,
St. Monica**
Groth + Graalfs, Berlin
64   **Seidel, Berlin**
Groth + Graalfs, Berlin

Münchehagenstrasse (odd numbers)
43   daycare center; Weissensee
District Authorities
55–57   **KSV, Berlin**
Groth + Graalfs, Berlin
59   daycare center; Weissensee
District Authorities
65   **Seidel, Berlin**
Groth + Graalfs, Berlin
67–89;
91–113   **v. Beulwitz, Berlin**
Groth + Graalfs, Berlin

Hofzeichendamm (odd numbers)
1   daycare center; Weissensee
District Authorities
3–7   **Neumeyer + Schönfeld,
Berlin**
Groth + Graalfs, Berlin
9–11   **Heueis + Fritzsche, Berlin**
13   daycare center; Weissensee
District Authorities
15–21   **Hermann + Valentiny**
Groth + Graalfs, Berlin
23–31   **Thomas Sieverts, Bonn**
Groth + Graalfs, Berlin
35–37   **Faskel + Becker, Berlin**
Groth + Graalfs, Berlin
39   **Thomas Sieverts, Bonn**
41–47   **Faskel + Becker, Berlin**
Groth + Graalfs, Berlin

Hofzeichendamm (even numbers)
36   **v. Beulwitz, Berlin**
Groth + Graalfs, Berlin

Strömannstrasse (odd numbers)
93–99   **Kammann + Hummel, Berlin**
Groth + Graalfs, Berlin

*Strömannstrasse (even numbers)
72, 74a–e, 76, 78, 80a–e*
Projekt GmbH

Achillesstrasse 1, Karestrasse 2–4
Apartment Building
Schmidt-Thomsen & Ziegert, Berlin
Client: Wohnungsbaugesellschaft
Weissensee mbH
Corner building, 4 stories,
39 housing units
gross floor area 4,217 sq. m,
cost DM 7.03 mill.,
built 1995–1996

(end of housing area Neu-Karow)

Berliner Allee 235, 237
Apartment and Commercial Building
Martin and Pächter, Berlin
Client: Wohnungsbaugesellschaft
Weissensee, Berlin
6 stories, 20 housing units,
4 commercial units,
gross floor area 2,582 sq. m,
cost DM 6,9 mill.,
completion March 1997

Gürtelstrasse 6, Meyerbeerstrasse 1–9
Apartment Buildings
Dieter Meisl, Berlin
Client: Wohnungsbaugesellschaft
Weissensee, Berlin
Urban infill, 3, 4, 5-story apartment
buildings, 48 housing units,
cost approx. DM 17 mill.,
completion July 1997

*Gustav-Adolf-Strasse 6,
Lehderstrasse 57, 58*
Apartment Building
Werkplan GmbH, Berlin
Client: Wohnungsbaugesellschaft
Weissensee, Berlin
5 stories, 34 housing units,
3 commercial units, green roof,
cost DM 11.1 mill.,
completion May 1997

Jacobsohnstrasse 27
Apartment Building
Metz + Partner, Berlin
Client: Eugen Klenk, Berlin
Block alignment,
14 subsidized housing units,
2 commercial units
cost DM 3 mill.,
built March 1996–May 1997

*Jacobsohnstrasse 29–33,
Pistoriusstrasse*
Apartment Building
**Rolf Backmann and Eugen Schieber,
Berlin**
Client: Kettler Liegenschaften GmbH
Corner building, 34 housing units,
3 shops, housing space 4,400 sq. m,
cost DM 8.2 mill.,
built 1996–1997

Streustrasse 58/59
Apartment Building
Büro Werkplan GmbH, Berlin
Grundstücksgesellschaft Dii-Fonds B99
5 stories, 25 housing units,
housing space 1,665 sq. m,
construction cost DM 8.78 mill.,
built March 1995–June 1996

Wigandstaler Strasse 1–7
Apartment and Commercial Building
"Wohnanlage Weissensee"
STORR Consulting, Munich
Client: Concordia Bau und Boden AG,
Berlin/Cologne
72 housing units (partly privately
owned, partly for rent),
7 commercial units,
the residential complex is part
of the large-scale
"Office-City Berlin-Weissensee"
completion January 1997

Wilmersdorf

Babelsberger Strasse 6
Apartment and Commercial Building
Barkow Leibinger Architekten, Berlin
Client: Texxky
Grundstücksverwaltung GbR, Stuttgart
Shops, offices, apartments,
gross floor area 1,450 sq. m,
built 1994–1996

*Barstrasse 35–39A,
Mecklenburgische Strasse 16–18*
Apartment Building
**Dagmar Bernardy, GEHAG
Dept. Technik, Berlin**
Client: GEHAG Gemeinnützige
Heimstätten-AG, Berlin
(Gehag Fonds 18 GbR)
Corner building,
6 to 7 stories, plus roof story,
161 housing units in all,
30 senior's apartments,
2 experimental dwelling communities,
10,685 sq. m housing space, 7 shops,
built summer 1995–January 1997

*Emser Platz 1–2
(former Hohenzollerndamm 188)*
Apartment and Commercial Building
Nalbach Architekten, Berlin
Client: Treu-Bau Kries GmbH & Co KG
Addition to an existing building,
urban infill with doorway,
colonnades to Emser Platz,
10 housing units, 8 commercial units,
net floor area 2,630 sq. m,
investment DM 16.5 mill.,
built December 1995–April 1997

Franzensbader Strasse 16
Multipurpose Sports Hall
Bezirksamt Wilmersdorf von Berlin
Client: Wilmersdorf District Authorities
gross floor area 2,051,
cost DM 8.8 mill.,
built November 1993–December 1996

Hohenzollerndamm 134
Weberbank Office Building
Hanno Hübscher, Berlin
Client: Weberbank Berliner
Industriebank KG a.O.
Office building with banking hall,
3,625 sq. m gross floor area,
cost DM 26.6 mill.,
built March 1995–February 1997
opening February 17th, 1997

Hohenzollerndamm 208
Extension Wilmersdorf Pumping Plant
Ackermann and Partner, Munich
Client: Berlin Water Works
Industrial building, 3 subterranean
stories, 2-story hall building
gross floor area approx. 1,560 sq. m,
built 1993–1997

Rudolstädter Strasse
Gym Hall
Axel Finkeldey, Berlin
Client: Wilmersdorf District Authorities
Hall over a 22 x 44 m sports ground,
built-in public gallery for 500,
cost DM 14.2 mill.,
completion 1997

Zehlendorf

Eilertstrasse 1
Apartment Building
Höing Architekten, Berlin
Client: Höing Architekten, Berlin
Small building with housing units
and one office,
built 1996–1997

Kiebitzweg 13–15
Free University Students Center
Wolf & Partner, Berlin
Client: Free University of Berlin
Offices, auditorium for the
students' self-government,
rooms for counselling,
gross floor area 1,200 sq. m,
built 1995–97

Königsweg 222
Apartment Houses
Ernst Bergmann, Berlin
Client: BFE – Bauträger für Eigenheime
GmbH
7 apartments and
2 semi-detached houses,
712 sq. m housing space in all
cost DM 2.3 mill.,
built winter 1995–spring 1997

Potsdamer Chaussee 70
Neuro-Psychiatric Clinic
"Waldhausklinik Zehlendorf"
**Cornelius Hertling, Berlin
(Project Management E. Brennecke)**
A loose building structure completes
and extends the clinic park from early
and mid-century, keeping the
characteristics of a garden city,
gross floor area 24,384 sq. m,
cost DM 140 mill.,
second building phase 1989–1996

Takustrasse 7
Konrad-Zuse-Center
Dähne-Dahl, Berlin
Client: Berlin Senate
for Research and Science
Research center for information
technology,
gross floor area 11,000 sq. m,
built 1994–1996

Erweiterung des Berlin Museums mit Abteilung Jüdisches Museum, D-Berlin, Architekt: Daniel Liebeskind Architectural Studio, D-Berlin

Das Material mit Zukunft

RHEINZINK® ist der Markenname für eine Zinklegierung mit Zusätzen aus Kupfer und Titan. Entwickelt für die besonderen Anforderungen moderner Bauklempnerei, zeichnet sich das Material durch seine hervorragenden Verarbeitungsqualitäten aus. Durch die sprichwörtlich lange Lebensdauer und Wartungsfreiheit sowie die ästhetisch anspruchsvolle Optik empfiehlt sich RHEINZINK® als Baumaterial mit Zukunft. Ein vollausgebautes Servicesystem unterstützt Handwerker, Bauherren und Architekten mit jeweils speziell auf ihre Bedürfnisse zugeschnittenen Leistungen. RHEINZINK® ist sowohl als „walzblankes" als auch schon ab Werk mit der typisch graublauen Optik der Patina versehenes „vorbewittertes" Material lieferbar. So verfügen Sie vom ersten Tag an über alle Qualitäten dieses wegweisenden Baustoffes.

RHEINZINK GMBH, Postfach 1452, D-45705 Datteln
Tel. 02363/605-0, Fax: 02363/605-209, Internet: http://www.rheinzink.de

Wir machen Bauwerke zu Bauwerten

Seit 1983 baut die Bauwert mit an der Zukunft Berlins.

Z.B. das TRIAS in Berlin-Mitte: 27.000 m² repräsentative Nutzfläche in exponierter Lage für Büros und Läden. Eine faszinierende Architektur, ideale Verkehrsanbindungen und ein qualifiziertes Raumkonzept schaffen optimale Arbeitsbedingungen. Mit der Fertigstellung war das Gebäude zu 100% vermietet.

Z.B. das *Charlotten-Palais* in Berlin-Mitte: Zwischen Unter den Linden und dem Gendarmenmarkt entsteht eines der repräsentativsten Büro-, Wohn- und Geschäftshäuser Berlins mit insgesamt 3.700 m² Nutzfläche. 70% der Büroflächen sind bereits vermietet, Fertigstellung wird im Frühjahr 1998 sein.

Die Bauwert errichtet in Berlin derzeit insgesamt über 118.000 m² hochwertige Büro- und Geschäftsflächen. Bei Übergabe weisen die Gebäude einen durchschnittlichen Gesamtvermietungsstand von über 90% auf. Ein Beweis für Qualität an hervorragenden Standorten.

Bauwert GmbH

Berlin hat Farbe verdient. Wo das Gesicht der Stadt für lange
Zeit erblaßt war, schaffen weiterentwickelte Bautraditionen
und moderne Architektur heute die Voraussetzungen für das
neue Leben in einer Metropole von morgen.

Die Anforderungen an die verwendeten Baustoffe sind
entsprechend hoch. Dauerhafte und bewährte Materialien sind
gefragt, die gleichzeitig modernen Ansprüchen genügen.
Zum Beispiel TECU®-Patina: Kupfer für Dach und Fassade in
einer zeitgemäßen Definition. TECU®-Patina ist von Anfang an
natürlich grün patiniert – eine Farbe, die nicht nur Berlin gut
zu Gesicht steht. Und alle bekannten positiven Eigenschaften
von klassischem Kupfer bleiben uneingeschränkt erhalten.

TECU®-Patina ist sofort und für immer grün –
dauerhafte und lebendige Farbe für Berlin
und andere interessante Orte dieser Welt.

immergrün

KM Europa Metal
Aktiengesellschaft
Postfach 33 20
D - 49023 Osnabrück

Internet http:// www.kme.de

Unser Auftrag –
Förderung der Berliner Stadtentwicklung

Unsere Aufgaben –
Entwicklung landeseigener Flächen für
zukunftsorientierte Investitionen,
Technologien und Unternehmensgründungen

Unsere Stärke –
Zuverlässigkeit und Kompetenz
„One-stop-agency": Vermittler
zwischen Investoren und
dem Land Berlin

für Ihren Erfolg

Berlin
B LEG

WIR
SCHAFFEN
VORAUSSETZUNGEN

Das TGS • Technologie-
und Gründerzentrum Spreeknie

Neu eröffnet
im November 1997

Der Wilhelminenhof

Helle Räume für
Handwerk und Gewerbe

Gewerbeflächen in Berlin

Schneller Baubeginn
mit unserem Know-how

BLEG • Berliner Landes-
entwicklungsgesellschaft mbH
Spreebogen Plaza
Pascalstraße 10c
10587 Berlin
Tel.: 0 30/39 91-40 00
Fax: 0 30/39 91-40 01

TGS • Technologie- und Gründer-
zentrum Spreeknie GmbH
Ostendstraße 25
12459 Berlin
Tel.: 0 30/53 04 10 00
Fax: 0 30/53 04 10 10

SACHLICHKEIT UND FUNKTIONALITÄT

Architekt: Prof. Rainer Oefelein

Ein klassisch schönes Haus im günstigen Preisleistungsverhältnis

Ihr Traum kann in Erfüllung gehen: Das Eigenheim in der Gartenstadt Rudow. Haus und Grundstück ab 307.000 DM. **Die Lage:** Im Süden Berlins gelegen, gilt Rudow den Berlinern seit Jahren als attraktive Wohngegend. Kleine Siedlungsgebiete und Gartenkolonien prägen das Bild. Rudow gilt als einer der schönsten Teile von Neukölln. Parkanlagen prägen das Stadtquartier. **Adresse:** Elisabeth-Selbert-Straße / Ecke Friederike-Nadig-Straße, 12355 Berlin-Rudow. **Infrastruktur:** Eine gewachsene Infrastruktur mit guter Verkehrsanbindung. **S- und U-Bahn:** U7, U-Bahnhof Rudow. Buslinien 171,

260, 271, 738 und für die Autofahrer bieten sich wie selbstverständlich Wege in die City. Die Stadtautobahn sowie die Zubringer zur Autobahn sind in wenigen Minuten erreicht. • Kitas, Schulen, Einkaufen, Gaststätten • Medizinische Versorgung • 20 Minuten bis zum Krankenhaus Neukölln • 30 Minuten bis zum Krankenhaus Britz. **Wir beraten Sie gern.** Bitte rufen Sie uns an. Kommen Sie zu uns, unser Immobilienteam berät Sie bei der Realisierung Ihrer Pläne. Von der Finanzierung bis zum Fullservice, wir beraten Sie gern: **Telefon: 6892-345**

STADT UND LAND

WOHNBAUTEN-GESELLSCHAFT MBH

Werbellinstraße 12 · 12053 Berlin · Sammelrufnummer: 68 92-0 · Telefax: 68 92-206

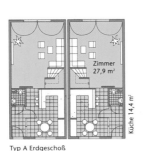

Typ A Straßenansicht

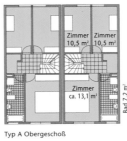

Typ A Erdgeschoß

Zimmer 27,9 m²

Küche 14,4 m²

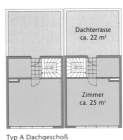

Typ A Obergeschoß

Zimmer 10,5 m² Zimmer 10,5 m²

Zimmer ca. 13,1 m²

Bad 7,2 m²

Typ A Dachgeschoß

Dachterrasse ca. 22 m²

Zimmer ca. 25 m²

Typ A Gartenansicht

Architektur: Patzschke, Klotz & Partner, Berlin; Innenarchitektur: Ezra Attia, London und Lars Malmquist, Living Design, Stockholm; Lichtplanung: Licht Kunst Licht, Bonn/Berlin.

Empfang im
Hotel Adlon in Berlin.
Licht von Erco.

ERCO

Die vierte Dimension
der Architektur.

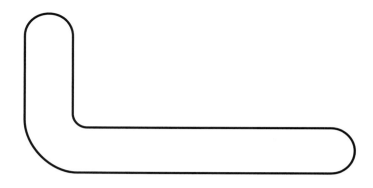

Handbuch 98/99

FSB-Beschläge für Türen und Fenster

Bestell-Fax
(0 52 72) 60 83 00

....
Name

....
Firma

....
Postfach/Straße

....
PLZ/Ort

.... kostenlose Exemplare

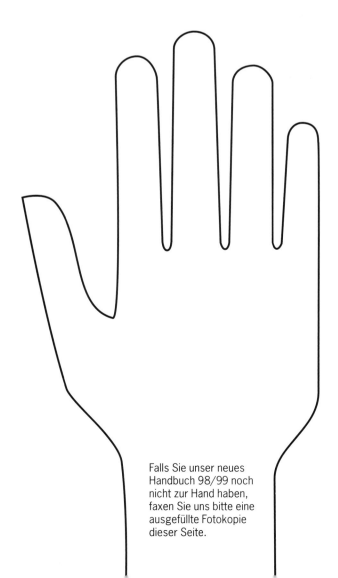

Falls Sie unser neues Handbuch 98/99 noch nicht zur Hand haben, faxen Sie uns bitte eine ausgefüllte Fotokopie dieser Seite.

Ökosozialer Wohnungsbau.

Architekten:
Torge Gaa Wercker
mit T. Langenfeld

Das »Karl-Philipp-Moritz-Haus« in Berlin-Kreuzberg vereint soziales und ökologisches Bauen unter einem Dach. Es beherbergt ein umweltorientiertes Beschäftigungsprojekt für Jugendliche und 46 Wohnungen im 1. Förderweg, von denen ein weiterer Teil für Jugendliche in betreuten Wohnprojekten reserviert ist.

Die Architektur baut auf eine Vielzahl umweltgerechter Komponenten: Wintergärten an der Südfassade schützen vor dem Lärm der stark befahrenen Straße und fangen zugleich die Sonnenwärme ein. Die Nordfassade öffnet sich über begrünte Terrassen in den ruhigen Park des

Blockinnenhofs. Ein gasbetriebenes Blockheizkraftwerk versorgt das gesamte Haus mit emissionsarm erzeugtem Strom; die Nutzung seiner Abwärme reduziert den Heizenergiebedarf aus dem Fernwärmenetz. Eine vorbildliche Wärmedämmung und die Verwendung von energiesparenden Geräten tragen zusätzlich zum rationellen Einsatz von Energie bei.

So sollte sozialer Wohnungsbau heute aussehen. Ein Beispiel für engagiertes Bauen – ein Projekt der GSW, eine der größten städtischen Wohnungsbaugesellschaften in Berlin.

Gut und sicher wohnen.

GSW

Gemeinnützige Siedlungs- und Wohnungsbaugesellschaft Berlin mbH
Kochstraße 22, 10969 Berlin

QUARTIER 206

FriedrichstadtPassagen

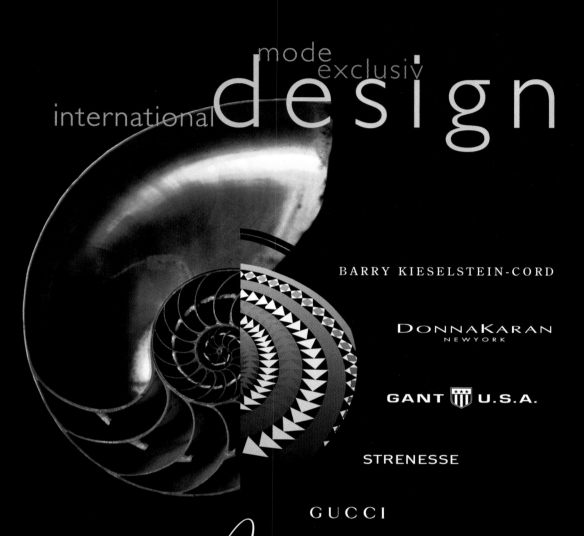

mode
exclusiv
international design

BARRY KIESELSTEIN-CORD

DONNAKARAN
NEW YORK

GANT U.S.A.

STRENESSE

GUCCI

Quartier
206
BERLIN

Mit dem Quartier 206 erhält die Friedrichstraße – zwischen Top-Hotels, Kunst und Kultur gelegen – wieder internationalen Flair. Mit der außergewöhnlichen Architektur im Stil des Art Déco der zwanziger Jahre und der gelungenen Mischung aus namhaften Modegeschäften, gehobener Gastronomie und repräsentativen Büros, ist das Quartier 206 der Friedrichstraße Mittelpunkt der zukünftigen Luxusmeile Berlins.

Jagdfeld
FriedrichstadtPassagen
Quartier 206
Vermögensverwaltung KG

Pascalstraße 10 b
10587 Berlin
Fon: (0 30) 39 91-01
Fax: (0 30) 3 99 61 80

Form. Farbe. Flair.

Aldo Rossi und Dr. Kottmair bringen italienisches Ambiente an ausgewählte Standorte Berlins.

Projekt am Leipziger Platz

Multifunktionaler Gebäudekomplex an
1A Standort mit ca. 212.000 m² BGF:
Büros/Dienstleistung, Wohnen,
Handel/Gastronomie, Hotel,
Showtheater „Cirque du Soleil",
Diskothek.

Blickfang ist eine Kuppel mit
70 m Durchmesser, größer
als die des Petersdoms.

– In Planung –

Landsberger Arkaden

Quartier Schützenstraße

Der berühmte Palazzo Farnese
von Michelangelo stand Modell
für eines der Gebäude.

Quartierbebauung nach historischem Vorbild mit zwölf
Wohn- und Geschäftshäusern in bester Innenstadtlage,
Nähe Checkpoint Charlie mit ca. 50.000 m² BGF:
Büros, Wohnen, Handel/Gastronomie.

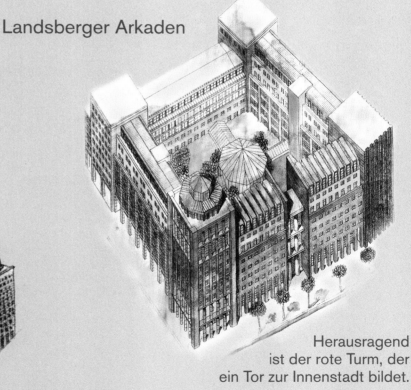

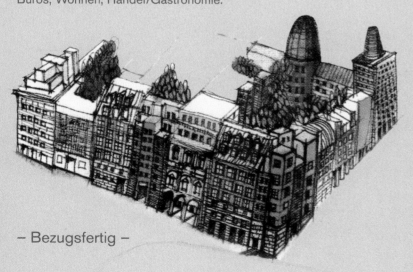

– Bezugsfertig –

Herausragend
ist der rote Turm, der
ein Tor zur Innenstadt bildet.

– Im Bau –

Farbenfroher Dienstleistungskomplex mit hervor-
ragender Verkehrsanbindung, direkt am S-Bhf.
Landsberger Allee mit ca. 45.000 m² BGF:
Büros/Dienstleistung, Handel/Gastronomie,
Hotel, Hotel-Akademie.

Projektentwicklungen der Dr. Peter und Isolde Kottmair GbR

Charlottenstr. 18 · 10117 Berlin · Telefon (030) 201 999 - 0 · Prielmayerstr. 1/VII · 80335 München · Telefon (089) 549 044 - 0

Wülfing Steiner

**Wir machen
Ihre Daten zum
Blickfang**

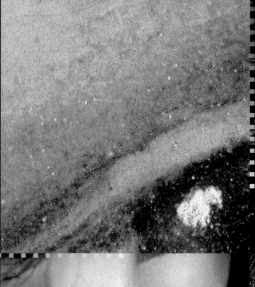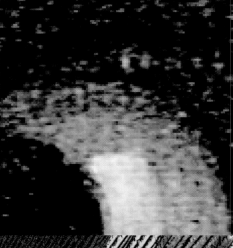

Architektur- und

High-End-

Präsentationen

Messetafeln

Displays

Leuchtkästen

Digital Drucke

Digital Fotografie

Cibachrome

Fachvergrößerungen

Reproduktionen

FineArt Printing

Diaduplikate

Scans

Overhead Filme

Kopien

Finishing

Acrylversiegelung

WoGeHe

Stadt(t)räume

Bei der Entwicklung Hellersdorfs zu einer attraktiven Adresse stehen die Interessen der Bewohner im Mittelpunkt. Eine der Hauptaufgaben ist es dabei, wohnortspezifische Merkmale zu entwickeln und Wohnadressen ein neues Ambiente zu geben, um die Identifikation mit dem Zuhause zu stärken.

Modernisierung und Instandhaltung in und an den Häusern wird dabei verbunden mit einer systematischen Neugestaltung sowie Aufwertung des Wohnumfeldes. Über 150 Projekte wurden in den letzten fünf Jahren realisiert.

Dazu gehört die Gestaltung von neuen Stadträumen und Stadtplätzen sowie die Einbindung von Kunst im öffentlichen Raum. Die Großsiedlung Hellersdorf ist so zu einer akzeptierten Heimat für über 100.000 Bewohner geworden.

Hellersdorf gestaltet seine Zukunft, nicht morgen, sondern heute.

Treffpunkte für Freunde

Hellersdorf bietet gerade für junge Familien ein attraktives Wohnumfeld. Um ihren speziellen Bedürfnissen gerecht zu werden, bietet die WoGeHe heute über 140 neugestaltete Spielplätze, zusätzlich laden rund 30 Bolzplätze zum Kickvergnügen ein.

Das Lichttor – Platz mit Atmosphäre

Einer der interessantesten Plätze Hellersdorfs ist der Stadtplatz zwischen Louis-Lewin-Str. und Schkeuditzer Str. Zu dem Ensemble gehört eine "grüne Mitte" von locker gruppierten Bäumen und das die Stadtachsen "verbindende" Lichttor mit zwei markanten Granitsäulen.

Das Balkonkino – Ort zum Wohlfühlen

Das Hellersdorfer Tor ist eines der neuen Hellersdorfer Entrees. Die Hauptattraktion jedoch ist das Balkonkino. Zwischen zwei Stahlmasten wird eine Leinwand gespannt, und schon sitzt man in der ersten Reihe.

Weitere Informationen erhalten Sie bei der Wohnungsbaugesellschaft Hellersdorf mbH, Öffentlichkeitsarbeit
Adele-Sandrock-Straße 10, 12627 Berlin
Telefon: 030/9 90 10
Telefax: 030/9 91 80 00

Public-Press GmbH

Wer in den **Himmel** will, sollte

1 x in der Woche

in die **Kirche** gehen ...

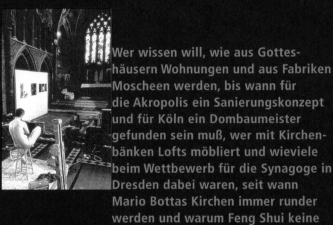

Wer wissen will, wie aus Gottes-
häusern Wohnungen und aus Fabriken
Moscheen werden, bis wann für
die Akropolis ein Sanierungskonzept
und für Köln ein Dombaumeister
gefunden sein muß, wer mit Kirchen-
bänken Lofts möbliert und wieviele
beim Wettbewerb für die Synagoge in
Dresden dabei waren, seit wann
Mario Bottas Kirchen immer runder
werden und warum Feng Shui keine
Sekte, sondern eine asiatische Art der
Raumgestaltung ist, der sollte
1 x in der Woche Bauwelt lesen.

Bauwelt

Seit 4546 Wochen:
jeden Freitag Architekturkritik etc.

Wo mit Weitblick gebaut wird,
sind die Aussichten am besten

G roth + Graalfs leistet seit über 15 Jahren seinen Beitrag bei der Gestaltung der Region Berlin-Brandenburg. Hier entstehen städtebaulich bedeutende Projekte wie das Kirchsteigfeld in Potsdam oder Neu-Karow in Berlins grünem Norden.

Kompetenz zeigt Groth + Graalfs aber nicht nur beim Wohnungsbau: Groth + Graalfs entwickelt und verwirklicht auch attraktive Standorte für Verbände, Botschaften oder Dienstleister.
So entstehen in der neuen Mitte Berlins die zukunftsweisenden Gebäude für die deutschen Spitzenverbände DIHT/BDI/BDA oder für die CDU Deutschlands.

WDR

BVG

| 24 | Ankunft | Arrivals 1 | ✈ | → |

www.audi.de/audi.com

www.bosch.de

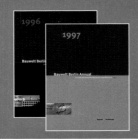

The book design is based on a concept by MetaDesign.

MetaDesign

Worldwide Corporate Design

Worldwide Corporate Design

Corporate Design
for Germany's largest State Run
TV and Radio Station

Corporate Design and Editorial Design
for a scientific Publisher

Corporate Design and Orientation System
for Berlin Public Transport

Corporate Design and Orientation System
for Düsseldorf Airport

Audi Homepage

Bosch Homepage

www.metadesign.com

MetaDesign Berlin
Bergmannstraße 102
D-10961 Berlin
+49·30·695 79·200
fax +49·30·695 79·222
mail@metadesign.de

MetaDesign London
5–8 Hardwick Street
GB-London EC1R 4RB
+44·171·520 1000
fax +44·171·520 1099
mail@metadesign.co.uk

MetaDesign San Francisco
350 Pacific Avenue
USA-San Francisco CA 94111
+1·415·627 0790
fax +1·415·627 0795
mail@metadesign.com

How about an

Island
of Love?

The Wasserstadt GmbH is
transforming old industrial
and harbour areas into
beautiful waterfront sites
for living and working
at Rummelsburg Bay,
Lake Spandau and elsewhere.
Berlin's development areas even
have two Islands of Love.

WASSERSTADT

Wasserstadt GmbH • Berlin's Waterfront Development Corporation • Managing directors: Uli Hellweg, Juergen Nottmeyer
Eiswerderstrasse 18 • D 13585 Berlin • Telephone +49-30-355 901 20 • Telefax +49-30-355 901 99 • http://www.wasserstadt.de

Wer Großes leistet, braucht einen starken Partner.

Unsere Bank ist kompetent in allen Fragen der Finanzierung
von Wohn- und Gewerbebauten in ganz Deutschland.
Die Berlin Hyp ist eine der großen deutschen Hypotheken-
banken und bietet mehr als nur günstige Zinsen: Mehr
Erfahrung, mehr Service und mehr Sicherheit.

Berlin Hyp

IHRE HYPOTHEKENBANK
ein Unternehmen der Bankgesellschaft Berlin

Budapester Str. 1 · 10787 Berlin · Tel. (030) 25 999-0 · Fax (030) 25 999-131
Landschaftstr. 8 · 30159 Hannover · Tel. (0511) 30 11-0 · Fax (0511) 30 11-384
Internet: http://www.BerlinHyp.de · E-Mail: Kommunikation@BerlinHyp.de

Auf Deutschland bauen

Berlins Architektur

beim Birkhäuser Verlag

Berlin baut in rasantem Tempo, kaum eine Woche vergeht ohne eine Grundstein-legung oder eine festliche Eröffnung in Stadtmitte. Bis zur Jahrtausendwende wird ein neues Bild der Stadt entstanden sein, an dem fast alle Architekten von Rang aus der ganzen Welt mitgewirkt haben.

Foreign Affairs
Neue Botschaftsbauten und das
Auswärtige Amt in Berlin
Sebastian Redecke,
Ralph Stern (Hrsg.)

240 Seiten,
60 Farb- und 350 sw-Abbildungen.
24 x 33 cm Broschur
DM 98.– / öS 716.– / sFr. 88.–
ISBN 3-7643-5618-9
Leinen mit Schutzumschlag
DM 128.– / öS 935.– / sFr. 108.–
ISBN 3-7643-5629-4
deutsch / englisch

Kanzleramt und Präsidialamt der Bundesrepublik Deutschland
Internationale Architektur-wettbewerbe für die Hauptstadt
Berlin
Annegret Burg,
Sebastian Redecke (Hrsg.)

240 Seiten,
40 Farb- und 610 sw-Abbildungen.
33 x 24 cm. Broschur
DM 88.– / öS 643.– / sFr. 78.–
ISBN 3-7643-5203-5
Leinen mit Schutzumschlag
DM 128.– / öS 935.– / sFr. 108.–
ISBN 3-7643-5204-3
deutsch / englisch

Downtown Berlin Mitte
Die Entstehung einer
urbanen Architektur
Annegret Burg
Hans Stimmann (Hrsg.)

224 Seiten,
90 Farb-, 310 Strich- und 220 sw-
Abbildungen.
24 x 33 cm. Broschur
DM 98.– / öS 716.– / sFr. 88.–
ISBN 3-7643-5063-6
Leinen mit Schutzumschlag
DM 128.– / öS 935.– / sFr. 108.–
ISBN 3-7643-5062-8
deutsch / englisch

Hauptstadt Berlin – Stadtmitte Spreeinsel
Internationaler Städtebaulicher
Ideenwettbewerb 1994

212 Seiten, 40 Farb- und
320 sw-Abbildungen.
24 x 33 cm.
Leinen mit Schutzumschlag
DM 128.– / öS 935.– / sFr. 118.–
ISBN 3-7643-5041-5
deutsch / englisch

Neue Berlinische Architektur:
Eine Debatte
Annegret Burg (Hrsg.)

172 Seiten,
66 sw-Abbildungen.
16,8 x 22 cm. Broschur
DM 39.80 / öS 291.– / sFr. 35.–
ISBN 3-7643-2998-X
deutsch

Babylon, Berlin etc.
Das Vokabular der europäischen
Stadt
Hans Stimmann (Hrsg.)

256 Seiten,
70 sw-Abbildungen.
Broschur
DM 39.80 / öS 291.– / sFr. 35.–
ISBN 3-7643-5211-6
Vorträge in deutsch und Original-sprache

Birkhäuser – Verlag für Architektur
Klosterberg 23 · CH – 40 10 Basel
http://www.birkhauser.ch